*Fashioning the Female Subject*

# Fashioning the Female Subject

The Intertextual Networking
of Dickinson, Moore, and Rich

*Sabine Sielke*

Ann Arbor
THE UNIVERSITY OF MICHIGAN PRESS

2000   1999   1998   1997      4   3   2   1

*A CIP catalog record for this book is available from the British Library*

Library of Congress Cataloging-in-Publication Data

Sielke, Sabine, 1959–
     Fashioning the female subject : The intertextual networking of Dickinson,
     Moore, and Rich / Sabine Sielke.
          p.   cm.
     Includes bibliographical references and index.
     ISBN 0-472-10788-7 (alk. paper)
          1. American poetry—Women authors—History and criticism—Theory,
     etc.   2. Women and literature—United States—History—19th century.
     3. Women and literature—United States—History—20th century.
     4. Feminism and literature—United States—History.   5. Subjectivity
     in literature.   6. Women in literature.   7. Dickinson, Emily,
     1830–1886—Criticism and interpretation.   8. Moore, Marianne,
     1887–1972—Criticism and interpretation.   9. Rich, Adrienne Cecile—
     Criticism and interpretation.   10. Intertextuality.   I. Title.
     PS152.S54   1997
     811.009'9287—dc21                                              96-45813
                                                                         CIP

*In memory of my grandmother, Gertrud Rotschinski*

# Acknowledgments

Slimmed down and dressed up, this is the revised version of the Ph.D. thesis I submitted to the Fachbereich Neuere Fremdsprachliche Philologien of the Freie Universität Berlin in 1992. Like most books of this particular genre, this one would never have seen the light of day, if it were not for the people who have inspired me and who helped sustain that inspiration, be it by providing emotional, intellectual, or financial comfort. I therefore take this occasion to thank all those who, in one way or another, have been involved in this project. Among them I would like to mention a few.

I received generous funding through scholarships and research grants from the School of Criticism and Theory at Dartmouth College, the German Academic Exchange Service, Brandeis University, the Förderkommission Frauenstudien of the Senatsverwaltung für Arbeit und Frauen in Berlin, and the Freie Universität Berlin. To all of these institutions I owe much. The Rosenbach Museum and Library assisted my research with great care and concern. The John F. Kennedy–Institut für Nordamerikastudien has been my academic backbone (and more) for many years. I thank all of its members, and especially those who make its library what it is, for buttressing my work. My particular gratitude and respect belongs to Heinz Ickstadt for his engaging teaching, writing, and thinking, as well as his intellectual and personal charisma, and for his continuous faith in and support of my work. Evelyne Keitel has always had a miraculous sense of the right direction, and her advice in crucial intellectual and pragmatic matters has been invaluable. Allen Grossman's interest in my writing has been as genuine as his council and backing have been compelling and pivotal. Cristanne Miller has done much; reading more than one version of my manuscript and providing her poignant and productive commentary so generously, she has shaped this book significantly. Many dear friends have helped this project evolve, and I hope they know they're the ones "without whom nothing." In their stead I want to thank Michelle Walker, feminist philosopher and fellow sufferer, for sending the most compassionate and upbeat postcards from "down under"—lines that made many a day at the desk—and for being there in crucial moments.

To the friends and colleagues who have read various fragments of what came to be this book, I am indebted for all the intelligent and perceptive comments and suggestions as well as for the encouragement they have offered. I thank Michelle Walker, Eva Boesenberg, Denise Donnelly, and Farina Boltersdorf for attentive proofreading and Harold Veeser for night shifts of expert advice in matters of publication and publicity. My gratitude also belongs to LeAnn Fields, executive editor at the University of Michigan Press, and to Team X, for their much appreciated editorial advice and assistance. The bottom line of my thankfulness belongs to Edgar Muschketat, who is part of this book in ways that resist representation.

I gratefully acknowledge permission to reprint the following material: Emily Dickinson's poems, reprinted by permission of the publishers and the Trustees of Amherst College from *The Poems of Emily Dickinson,* Thomas H. Johnson ed., Cambridge, Mass.: The Belknap Press of Harvard University Press, Copyright © 1951, 1955, 1979, 1983 by the President and Fellows of Harvard College; and from *The Complete Poems of Emily Dickinson,* by T. H. Johnson, ed., Copyright © 1929, 1935 by Martha Dickinson Bianchi; copyright © renewed 1957, 1963 by Mary L. Hampson. By permission of Little, Brown and Company. Marianne Moore's poem "A Face," reprinted with the permission of Simon & Schuster from *The Collected Poems of Marianne Moore.* Copyright © 1951 by Marianne Moore, renewed 1979 by Lawrence E. Brinn and Louise Crane. Marianne Moore's poem "The Paper Nautilus," reprinted with the permission of Simon & Schuster from *The Collected Poems of Marianne Moore.* Copyright © 1941 by Marianne Moore, renewed 1969 by Marianne Moore. Unpublished material by Marianne Moore, used by permission of Marianne Craig Moore, Literary Executor for the Estate of Marianne Moore. All rights reserved. Anne Sexton's poem "Housewife," from *All My Pretty Ones,* Copyright © 1962 by Anne Sexton, Copyright © renewed 1990 by Linda G. Sexton. Reprinted by permission of Houghton Mifflin Co. All rights reserved. Quotations from the letters of Elizabeth Bishop are used here by permission of her Estate and Farrar, Straus & Giroux, book publishers. Copyright © 1996 by Alice Helen Methfessel. Excerpts from the letters of H.D. to Marianne Moore, Copyright © 1997 by Perdita Schaffner, used by permission of New Directions, agents. Excerpts from the letters of John Ashbery to Marianne Moore, reprinted by permission of John Ashbery. Excerpts from the letters of Louise Crane to Marianne Moore, reprinted by permission of Louise Crane.

# Contents

# Abbreviations

CPMM    *The Complete Poems of Marianne Moore* (New York: Viking, 1981)

J    refers to the Johnson edition of Emily Dickinson's poems (*The Poems of Emily Dickinson,* ed. Thomas H. Johnson, 3 vols. [Cambridge: Harvard University Press, 1955]) and is followed by the numbers Johnson assigned to the poems

L    refers to the Johnson and Ward edition of Dickinson's letters (*The Letters of Emily Dickinson,* ed. Thomas H. Johnson and Theodora Ward, 3 vols. [Cambridge: Harvard University Press, 1958]) and is followed by the numbers assigned to the letters

Rosenbach    refers to the materials located in the Moore Archives at the Rosenbach Museum and Library, Philadelphia

# Introduction

Just imagine, for a moment, that "Shakespeare's sisters" had a dinner party.[1] Emily Dickinson, Marianne Moore, and Adrienne Rich got together for one "Wild night" (J 249), at some place where, as Dickinson would have insisted, "Period exhaled" (J 1159). Dickinson finally left the house for some other than "her own Society" (J 303). Moore "c[a]me flying" from Brooklyn (Bishop, *Poems* 82). And Rich, excited to encounter her "foremother" Dickinson (*On Lies* 167) and with a strong "drive / to connect" (*Dream* 7), overcame her dislike of Moore's "fiddle" and formality (*CPMM* 266). Seated "Face to Face"— "starved, intense," "behind dry lips / a loaded gun" (Rich, *Necessities* 49)—what would, what could, they say to one another? On what issues would they agree; where would they connect and comprehend one another? Would there be open conflict or, rather, innumerable "Unsaid Word[s]" (Rich, *Change* 51)? And where would difference and silence begin?

"Women talk: men are silent: that is why I dread women," Thomas Wentworth Higginson recorded Dickinson saying (L 342a). She would have found Moore an unusually agreeable woman. "One is a pleasanter companion," Moore claimed, "if one does not interrupt each statement with an anecdote livelier than the one related. Brevity is an art; the best conversationalist is the best listener" (*Prose* 597). Recalling meeting Denise Levertov at a dinner party once, Moore reminisced: "Denise is a very good writer, I think . . . She is so urgent . . . and had so many urgent thoughts that it made the whole thing lively. I didn't say a word—I just listened, with all ears" (qtd. in Schulman, "Conversation" 163). And maybe both Dickinson and Moore would listen "all ears" to Rich's accounts of "the urgency of struggle for survival itself," which, according to Levertov, is a shared concern of all contemporary political poetry ("Edge" 167). In the habit of "taking into [her]self the language of experience different from [her] own—whether in written words or in the rush and ebb of broken but stubborn conversations" (*Doorframe* xvi), Rich would in turn be silenced by the laughter Dickinson and Moore were suspected to share, the "kind of humor . . . which is dependent on the quick perception of the local, the particular, the small which is frequently ignored by the Large, the Mighty, and Important" (Garrigue, "Notes" 55).

Undoing the limits of linear time, this fictive scenario provides plenty of food for fantasies about an "actual" encounter of the poets: Dickinson, "one of American literature's most expert poseurs," posing in white (Gilbert and Gubar, *Madwoman* 583); Moore, no less theatrical, yet more comfortable with companions other than her "Lexicon" (Dickinson, L 261), in dark suit, tricorn hat, and gloves in hand; and between them Rich, leisurely and an anachronism. None of them would care much for the menu, of course, for all knew well "how to starve" (J 690). Instead of repeating familiar myths, however, instead of projecting a "no-man's land" of female discourse (Gilbert and Gubar), I mean here to suggest another way of reading the poets' texts. Letting the poets "talk" to one another intertextually, I want to show how American women's poetry fashioned the female subject and how they evolved her historically as a negotiation of subjectivity, identity, and the body and as a process of past and present over the last 150 years.

Much has already been said and speculated about female subjectivity, and yet, for better or for worse, the concept has remained nebulous. Still, my argument can be based on three assumptions that literary theory and cultural criticism have made over the last decades. First, I take it that subjectivity is a position fashioned—or, to use the more fashionable term, constructed—in discourse. Second, I argue that this understanding applies particularly to female subjectivity, which historically, in life as in letters, has been denied existence or has been fashioned, and objectified, by others in order to ascertain their own subject position. And, third, I return to Nancy Miller's "working hypothesis," or metaphor, which assumes "the location of female subjectivity in female authorship" ("Changing" 107). Female subjectivity is a "question of authority" indeed (Miller).[2] In fact, it depends on authority, as I will argue, and not its denial.

Built on these hypotheses, my book unfolds the constructions of female subjectivity in the work of the three paradigmatic American poets Dickinson, Moore, and Rich and traces the historical transformations they have undergone since the middle of the nineteenth century. Such a project calls for a perspective that mediates a focus on lyric forms and fashions with both psychoanalytic approaches to poetic language and historical analysis. The path I have chosen is to involve the poets in dialogues with one another. Based on a Bakhtinian sense of the dialogic and Julia Kristeva's conception of intertextuality, my readings engage Dickinson with Moore (chap. 1), Moore with Rich (chap. 2), and Rich with Dickinson (chap. 3). Central to my argument about the development of female subjectivity is a revisionist perspective on poststructuralist theories of the subject that concentrates on the work of Kristeva, Luce Irigaray, and, to a lesser degree, Hélène Cixous. To my mind, this work continues to be important because it has acknowledged subjectivity as a position in language *and* recognizes the function of the material body in subject constitution. Moreover, it remains crucial because, despite all claims to the contrary, it enables historical analyses that have not yet been put into critical practice. This book is consequently both a rereading of American women's poetry and part of the revision of French feminist theory presently on its way.[3] Starring three "Foreign Lad[ies]" (J 593), our dinner party is consequently neither an intimate ménage à trois nor an "American triptych" (Wendy Martin) but, instead, a transatlantic affair.

Both American women's poetry and French feminist thought are, of course, more diverse than my choice of Dickinson, Moore, and Rich and my focus on Kristeva, Irigaray, and Cixous could ever suggest. Yet my choice is, of course, not an arbitrary one. Even though we can no longer argue the representativeness of a few canonical authors for particular moments in (literary) history, certain authors have become representative for our readings and representations of that history. Dickinson, Moore, and Rich are such authors. Not only does each of their names stand for a body of comparatively familiar, though fairly distinct, texts. They also embody noteworthy histories of reception. All of them have had a strong impact upon their audiences, whether they have been poets themselves, literary critics, or just readers of poetry. All of them are innovators of their own kind—so innovative, in fact, that Dickinson had to invent an alternative sense of publication, as Martha Nell Smith has convincingly argued;[4] that Moore's idiosyncracies excited as much as it infuriated her readers;[5] and that Rich, who started out highly aware of her modernist "family tree" (Auden, Foreword 10), has turned into *the* central figure of a radically feminist poetics. Most important for my reading, however, is that Dickinson and Moore, just like Rich, are innovators in matters of gender and subjectivity as much as in poetics. This is so, even if gender politics has not always been their primary agenda, or indeed, an agenda at all.

Engaging Dickinson's, Moore's, and Rich's lyric texts in dialogue with one another, my reading approaches female subjectivity through literary affiliations. In this way it necessarily reconsiders those lineages among American women poets that preoccupied early feminist literary criticism before poststructuralist theory provoked a renewed interest in modernist writing. In the female poetic tradition claimed during the 1970s and 1980s Dickinson was assigned the central position Whitman and Emerson have occupied within the traditional canon of American poetry and poetics.[6] Metamorphosed from "freak of the Valley" (K. Keller, "Notes" 75) to fierce female voice, the American woman poet whose work most obviously attests to the fragility and discontinuity of poetic utterance and identity, to the drama of self and subjectivity, became "a source of strength" (Juhasz, *Naked* 31) and a "foremother" to women readers and writers. Due to the new emphasis placed not on Dickinson's self-denials and renunciations but, rather, on her self-determination, she turned into the heroine of American women's poetry whose concerns seemed to reach all the way to contemporary women's texts.

By privileging content over poetic construction, "female experience" over formal experimentation, feminist revisions of the American poetic tradition have managed to draw a line from Dickinson's venturesome poetics to Rich's straightforward feminist politics. Such politically motivated readings have necessarily had to attune the dissonances within women's verse to harmony.[7] At the same time, it has downplayed the affiliation between Dickinson's and other modernist women poets' work. Due to a supposed "enigmatic self-effacement" (Van Dyne 468) and "fiddle" with form, modernist poetry by women—and Moore's work, in particular—has appeared a stumbling block on the way from Dickinson's premodernism to the political poetry of the postmodernist era.[8] As a consequence, the parallels between Dickinson's and Moore's work have for a long time received little attention, even though—or just because—New Criticism repeatedly associated the poets. Analogously, the scarcity of studies on Rich *and* Moore seems to testify to an incompatibility of High Modernist and contemporary political poetry. Mimicking both feminist and political poets' denials of their modernist aesthetic roots, feminist critics frequently dismissed the links between modernist and contemporary female poets. Women's texts that negotiate gender in more mediated, indirect manners and whose discontinuous discourse calls into question the very sense of continuity, coherence, and identity that feminist literary history was trying to establish were frequently excluded from that tradition.[9]

As the disruptiveness of modernist poetry called upon—and partly produced—poststructuralist modes of literary analysis, it became evident that feminist skepticism against modernist poetry was closely entangled with the resistance to theory that characterized much feminist analysis in its beginnings.[10] Once this resistance gave way, feminist critics turned to modernist poetry by women. Yet, while the feminist revision that the work of Moore, H.D., Mina Loy, and Gertrude Stein has been subjected to in the 1980s and 1990s has challenged our sense of American modernism as a whole, the few existing diachronic poststructuralist approaches to American women's poetry often made Dickinson or, less often, Moore the touchstone by which to measure contemporary political women's poetry (see Burke, "Supposed Persons" 134). And, while early feminist readings tended to iron out the stylistic unorthodoxies in women's modernist lyrics, deconstructive analyses have frequently surrendered when confronted with a poetics that is political in a more conventional sense. Thus, just as the concepts of a continuous female tradition and of the specific female self it seems to express have been founded on principles of exclusion, the revaluation of the negativity and subversiveness of women's writing could render yet another partial picture of the sense of subjectivity expressed in women's poetry.

I am by no means suggesting that we could ever derive a full picture. The fact that Dickinson's poetry, for instance, could be claimed by both feminist literary criticism and poststructuralist approaches, that her texts reflect an "integrated, transcendent sense of self" to one critic (Bennett 73), "a nineteenth century anticipation of possibilities for an *écriture féminine*" to another (C. Miller, *Dickinson* 184), proves that our readings manipulate textual ambiguities. Overdetermined as they are by our present (dis-) positions, questions, and concerns as well as by our (mis-) conceptions of the past, our readings cannot be anything but partial. My dialogues are necessarily triangulations. In some sense we do cherish our dinner party fantasy, creating for ourselves a space to fix literary figures in one place and time, if only for this imaginary moment. Aware of the fact that, as Bakhtin puts it, "the authors do not invite the literary critics to share the table at their banquet" (*Ästhetik* 349),[11] we authorize ourselves as masters of ceremonies. Our mastery, though, always depends upon the current fashions of our trade, even—or all the more so—if we distance ourselves from them.

Limited by my own partialities, what I intend to show by engaging the lyric texts in dialogue with one another and with French feminist theory is that Dickinson's, Moore's, and Rich's poetry is not simply divided, as it has seemed under both poststructuralist feminist and early feminist perspectives, between a subversive modernist aesthetics, on the one hand, and a direct political discourse, on the other. Reading the poets' texts dialogically, Dickinson, Moore, and Rich instead interrelate with one another but do so on three different, though interdependent, levels of textual practice. Dickinson and Moore share a passion for language and a concern with form whose predominant effect is not conformity but a transgression of discourse and a destabilization of the speaking subject. Moore and Rich, on the other hand, compare by the ways in which they interrogate matters of voice and reproduction. While their early texts use a high degree of quotation from other discourse and in this way fragment the traditional lyric voice and problematize women's exclusion from language, their later poems, in turn, explore the maternal as a realm of a possibly other female economy of discourse. Dickinson and Rich finally affiliate by a simultaneous attraction to and rejection of powers that are historically conceived of as patriarchal. Appropriating such powers of discourse and rhetoric, both poets engage in strategic constructions of subjectivity, in a poetic practice from which emerges a multiple, shifting sense of the subject, two entirely distinct versions of a subject-in-process.

By producing three distinct levels of affiliation, a dialogic approach to women's poetry underlines that neither the concept of a continuous female literary tradition nor that of a "feminine discourse" could render the complex relation between Dickinson's, Moore's, and Rich's texts. Instead, their affiliation presents itself as an *intertextual network,* a structure with spatial and temporal dimensions, with connections, reconnections, and parallels at some, disconnections and divergence at other, points. In such a configuration continuity becomes interconnection, hierarchy interrelation, progression interdependence—assets that characterize female subjectivity as well. Therefore, in addition to redefining our sense of affiliation among women poets, a dialogic analysis of Dickinson's, Moore's, and Rich's poetry has significant repercussions for the sense of self and subjectivity developed by feminist literary criticism and theory.

While feminist literary criticism has focused on the assertion of a female self in women's writing, poststructuralist feminist theory, by contrast, has foregrounded the constitution and, even more so, the subversion of subjectivity in language. Following Lacan, Kristeva describes the subject's entrance into the symbolic order "as a separation from a presumed state of nature, of pleasure fused with nature," a violent breaking away from identity that is "the common destiny of the two sexes, men and women" alike. Language constitutes, she claims, "an articulated network of differences, which refers to objects henceforth and only in this way separated from a subject, may constitute *meaning*" ("Women's Time" 23). At the same time, Kristeva's own sense of subjectivity as a dialectic process of the symbolic and the semiotic calls into question the Lacanian view that the subject constitutes himself by successfully suppressing the maternal body. More than that: defined as a heterogeneous flow of pre-oedipal energies and drives that re-traverse the symbolic, return in poetic language, and manifest themselves in syntactic disruptions, semantic inconsistencies, and "rhythmic constraints" (*La révolution* 210), Kristeva's conception of the semiotic revaluates the destabilizing elements of poetic language, or what she termed the *dispositif sémiotique du texte,* as a fundamental part of the processes of subjectivity.

In the early 1980s the juxtaposition of a "strong core of self" and a "subversion of the subject," which Jane Gallop identified as the fundamental difference between Anglo-American and French feminist perspectives, seemed to present two *alternative,* if not mutually exclusive, conceptions of subjectivity ("Psychoanalysis" 106). Since then these apparently incompatible conceptions of self and subjectivity have been put into historical perspectives. Nancy Miller, among others, has defended the supposedly naive feminist faith in the possibilities of a "true," or "full," female self. Women, she insists, never had an Enlightenment, never "had the same historical relation of identity to origin, institution, production, that men have had," never had a self to lose or to escape from. Due to the fact, she argues, that "the female subject has juridically been excluded from the polis, and hence decentered, 'disoriginated,' deinstitutionalized, etc., her relation to integrity and textuality, desire and authority, is structurally different" ("Changing" 106). Her texts may therefore subvert, claim, and reconstruct authority all at once.

In addition, this structural difference vis-à-vis "integrity and textuality, desire and authority" has changed over time as these concepts themselves, and women's positions, have changed. The constructions of female subjectivity produced here are necessarily dialogues between different historical moments. Aware of the limits of French feminist thought, I intend to explore a part of its historical potential that has frequently been passed over. Such enterprise needs, first of all, to reinterpret the supposed opposition between self and subjectivity as interdependence. Self and subjectivity are interrelated concepts in the sense that the "building of a 'strong core of self'" (Gallop, "Psychoanalysis" 106) requires a notion of subjectivity as both a place in language and a performative act. Or, to put it differently: only the insight that subjectivity is a position and performance in discourse allows one consciously to construct subject positions. Accordingly, the lyric texts lay claim to selfhood while at the same time acknowledging that any version of the self remains a projection, a construction, a subject-in-process. More than that, however, the textual analyses show that the concepts of subversive subjectivity and assertive selfhood can be related to two different yet interdependent and partly parallel historical processes: the crisis of the philosophical male subject, on the one hand, and the emergence of a historical female subject, on the other.[12]

Concerned with the fin de siècle subject-in-crisis, Kristeva's subject theory captures that historical moment in modern subjectivity at which the male philosophical subject had become increasingly destabilized. The frequent objection, on the part of feminist criticism, that, lacking a sense of female subjectivity, Kristeva's subject theory remains inadequate for feminist analyses is thus only partly to the point. Female subjectivity, after all, evolves in relation to male subjectivity, which itself is transformed in the process. In addition, Kristeva's sense of subject constitution and intertextuality offers a dynamic, transhistorical concept of subjectivity, text, and cultural context that allows us to conceptualize the intertextual and intersubjective affiliations between different authors' work and their designs of subjectivity. In order to account for a text's multiple, oftentimes contradictory, voices, the analytical focus would have to shift, however, from Kristeva's tendency to privilege the transgressive elements in discourse to an exploration of the dialogic interplay between the semiotic and the symbolic, between the deconstructive and (re-) constructive moments inherent in all textual practice.

Such a shift restores agency to Kristeva's sense of the text as a "mosaic of quotations" (Kristeva, "Word" 37) and of disruptions as a return of the body in language to a conception of discourse that "den[ies] the subject's ability to reflect on the social discourse and challenge its determination" (Alcoff 417) and diminishes the importance of a semantics of the (female) body. It allows us to show that language is "an instrument for changing subjectivity rather than accepted as a given medium" (Ross 76) and that "literary texts," as Evelyne Keitel puts it, "open possibilities which transgress those of theoretical texts" (166).[13] Literary practice has allowed women to claim subjectivity in the very act of writing and to challenge discourse and gender in the process. At the same time, due to cultural constraints of gender and discourse, the poets' designs of (female) subjectivity remain contingent upon cultural conventions of femininity. Dickinson's poem "Except to Heaven, she is nought" (J 154), for instance, acknowledges the limits of gendered subjectivity by projecting visions of women's identity into a realm "Nicknamed by God - / Eternity -" (J 453). Rich, who in contrast insisted that women need to repossess their bodies as "the grounds from which to speak with authority *as* women" (*Blood* 213), in her own poems eventually accepts the female body as a locus of silence and disempowerment.

Likewise, based on an awareness that women are "regarded as belonging necessarily to either of two classes—that of the intellectual freelance or that of the eternally sleeping beauty" (*Prose* 82), Moore's sense of female subjectivity accommodates such bias. Consider, for instance, her poem "To Be Liked by You Would Be a Calamity" (1916).

> "Attack is more piquant than concord," but when
> You tell me frankly that you would like to feel

My flesh beneath your feet
I'm all abroad—I can but put my weapon up and
 Bow you out
Gesticulation—it is half the language.
Let unsheathed gesticulation be the steel
Your courtesy must meet
Since in your hearing words are mute, which to my
 senses
Are a shout.

This disengendered, combative speaker clearly reflects Moore's favor for intel-
lectual freelancing. The single-mindedness gestured here becomes most evi-
dent, though, when we take the frame in which this poem first appeared into
account. Preceded by a piece on Samuel Butler, whose determination to write
as he pleases is praised by Moore, "To Be Liked by You" is trailed by Laura
Benet's poem "'She Wandered after Strange Gods . . .'" and Helen Hoyt's
"Remonstrance with Sleep." Conventional in form and diction, both of these
texts are—literally as well as figuratively—voiced by sleeping beauties. In
Benet's poem the female mourns the loss of a "fairy steed," a fairy-tale lover or
animus figure:

And there his wings they waved so bright
Before my eyes, I drooped and slept;
When I woke up it was dark night
I raised my voice and wept.

Hoyt's poem, in contrast, mourns the loss of precious time, that is, youth and
beauty in sleep: "Each night to step, to erase, to die; / Each night, hour after
hour to lie." Among such weeping women's voices Moore's voice is indeed, as
Pound puts it, a "mind cry, more than a heart cry" ("Moore and Loy" 46). As
such, it cannot help but reinforce the supposed binarism of heart and mind. At
the same time, however, it is also a shout, a call to arms, a rebel yell in a com-
bat against conventional—and conventionally engendered— categorizations.
 In this way the poets' various notions of female subjectivity circumscribe
what Teresa de Lauretis describes as a "subject in two senses of the term: both
subject-ed to social constraint and yet subject in the sense of the maker as well as
user of culture, intent on self-definition and self-determination" ("Feminist
Studies" 10). From a dialogic reading of Dickinson's, Moore's, and Rich's poetry,
female subjectivity therefore emerges as an ambivalence, as a variable position of
"in-betweenness" and double-voicedness.[14] This position is neither wholly

opposed to nor wholly reliant on the symbolic order but is, rather, a process that oscillates between a negation and deconstruction of conventions of discourse, subjectivity, and femininity, on the one hand, and their appropriation and reconstruction, on the other. This in-between position, I argue, is a fundamental aspect of female subjectivity. It gets reflected on various levels of the poets' texts; it recurs in the duality of Moore's and Rich's poems on the maternal, in Rich's and Dickinson's ambivalence toward power as well as in Dickinson's and Moore's restrained disruptive aesthetics. And, curiously enough, when Kristeva, in her analysis of syntactic deletions, borrows her terminology from Samuel R. Levin's article on compression in Dickinson and distinguishes the American poet from the French writers by the lesser "significance" of her elisions (*La révolution* 281), she herself implies such sense of in-betweenness, of reluctant radicalism.

A dialogic analysis, moreover, foregrounds that the difference between deconstructive and reconstructive writing practices is a difference within rather than between texts. It is a tension that structures each of the author's work, as it does individual poems, in specific ways. The texts therefore need to be distinguished by the degree to which one or the other tendency dominates and not upon whether they subvert the subject or center a self. From the late 1960s on Rich, for instance, has continuously attempted to locate and represent her own (speaking) position in a self-conscious "identity politics," or practice (de Lauretis, "Feminist Studies" 9).[15] Such a practice, however, does not attest to a "strong core of self" but, instead, defines identity as a process that constantly dismantles and reauthorizes the subject. Though Moore's idiosyncratic discourse destabilizes representation and subjectivity, the dazzling surfaces of her poems also, somewhat paradoxically, further the physical integrity of the female subject delineated in her texts. Dickinson, by comparison, evolved "Columnar Sel[ves]" (J 789) in highly fragmented lines and turned her visions of a supposedly whole identity located beyond subjectivity into the ultimate challenge of her disruptive aesthetics.

The following three dialogues thus illustrate that "the female voice," as Barbara Johnson aptly puts it, "may be universally described as divided, but it must be recognized as divided in a multitude of ways" (*World* 170). They, moreover, foreground that issues and representational forms of female subjectivity recur throughout history while also being constantly reshaped by the particular cultural contexts in which they are (re)produced. Never is female subjectivity a place apart from the so-called symbolic order, always a position of in-betweenness dependent upon *and* constitutive of cultural discourse. And neither the symbolic order nor female subjectivity has ever been a fixed entity. Instead, as women's position within culture has changed, the designs of female subjectivity in American women's poetry have changed. More specifically, the poets' double-voicedness is produced by the tension between the increasing destabilization of the male, philosophical subject and the emergence of a politically enfranchised female subject and its history. Accompanied by a subsequent loss of faith in institutions such as orthodox religion and marriage, the crisis of the subject manifests itself most evidently in the poetry of Dickinson and Moore. Their texts disrupt poetic discourse much more persistently than their male American contemporaries do and thus put the subject in process/on trial. At the same time, unlike their contemporaries Whitman and Williams, Dickinson and Moore do not abandon conventional formal patterns entirely. Adapting ballad meter and syllabic verse, Dickinson and Moore insist that female subjectivity requires structural authority. Becoming significant in Moore's work, the emergence of the female historical subject culminates in Rich's reconstructions of female subjectivity as a process in history. Central to this gradual inscription and authorization of the female subject is a successive revaluation of the female body.

Both the intertextual network among the poets and their sense of subjectivity can, to a certain degree, be framed by Kristeva's and Irigaray's poststructuralist subject theories. In the first chapter, "Emily Dickinson and Marianne Moore: Select Defects—Disrupted Discourse and the Body," I appropriate Kristeva's sense of the *sujet en procès* and her conception of the *dispositif sémiotique du texte* to investigate subjectivity as expressed in Dickinson's and Moore's modernist aesthetics and to redefine the poets' transgressive poetic designs as part of subject constitution processes. Both poets' texts display, for instance, what Kristeva has called a "fluctuation du sujet de l'énonciation," which "integrates" the three persons in charge of enunciation (*La révolution* 316). Projecting the first-person singular as "we," "ourself," "me," and "myself," Dickinson delineates the subject as multiple and fluent. Likewise, in Moore's poem "Poetry" (1919) the subject switches from an "I, too," that is, an "I" aligned with others, to a communal "we" and an unspecific "one" before disappearing in face of a "you," thus transforming from "I, too, dislike it" into "you are interested in poetry."

By adding a third term, be it an indefinite "one," the addressee of an apostrophic poem, or the double of the "I," Dickinson and Moore construct speaking positions, comparable to those Kristeva observes in Lautréamont's *Les Chants de Maldoror,* in fiction as well as in phantasms and psychic hallucinations. Only fiction, though, Kristeva argues, maintains the symbolic *and* creates a new matrix of enunciation. Occupying various instances of discourse at once, the subject is divided and multiplied, the selective and localizable subjectivity of normative language usage pulverized. At the same time, my own focus on the interdependence of disrupted discourse and female subjectivity raises questions that exceed Kristeva's theoretical framework—a theory that conceptualizes the crisis of the subject reflected in Dickinson's and Moore's deconstructive aesthetics yet fails to capture reconstructive elements indicating the emergence of a historical female subject. What, then, are the differences between the semiotic practice of the avant-garde writers Kristeva investigates and that of the female modernists, and in what ways are these differences gender related? How are we to interpret the conflict between a foregrounding of the corporeality of language and the renunciation or, respectively, deflection of matters of the body in Dickinson's and Moore's poetry? And if, in view of the fact that matters of the body materialize in discourse only in highly mediated ways, we resist reading poetic disruption as a return of the body in language, what exactly is the relation between poetic disruption, female body, and female subjectivity?

In Dickinson and Moore the tension between the crisis of the male subject and the emergence of a female subject surfaces as a textual practice that I want to call, with Cixous, a "working (in) the in-between" ("Medusa" 287). Dickinson and Moore neither adapt a traditional aesthetics nor take their deconstructive textual practice to Mallarméan extremes but, instead, mediate transgression with the construction of new kinds of authority. This difference shows in the degree to which they incorporate deconstructive elements and the particular functions Dickinson and Moore assign to them. Their poetry correlates an emphasis on discursive materiality with the figurative equivocations and displacements of matters of the (female) body in their texts. Aware that women's exclusion from the symbolic order has always been substantiated with reference to their biological difference, the poets like-mindedly reject traditional identifications of woman, body, and nature. Instead, they use poetic disruption both to escape (Dickinson) or disguise (Moore) the female body and to bring their powers of imagination and intellect to the fore. This aesthetics signifies a historical transition in the conception of female subjectivity, a transition due to the opening up of women's spheres and changing ideas about female sexuality.

The link between Moore and Rich (and their distance to Dickinson), by comparison, is based on two parallel textual practices: on the destabilization of poetic voice by means of quotation and the revalorization of the maternal. Chapter 2, entitled "Marianne Moore and Adrienne Rich. Daughters-in-Law or Outlaws?" conceptualizes this affiliation by way of Irigaray's writing. According to Irigaray, quotation and mimicry are deliberate though interim strategies through which women act out the function that they historically have

been assigned—that of reproduction—while at the same time ironically under-
mining the functions they expose. Moore's poem "Silence" exemplifies the
ways in which such mimicry works.


My father used to say,
"Superior people never make long visits,
have to be shown Longfellow's grave
or the glass flowers at Harvard.
Self-reliant like the cat—
that takes its prey to privacy,
the mouse's limp tail hanging like a shoelace from its mouth—
they sometimes enjoy solitude,
and can be robbed of speech
by speech which has delighted them.
The deepest feeling always shows itself in silence;
not in silence, but restraint."
Nor was he insincere in saying, "Make my house your inn."
Inns are not residences.

(Poems 82)

As a poem about self-reliance, "Silence" relates to Moore's poem "Peter"
(1924). Without a single quoted phrase "Peter" portrays an individualist (cat)
that does as he pleases. "Silence," by contrast, uses quotation to put forth an
understanding of self-reliance based upon restraint and lack of voice. As
Moore's notes indicate, the poem does not simply present a particular person's
view on life but lets the principles of one person, the father, be echoed by
another, the daughter.[16] Having the female be "robbed of speech / by speech"
of the father, the poem performs the very operation that imposes silence upon
women: mimicry. At the same time, the speech of the father is itself borrowed
from another. Preying upon James Prior's *Burke's Life* (1873), the father, unlike
the daughter, however, does not give credit to his source.

Cherishing the subversive potential of such textual travesties, we still have
to ask what exactly is being deconstructed, what is reinforced by Moore's and
Rich's mimic performances? In Rich's "Snapshots of a Daughter-in-Law," for
instance, woman's mimicry is less a subversive than a self-destructive force
whose effect gets reproduced among women as their communication gets dis-
placed by prefabricated misconceptions. The poem's third section depicts this
pattern in a portrait of "Two handsome women, gripped in argument,"

each proud, acute, subtle, I hear scream
across the cut glass and majolica
like Furies cornered from their prey:
The argument *ad feminam,* all the old knives
that have rusted in my back, I drive in yours,
*ma semblable, ma soeur!*

(Snapshots 22)

Delineating women as fighting furies, fussing animal-like ("prey") about sup-
posedly trivial matters, the passage echoes common associations of femininity
and hysteria, the latter being, itself, a form of mimicry. In the process, between
her first and second appearance, the lyric "I" switches positions; the spectator
comes to participate in the "argument *ad feminam,*" turns impersonator. As she
addresses another woman by adapting a fragment from Baudelaire's "Au
Lecteur," previously adapted by T. S. Eliot and Robert Lowell—a dialogue that
C. K. Williams picked up more recently[17]—the first-person speaker confirms
that neither her "words nor music are her own" (*Snapshots* 22). Attempting to
speak to women by way of a text that excludes them as speakers and listeners
alike, Rich's poem underscores that the effect of women's mimicry is not only
to parody and expose the dominant symbolic system but also to reinforce the
distance among women.

Woman's own voice, in contrast, may be retrieved, so Irigaray argues, by
reactivating the maternal economy, the matrix that underlies signification and
established power structures. Significantly enough, however, it is Moore and
not Rich whose poems on the maternal explore the floating discourse that Iri-
garay assigns to the female voice. Yet, while Moore's poem "The Paper Nau-
tilus," for instance, aligns creativity with procreation, nurture, and identity, it
lacks references to the female body and in fact echoes male fears of female
reproductive powers and female sexuality. Rich's poems, by comparison, make
it quite explicit that a new female self-conception requires, on the one hand,
the death of the mother. In her poem "The Mirror in Which Two Are Seen as
One" (1971), for instance, the mirror image of female identity emerges from the
mother's dead body through a process in which the newborn woman becomes
her own midwife.

your mother dead and you unborn
your two hands grasping your head
drawing it down against the blade of life

> your nerves the nerves of a midwife
> learning her trade
>
> (*Diving* 16)

Rich's collection *Dream of a Common Language* (1978), on the other hand, turns to the maternal body in order to ground in it a female voice and sexual identity. Pondering the realm of the unnameable, Rich soon comes up against the limits of language, though. The final lines of the collection's first poem, "Power" (1974), which assesses the achievements of the radiation scientist Marie Curie, in some sense reflects upon Rich's own admittedly much less dramatic and lethal position. Whereas Moore still considered Curie a figurehead of women's emancipation (*Prose* 678), Rich's poem concludes that

> She died    a famous woman    denying
> her wounds
> denying
> her wounds    came    from the same source as her power
>
> (*Dream* 3)

The poet, by comparison, will have to acknowledge that her power depends on language, that is, on structures that cut the connection with the silent maternal body. The question that consequently remains to be answered is twofold: How do the poets manage to reinscribe the maternal economy, a space that has traditionally served to justify women's exclusion from the contexts of cultural production? And how can a sense of subjectivity possibly be established upon a realm that precedes signification?

Kristeva and Irigaray take my reading of female subjectivity a certain way. The poetic texts in turn imply that French feminist theories of subject formation are not as ahistorical as has commonly been assumed. Instead, Kristeva and Irigaray turn out to provide theoretical and methodological perspectives on distinct historical moments within the development of poetic designs of female subjectivity. Due to their basic Lacanian premise of woman's exclusion from the symbolic order, however, neither Kristeva's notion of the subject-in-process/on trial nor Irigaray's sense of the female between mimicry and maternal voice can account for the historical transformations the poetic designs of female subjectivity have undergone. The transformation of Irigaray's own perspective, however, which moved from an earlier faith in the subversive force of mimicry and the postulate of an "other" maternal discourse to an ethics of gender-differentiated legislation serves to describe the shift within Moore's and Rich's work. Whereas Dickinson's writing consistently rejects the maternal and "mother figures" (such as "Mother Nature"), Rich's and Moore's work moves from a practice of mimicry to symbolic explorations of the maternal that need to be distinguished in poetics and perception of the female body. Only Rich follows Irigaray's third step, her claim to a "legitimate" female subjectivity. By defining the female body as a fundament of female subjectivity, as a difference within the symbolic order, the focus of Rich's feminist poetry in particular, like that of Irigaray's theory, has shifted from an exploration of female difference to a reinscription of this difference into cultural discourse. Irigaray, however, has come to argue the case for gender-related (legal) laws, while Rich's more recent poetry rewrites female subjectivity as a process in history that mediates a "living memory" (*Time's Power* 46) of one's own and other women's past with a "power to forget" (Dickinson, J 1464). The lyric texts consequently suggest that the theory be revised.

What French feminist theory lacks, indeed, is a sense of the position of the female subject as an agent of history. It is this concern that simultaneously aligns and distances Rich and Dickinson and locates a blind spot in feminist theory itself. Lacking an approach that accounts for the affiliation of Dickinson and Rich, I derive this theoretical position from the dialogues between the poets themselves and from Rich's writing in particular. For Rich, as I argue in the third chapter, "Adrienne Rich and Emily Dickinson: From Absence to Feminist Transcendence—Female Subjectivity as Process in History," takes a significant and so far unacknowledged part in poststructuralist feminist theory, not necessarily by what she advocates rhetorically but, rather, by what her poetry and prose practice. Both Rich's and Dickinson's poems claim subjectivity by rhetorically dismissing their paternal heritage and privileging an other, a female tradition, the shape and temporality of which they themselves imagine, though rather differently. At the same time, both poets acknowledge that their own designs of (female) subjectivity cannot be but inextricably entangled within and thus reproduce their particular cultural contexts—or, to put it differently: that to some degree all speech is mimicry. In Dickinson's poem "I'm Ceded—I've stopped being Theirs—" (J 508), for instance, the speaker rejects her ("Crowing") religious background and inherited birthright and claims a second "Adequate—Erect" identity. Choosing "just a Crown," she establishes that new sense of self *on* her own terms, though *with* terms whose Calvinist connotations seem to exceed the very cultural conformity she means to dismiss. Similarly, the poem "I am ashamed—I hide—" (J 473) erects a sense of superior subjectivity upon the posture of the bride.

Fashion My Spirit quaint—white—
Quick—like a Liquor—
Gay—like Light—
Bring Me my best Pride—
No more ashamed—
No more to hide—
Meek—let it be—too proud—for Pride—
Baptized—this Day—A Bride—

Adopting "Far Fashions—Fair—" "as Feudal Ladies wore—," using this or that "Trinket—to make [her] beautiful" yet keeping her ironic distance, this speaker appropriates conventional costumes to come out "No more ashamed— / No more to hide—."

In this way Dickinson from early on, as Rich will eventually come to do, recognizes subjectivity and history as constructs and rhetorical strategies, as ongoing and open-ended processes based on appropriations and transformations of concepts, terms, and "dress codes" fundamental to the culture one is engaged in. Both poets have their speakers change costumes frequently and thus engage in a literary practice that projects the subject as a subject-in-process. The processes their subjects go through are quite distinct, though. Dickinson appropriates dominant cultural rhetoric to invest it with new meanings. This enables her to act symbolically, to perform a variety of conflicting postures unattainable in "real life" experience as symbolic acts, instead.[18] Rich, in contrast, uses her insight into the fictionality of language constantly to revise and rewrite female subjectivity and her own self-image from her ever-changing political positions.

Part of Rich's strategy is to construct her own identity and history by engaging with other women's texts, and Dickinson has played a major part in her dialogic identity practice. In fact, Dickinson's texts have served Rich as a kind of matrix, a ground against which she projected her own poetic figures. Aligning Dickinson's work with particular stages of her own, Rich makes her personal history frame her analysis. In this way the process of reading an other does not only engage Rich with another woman's work. It involves a constant revision that forces her to put her own poetic and political development into historical perspectives. Reinscribing the female subject as a process between past and present, she comes to accept the fragmentation of subjectivity in history. As she continues striving to "piece together" the "still-fragmented parts" in herself (Blood 176), to achieve identity in time, if necessary by acts of forgetting, Rich's poetry constitutes a feminist practice that insists upon its ethical responsibility and highly moralistic stance. This implies a revision, a retheorization, of the concept of female subjectivity that has been waiting to be explored. Fashioning the female subject is an act of making, shaping, and molding, a matter of personal styles and predilections that is never independent, though, from prevailing customs, from "Far Fashions—Fair—" and from latest fads. And part of female subjectivity as fashioned by Dickinson, Moore, and Rich is a feast indeed.

# Emily Dickinson and Marianne Moore: Select Defects—Disrupted Discourse and the Body

The great modernisms were . . . predicated on the invention
of a personal, private style, as unmistakable as your finger-
print, as incomparable as your own body.
                                            — Fredric Jameson

"Soto! Explore thyself!" reads one of Dickinson's poems written in 1864, "Therein thyself shalt find / The 'Undiscovered Continent'—No Settler had the Mind." (J 832). The self, this "undiscovered continent" is central to Dickinson's mind, making much of her poetry, as Roland Hagenbüchle convincingly argues, "a sort of 'phenomenological reduction.'" As she "bracket[s] reality," Hagenbüchle observed, "the poet does not try to account for *what* appears, but *how* it appears and affects the mind. Instead of focusing on the world of objects, she concentrates on consciousness as such" ("Precision and Indeterminacy" 34).[1] Moore's poetry, in contrast, is marked with what Geoffrey Hartman reads as "an extreme reverence for created things coupled with an extreme distrust of the self" (111). Preoccupied with animate or inanimate objects, multifaceted surface structures, and freewheeling images, her poems prompt comparisons to "overstuffed cupboards, full of irrelevancies and distractions" (Costello, "Feminine Language" 223). For many of her readers Moore's poetry has not been a place where the self is openly encountered but, rather, "a selfless assertion of the self" (Hartman 111).

Despite their distinct perspectives on the relation between self and world, between subject and object, the poets have been associated with each other for a variety of reasons, be it the notion that both were "incontrovertibly American" (Gifford 173) or the more dubious sensation that both women "looked like" their verse (Gregor 151). Most frequently, critics pointed to their similarly unorthodox poetics. Like Dickinson's poetry, which Higginson found "wayward and unconventional in the last degree" ("Portfolio" 26), Moore's texts represented a "break through all preconceptions of poetic form and mood and pace, a flaw, a break in the bowl" (Williams, "Moore" 52). Yet, to my mind, Jean Garrigue captured the poets' relationship most poignantly. "Both," she wrote, "have the laconic abruptness of decisive daring." She found "[a]n asceticism in each," "rectitudes of being," and "a trenchant authority with language." Both "have," she claimed, "no conventional smoothness, sweetness, sleekness," "are startlingly original," and

> wrote what bursts the seams of the poem with thought. Both with a penchant for the pith of the brief, the grief, the quick, the wit. For each—no threadbare questions, let alone answers. . . . The modesties of both—or their restraint—more powerful than, more suggestive of undying intensities than any forthright ex-pressing, con-fessing of them. Both alike in that they are prone to enigmatical brilliances, audacious impertinences and leaps of wit. ("Notes" 52–57)

I quote at length here because, more than anyone else (before Joanne Feit Diehl), Garrigue appreciated the reluctant radicalism common to both Dickinson's and Moore's poetics and personality. For both poets silence and certitude are equally impossible. For both writing was an act of "decisive daring" and rectitude as well as restraint; it afforded authority and "enigmatical brilliance" at once. "Working (in) the in-between," both poets are radicals with restrictions. What Garrigue sensed, but did not theorize, is that both their radicalism and their restraint are gender-related strategies and not, as some of their readers assumed, defects dependent on a biological lack. At the same time, their writing reflects a sense of subjectivity that is highly ambivalent toward matters of the female body. Taking off from a Kristevan reconsideration of Dickinson's and Moore's disrupted discourse, I will, in the following, explore the ways in which their radical modernist aesthetics signifies the crisis of the male subject, interrogates dominant representations of the female body and the female *as* body, and contributes to the construction of the newly emerging female subject. Both poets projected this subject as a third way, or a "third event," as Dickinson has it in one of her last poems (J 1732), a somewhat disengendered or in-between subject that, due to the poets' historical distance, comes in two rather different designs.

## Reading Disruption

As part of women's texts, transgressive forms and figures have for a long time been ascribed to the author's ignorance of appropriate technique, her incapability to assert control over feelings and material, or, as in Moore's case, an overkill of, an excessive zeal for, control that eventually turns into its opposite. Moore's syllabic verse patterns and the idiosyncracy of her diction and punctuation, her contrapuntal rhythms and curious enjambments, were frequently depicted as mere marks of obscure mind games. Dickinson's texts, in contrast—cryptic, compressed, and with little concern for conventions of grammar and genre— were subjected to criticism and censorship. Practicing what Mabel Loomis Todd called "creative editing" (Franklin 23), Dickinson's first editors did what could be done to accommodate Dickinson's violations of poetic decorum and to please stylebook and reader alike. Still, critics complained. "There is hardly a line in the entire volume, and certainly not a stanza," Arlo Bates wrote in 1890, "which cannot be objected to upon the score of technical imperfection" (12–13). An anonymous critic found "no words that can say how bad poetry may be when it is divorced from meaning, from music, from grammar, from rhyme; in brief, from articulate and intelligible speech" ("The Newest Poet" 27). Yet another felt that "after reading two volumes of Miss Dickinson's verse one gets exhausted, and a healthy mind begins to fear paralysis" ("Recent Poetry" 50). In 1925 Harold Monro called Dickinson "intellectually blind, partially deaf, mostly dumb, to the art of poetry" (121). And Allen Tate simply claimed that she "cannot reason at all" (87).[2]

Reviewing Todd's 1931 edition of Dickinson's letters, Moore herself opposes the ambitious attempts of "'so enabled a man' as the twentieth-century critic" to reveal "Dickinson's notable secret" and, instead, opts for a more sophisticated reader who cherishes the "frankness" of her precursor's textual transgressions. "The self-concealing pronoun . . . independence of the subjunctive, and many another select defect," she claims, "are, for the select critic, attractions" (*Prose* 292). Many of Moore's own critics were not select enough to be attracted to her experimental work, as it appeared from 1915 on in avant-garde magazines such as *Poetry, Others,* and *The Egoist.* At a time when anything original seemed welcome, Moore herself felt "a pariah" ("Art" 29). Her early work, these "curiously wrought patterns" and "quaint turns of thought," as H.D. put it in 1916 ("Moore" 118), were frequently dismissed as the work of "a poet too sternly controlled by a stiffly geometrical intellectuality" (Monroe 213), as intellectual poetry that, according to Margaret Anderson, "is NOT

POETRY" (187). In retrospect, Anderson favored Eliot, who "uses his mind to reveal the life of his emotions," over Moore, who "uses the life of her mind as her subject-matter" (187). Along similar lines Mark Van Doren's review essay "Women of Wit" objected that Moore, Edna St. Vincent Millay, and Anne Wickham, who, "lack[ing] contracted marriages with wit, have committed themselves to careers of brains." Marion Strobel, associate editor of *Poetry,* "would rather not follow the contortions of Miss Moore's well-developed mind" (Monroe 210). And even Pound, who appreciated Moore's work from the very beginning, claimed that, like Loy's poetry, Moore's "would drive numerous not wholly unintelligent readers into a fury of rage-out-of-puzzlement" ("Moore and Loy" 58)—a statement deleted in Charles Tomlinson's edition of critical essays on Moore.

For both Dickinson and Moore the list of such commentary can be easily extended. These examples, however, suffice to suggest that the critics were biased against their gender just as against the radicalism of the poets' art. Dickinson's apparently "uncontrolled" forms seem to prove that women lack the intellectual capability to write; that, after all, "woman," as John Crowe Ransom put it in his essay on Millay, "lives for love" (*World's Body* 77). More than that, many a critic took Dickinson's transgressive aesthetics as a symptom of psychic disorder.[3] Moore's critics, conversely, do not only confirm that "too stern an intellectual emphasis on this quality or that / detracts from one's enjoyment" (Moore, *CPMM* 48). They also suggest that too much mental control and "fiddle" with form masculinizes femininity. Bryher, for instance, found "the spirit" of Moore's work too "robust, that of a man with facts and countries to discover and not that of a woman sewing at tapestries" (qtd. in Monroe 209). It was not women's writing as such that irritated the critics but the fact that their writing attacked the conventions and constraints of gender and genre, producing, instead, new and bolder notions of (female) subjectivity.

Yet how do poetic disruption and the construction of subjectivity relate in the first place? While neither Russian formalism and New Criticism nor Anglo-American feminist criticism pondered this question,[4] Kristeva did, though with little concern for women's writing. Equipped with a heritage of formalism, Marxism, linguistics, structuralism, and Lacanian psychoanalysis, she developed a theory of poetic language that reads ruptures in discourse neither as pure aesthetic effects nor as reflections of role conflicts but, rather, as traces of the processes of subject constitution and as subversions of the symbolic order. Focused on the textual practice of nineteenth-century post-symbolist avant-garde writers, her book *La révolution du langage poétique* (1974) mediates a political interpretation of poetic disruptions with a psychoanalytic conception of the subject as a dialectical process of the semiotic and the symbolic. Constituted by dominant, syntactically structured discourse and by social institutions that inscribe paternal law and cultural constraints, the symbolic provides a kind of scaffolding for the subject. The semiotic, in contrast, consists of a heterogeneous flow of preoedipal energies, drives, and rhythms, originating from what Kristeva termed the semiotic chora and from the dyadic phase, in which subject and maternal body are still united. As a kind of "pre-symbolic signification" and feminine force, she argues, these energies traverse the symbolic, return in language and manifest themselves in syntactic disruptions and semantic incoherences. Moving at the margins of discourse, the semiotic foregrounds the heterogeneity and materiality of a text while destabilizing its meaning. Due to this return of the body in language, the subject can no longer be understood as a fixed entity. It has turned into a subject-in-process and on trial ("mise en procès").

The signifying practice that most radically reactivates the semiotic, Kristeva claims, is poetic language, represented by the heterogeneous textual practice of fin de siècle literature as well as Joyce's stream-of-consciousness techniques. In Mallarmé's and Lautréamont's texts the semiotic crosses the morphonemic level, its syntax and composition, enunciations and intertextual context, thus changing the status of the subject and exploring the very operations of its constitution. Redistributing syntax and pulverizing meaning and subjectivity, this *dispositif sémiotique* of avant-garde texts subverts the symbolic order.[5] Viewed in its particular cultural context, the crisis of the subject delineated in Mallarmé's and Lautréamont's texts, Kristeva concludes, marks a resistance against the bourgeoisie under the Third Republic as well as the continuous development of industrialization, consumerism, imperialism, and chauvinism and reflects a general crisis of capitalist economy and religion. In this way, it follows, "an atomized subjectivity . . . is the motor of practice and therefore of social transformation and revolution" (Coward and Ellis 146). My reading of the poems "One need not be a Chamber—to be Haunted—" (J 670) and "People's Surroundings" shows that it is first of all this kind of cultural crisis, and not female subjectivity, that drives Dickinson's and Moore's texts—a crisis that their male contemporaries attempted to master in rather different ways.

## Dickinson's and Moore's Semiotic Textual Practice

"Poetry . . . is an assertion," Moore copied from a 1919 review by Williams. "The poet must use anything at hand to assert himself . . . . The proof that I am

I is that I can use anything, not a special formula but anything. That is the first necessity" ("Foreigners" 38). Moore may have shared Williams's notion of the function of poetry. His sense of self-assertion, which reformulates the Cartesian "I think, therefore I am" as "I am I, because I use anything," is foreign to her. The use Moore's poems make of "people's surroundings" hardly ever proves the identity of the speaker. In contrast to Williams's formula "'I' plus anything equals subject," Moore's attempts "to cope with the perceived world's multifarious otherness" (Kenner 114) led to a proliferation of objects, which destabilizes subjectivity.

In her writing indefinite subjects such as "one," "people," "we," "they," or a proverbial "you" predominate. The speaking subject rarely takes a stable position. Often Moore's poetry provides the subject only a "partial" presence, rendered by a possessive pronoun, an imperative, or an apostrophic address.[6] By investing another with a voice, these poems do not, however, silence but, in fact, authorize the speaker. As a turn aside from speech that evokes poetic presence, their speakers introduce a third term that works "less to establish an I-Thou relation . . . than to dramatize or constitute an image of self" (Culler, *Pursuit* 142). Moore's intentional avoidances of self-centeredness thus cannot help but revolve around matters of subjectivity while at the same time fragmenting the subject. Such fragmentations distinguish Moore's from Whitman's catalogue poems, to which they have often been compared. Unlike Whitman, Moore does not subsume multiplicity under one central though supposedly collective consciousness, as the final lines of "People's Surroundings" exemplify.

> there is neither up nor down to it;
> we see the exterior and the fundamental structure—
> captains of armies, cooks, carpenters,
> cutlers, gamesters, surgeons and armourers,
> lapidaries, silkmen, glovers, fiddlers and ballad-singers,
> sextons of churches, dyers of black cloth, hostlers and chimney-
>     sweeps,
> queens, countesses, ladies, emperors, travellers and mariners,
> dukes, princes and gentlemen,
> in their respective places—
> camps, forges and battlefields,
> conventions, oratories and wardrobes,
> dens, deserts, railway stations, asylums and places where
>     engines are made,

shops, prisons, brickyards and altars of churches—
in magnificent places clean and decent,
castles, palaces, dining-halls, theatres and imperial audience-
    chambers.

*(Conversations* 68)

Moore neither "sings" herself nor identifies with any of the figures she presents. Whereas Whitman features persons in harmony with their work, actions, and positions, Moore's text separates people from places, alienates subjects from objects.

Dickinson's speakers, in contrast, embody the figures, inhabit the places, and take the positions Moore was to depict from a distance. Her poems feature queens and ladies, carpenters and surgeons, travelers and mariners, inmates of prisons and asylums, residents of palaces and chambers. Like Whitman, Dickinson thus projects a multitude of positions, though with no attempt to unify diversity, to dissolve subordination. Figuring dukes, kings, and queens just as beggars, housewives, and daisies, Dickinson's verse delineates various psychic and physical states—conditions that are rarely stable but, rather, subjected to sudden changes. Dickinson's "Delinquent Palaces" (J 959) are conquered in one moment, lost in the next. "High" and "low" spirits, gains and losses, pains and powers are dynamic processes within a wide-ranging consciousness. Closer to Moore than to her "disgraceful" contemporary Whitman (L 261), Dickinson dispenses with notions of unity and center and presents pieces of a puzzle, which never form a full picture, partial portraits, which burst the frame and leave the fringes.

> One need not be a Chamber—to be Haunted—
> One need not be a House—
> The Brain has Corridors—surpassing
> Material Place—
>
> Far safer, of a Midnight Meeting
> Exernal Ghost
> Than it's interior Confronting—
> That Cooler Host.
>
> Far safer, through an Abbey gallop,
> The Stones a'chase—
> Than Unarmed, one's a'self encounter—
> In lonesome Place—

Ourself behind ourself, concealed—
Should startle most—
Assassin hid in our Apartment
Be Horror's least.

The Body—borrows a Revolver—
He bolts the Door—
O'erlooking a superior spectre—
Or More—

Like Moore's poems, this text displays a sense of subjectivity that is all but
"one." While using the lyric "I" much more frequently than Moore, Dickin-
son's representations of the first person delineate the subject as divided and
multiple. Though the subject is inseparable from its own other (J 642), this
other can be both friend or foe (J 683). "Horror's most," so to speak, happens
when, deprived of faith and certainty, "one's a'self encounter[s]." Dickinson's
use of the unorthodox reflexive pronoun *ourself* expands conventional gram-
mar to represent multiplicity ("our") in oneness ("self"). Repetitions of pro-
nouns ("ourself behind ourself, concealed") stretch the limits of language and
"cause difference to emerge from sameness" (Homans 211). More explicitly
than Moore, Dickinson thus identifies the crisis of the subject as a crisis of rep-
resentation, a moment at which language fails. Or, as Dahlen puts it: "'Our-
self behind ourself, concealed—' [is] the I and its double, another, the ghost
which begins to haunt literature in the middle of the last century, that ghost
which is the paranoid double of the ego, an omen of silence, of death" (11).
The poem's final lines indicate, though, that silence and death are not the end
of the story. Transgressions of conventional representation and physical exis-
tence "surpass . . . / Material Place" and open "a superior spectre— / Or
More—!" Dickinson does not dismiss the notion of identity. She projects it
beyond the poem's final line, beyond signification, into the white silence that
follows the last hyphen.

In addition to the "fluctuations of the subject of enunciation" I have
described in the introduction, subjectivity is compromised by ruptured syntac-
tical structures among which Kristeva, drawing on generative grammar, distin-
guishes two kinds. Recoverable—that is, suppressions of syntax that, like appo-
sitions, ellipses, passive transformations, and nominalizations—can be retrieved
through an analysis of a text's deep structure, produce a surplus of syntax, that
results in ambiguity and polysemy. Nonrecoverable deletions, in contrast, can-
not be reconstituted, because they modify deep structure and thereby rupture

the linearity indispensable to predication. In nonrecoverable deletions, Kristeva argues, processes of transposition and condensation, which usually complement contiguity, tend to reestablish presyntactic semiotic operations. Like the accumulation of sounds, they immerse the speaking subject in the semiotic chora. The effects of both kinds of deletion nonetheless compare: they constitute masked predication, lack of linear syntax, and a tendency toward spatialization. In Mallarmé's most experimental poem, "Un coup de dés," for instance, the noun predominates verb forms, the verb gets dissimulated into participles and present-tense forms, or, as in the case of *être,* frequently deleted by numerous transformations of nominalization. Destabilizing the subject by a suprasyntactic sense and new rhythms, such texts, according to Kristeva, liberate pleasure.

Many of Moore's poems display the kind of nominal style Kristeva observed in Mallarmé. The "squadrons of nouns in series" that "march" through Moore's poetry (Borroff 99) and its tendency toward spatialization displace copula and verb by passive transformations, participles, infinitive constructions, and gerunds, by a "coupling of nouns with adjectives or participles, without benefit of finite verbs or copulas" (121).[7] Since predication negotiates the relation between subject and object and, as has been argued, thus takes the same function as the phallus (Homans, *Bearing the Word* 7), its deletion or destabilization shakes the very grounds of subject constitution. This, however, does not necessarily liberate pleasure, Bishop suggests in a 1940 letter: "I have that continuous uncomfortable feeling of 'things' in the head," she wrote, "like icebergs or rocks or awkwardly shaped pieces of furniture—it's as if all the nouns were there but the verbs were lacking—if you know what I mean" (qtd. in Kalstone, *Becoming a Poet* 76).

Like Moore, Dickinson destabilizes the subject by unorthodox treatment of the verbal function and tense markers. "One need not be a Chamber—to be Haunted—" reflects the poet's favor for continuous forms ("surpassing," "Confronting," "Meeting," "O'erlooking"), which underscore present and process and signify acts while masking agency. The second stanza deletes the predication and equivocates the grammatical subject; the third omits the latter. Most noteworthy, however, has been Dickinson's predilection for uninflected verbs and the "independence" of her subjunctives, a long-obsolete mode that renders mood, tense, person, and subject-object relations indefinite and tends to dominate poems concerned with Dickinson's "Flood subject," immortality (L 319).[8] Depending on their context, these verb forms read as subjunctives, imperatives, or, assuming that auxiliaries were ellided, indicatives or forms of future tense. In the phrase "Be Horror's least," for instance, the auxiliary *would* could have been deleted in order to make the statement less conditional and to add a taste of timelessness to the scene.

As Moore dispensed with "the syntactic lubricants that slide us past a comparison" (Kenner 101), "despised connectives" (Williams, "Moore" 54), Dickinson frequently displaced syntactical coordination by contiguity. The second line of her chamber poem, for example, refrains from repeating the phrase "to be Haunted" and thus establishes the poem's oscillating line lengths, which align contraction with loss of signification, though, in this case, without severe damage to the poem's meaning. Erasing connectives and conjunctions, her poems frequently put clauses and phrases into indefinite relations. Missing pronouns in subject and object position, as in "'Tis Opposites—entice" (J 355); ambivalent references of preposition, as in "The Battle fought between the Soul" (J 594) or "The Soul unto itself" (J 683); and minor words, such as *to, of, as,* and *than,* add to the heterogeneity of Dickinson's texts. In addition, the second stanza of "One need not be a Chamber" uses an archaic form ("of a") to suggest that it is "Far safer meeting an External Ghost at Midnight." Inversion serves the rhyme scheme here and equivocates reference. Intensified by unorthodox punctuation (e.g., the apostrophe after *a*) and use of the dash—an earlier version fragments the text by no less than twenty-eight dashes—the overall effect of such strategies is discontinuity. For Dickinson "Cleaving[s] in [the] Mind" (J 937) translate into cleavings in the text.

In sum, one can say that Dickinson's and Moore's aesthetics and the *dispositif sémiotique* of avant-garde writing display significant similarities. Like Mallarmé—whom Moore, by the way, aligned with Dickinson[9]—Dickinson and Moore delete rather than dilute and frequently omit syntactical elements, conjunctions, copula, and verb forms. Moore's poems, in particular, tend strongly toward nominalization. In both poets' texts the reader finds the subject of enunciation fluctuating. Conventions of traditional meter, rhyme, and stanza form get compromised, as in Dickinson, or, as goes for Moore's syllabics, displaced by forms that do not correspond to the conventions of English verse at all. In addition, Dickinson as well as Moore, like Mallarmé, assign meaning to the typographic and visual appearance of their poems. On their own particular terms, but with strategies comparable to those of the avant-garde writers, Dickinson and Moore destabilize syntactic linearity, semantic coherence, and referentiality. They challenge conventional assumptions of poetic authority, representation, and meaning as such. They create spaces of signification excluded by orthodox rules of grammar and prosody and in various ways affect the representation of the subject in writing, marking it as troubled, divided, and scattered rather than unified.

While the destabilization and fragmentation of subjectivity characterizes avant-garde texts and modern American (women's) poetry alike, there are decisive differences between (Kristeva's reading of) the avant-garde texts and Dickinson's and Moore's poetry as well as within these two women's work. To my mind, Dickinson's and Moore's texts attest to the crisis of male subjectivity and mark the emergence of the female subject, though in undoubtedly distinct ways. An analysis of the particular function poetic disruptions take in such texts, however, evade Kristeva's theory, which "tends to halt at the point where the subject has been fractured and thrown into contradiction" (Eagleton 191). It rests soundly on the binarisms of male and female, order and chaos, speech and silence, body and mind, binarisms reinforced by her analysis of texts that immerse male speakers in female otherness. We look in vain for a concept of female subjectivity in Kristeva's work. Associating textual disruption, primary processes, and the maternal body, her work has tended to reduce femininity to the status of a reading effect, to collapse it with modernity, and to drop women out of the picture altogether.[10] Like Lacan and Derrida, she has repeatedly claimed that woman, defined as "something above and beyond nomenclatures and ideologies" and thus particularly dependent on the law ("Woman Can Never" 137), exists in her function as mother, as support of transcendence, and effect of the symbolic only yet never as a subject in and of discourse. Due to their particular relation to the maternal, women may touch upon borderline experiences in language. Discussing experimental women writers, Kristeva concentrates, however, not so much on the authors' work but on their lives and, most particularly, on the self-inflicted loss of their lives. In fact, Kristeva reads the suicides of Virginia Woolf, Marina Tsvetayeva, and Sylvia Plath as inevitable consequences of their unorthodox textual practice. When woman follows the maternal call, indulges in the semiotic, she subverts her only guarantee, the symbolic order. Without paternal law only her death drive prevails (*Die Chinesin* 269–72). Avoiding to identify woman explicitly with the semiotic, Kristeva allows woman no other place but otherness. Dickinson and Moore, by contrast, began to make room for her in the discourses of subjectivity.

## Rereading the Semiotic: Poetic Disruption and Gender Difference

Due to the conventional sexual binarism upon which Kristeva's subject theory is built, her sense of subjectivity could not simply be transferred into discussions of women's modernist writing, which tend to intertwine deconstructive processes with constructions of female subjectivity. This shows, for instance, in the self-assertions of Dickinson's and Moore's speakers, which, despite the fact that the poets associate otherness with femininity, are usually not carried out at the expense of female figures. Characterized by a "judgmental rhetoric" (Holley 26) ranging from high praise and a sense of indebtedness to uncompromising accusation and rejection, Moore's apostrophic poems turn first and foremost toward and against male addressees. Likewise, in Dickinson's poems figures and phenomena that constitute or threaten the speaking subject are usually imagined as male. Frequently, the position of the other is taken by a "mythical 'you'" (Hagenbüchle, *Dickinson* v), substituted by *it, he, me,* and *they* or by a third-person pronoun that projects a powerful male other of multiple identities, ranging from the fairytale prince of heterosexual romance to various personifications of patriarchy and uncanny phenomena such as death. Accordingly, the other in "One need not be a Chamber," figured as "Body," is referred to as "He."

Furthermore, Dickinson and Moore question Kristeva's claim that deconstruction of syntax and subjectivity correlates with the crisis of the ontological and historical subject and of political, economic, and social orders. In their poetry destabilized syntax and fluctuating subject positions do not necessarily correspond to the collapse of social hierarchies. The universe of Dickinson's poetry, in which dukes, kings, and queens confront beggars, housewives, and daisies, remains hierarchically structured, even if such hierarchies are locally subverted. Similarly, Moore's catalogues only seem antihierarchical. Though introduced by a critique of subordination ("sophistication has like 'an escalator, cut the nerve of progress'"), the final lines of "People's Surroundings" hardly read as "an ecstatic vision of a living, working community" (Slatin 134). Rendering a feudal society in catalogue rhetoric, they parody, rather, Whitman's project of a democratic discourse and indicate that deletions of syntactical subordination do not necessarily open "democratic vistas." Hierarchy persists in class and gender differences, embodied by the diverse persons and positions placed next to one another. "Cutlers, gamesters, surgeons, and armourers" occupy other "respective places" than queens, ladies, princes, and gentlemen. The first belong in workshops and battlefields, the latter in mysterious "magnificent places clean and decent." Unlike surgeons, sextons, emperors, and dukes, "queens, countesses, [and] ladies" lack profession, though they may have positions and power. As wives of kings, counts, and gentlemen, however, they can also be reduced to decoration for castles, palaces, and dining halls. Degrees of estrangement thus depend on gender. In contrast to the speaker's claim that there is "neither up nor down to" the final lines, "the fundamental structure" of social and sexual hierarchies shines through the democratic "exterior" of their catalogue rhetoric. Whitman's speaker, by comparison, singing his own multitude ("Of every hue and caste I am, of every rank and religion" [45]), finally dismisses the spinning girl and the squaw, the mothers and female mill workers he first called upon, thus reinforcing the very hierarchy he meant to abolish.

The marks of gender in Dickinson's and Moore's poems signify the different positions culture has assigned to male and female. Any reading of the *dispositif sémiotique* in women authors' texts thus has to take into account that femininity and womanhood have traditionally been identified as other. It has to acknowledge that female subjectivity emerges in conflict with both this sense of otherness and the established position of the male subject. Read with regard to the nineteenth-century myths of "true womanhood" or the ever-changing visions of a "new woman," fluctuations of subject positions in women's texts attest to both an "eclipse" of the male "I" and to ellipses of the first-person singular female. Having lived and written in the "age of the first person singular" (Emerson, qtd. in Matthiessen 5), "the new importance given to the single person" (Emerson, *Complete Works* 7: 68) manifests itself in Dickinson's use of the pronoun *I,* the most frequent word in her poetic work after *the, a, and, to,* and *of* (Lindberg-Seyerstedt 33)—in poems like "The Soul selects her own Society" (J 303), which Moore, by the way, copied into her reading notes, and in a single-mindedness, a "sense of privacy" (*CPMM* 81) and detachment Dickinson and Moore share. Since the first-person singular, the self-reliant individual, or the poet was generally projected as male while woman was defined by her "nature" and celebrated as "civilizer of mankind" (Emerson, *Complete Works* 11:340,345), it was a difficile and daring act to posit an "I" that was both an authority and female.

While notions of women's moral superiority lived on past the turn of the century, the cultural perception of the female body changed dramatically. The fragile Victorian female was displaced by the image of an energetic, intellectually and economically independent woman with "access . . . to experience" (Moore, *CPMM* 54), a person with sexual desires and social ambitions. Accelerated by Freud's theorization of the unconscious, man ceased to be the master in his own house. Women, however, became more outgoing, in all senses of the word. Yet, even though the new emphasis on female sexuality was paralleled by a continuous emancipation of women, fictions of a "new" femininity added to the notion of woman as sexual being the demand that this sexuality should also be expressed more freely (Hymowitz and Weisman 291).

Both Dickinson's and Moore's texts take issue with the conventional alliance of woman, nature, and body. Kristeva's reemphasis of the body is thus indeed crucial for a revision of women's poetry yet only if we acknowledge that the body figures in the processes of male and female subject constitution in fundamentally different ways. Due to the specific culturally inscribed functions of the female body, which has legitimated women's exclusion from subjectivity and history, women authors have tended to downplay matters of sexual difference for a long time and to assert their intellectual range instead. In both Dickinson's and Moore's texts we therefore find the materiality of discourse foregrounded, a semantics of the female body and sexuality equivocated—equivocated, though, in different ways.

"Sex," Moore copied into her reading notebook in 1921, "is a primal force in the world—it is real."[11] Reflecting her strong interest in the various publications on psychology flooding the market at the time, the tenor of the passages she reproduced is generally critical of the strong emphasis psychoanalysis puts on the function of sexuality in human development and creativity.[12] Likewise, her own work—poetry, prose, and editing practice alike—shows such ambivalence toward the sexual body. The female figures starring in her poems compare to the ladies of Renaissance literature, who are "clad in [the] complete Steel" of chastity (Milton, "Comus" l. 421). Though an admirer of e. e. cummings's poetry, Moore still objected to his "obscenities" (*Prose* 302; see also 395). Her translations of *The Fables of La Fontaine* tend to eliminate sexual allusions. And poems such as "People's Surroundings" reduce the human body to synecdochic bits and pieces ("pointed ears," "the eye") or to images that employ its "dry" parts ("This dried bone of arrangement") and celebrate the enchanted mind.

This ambivalence that governs Moore's representations of the body—and the female body, in particular—is due to the prevalent binarism according to which gendered identities get constructed and which are played out in Moore's poems. The "acacia-like lady" featured in "People's Surroundings" appears fearfully small and objectified,

> shivering at the touch of a hand,
> lost in a small collision of the orchids—
> dyed quicksilver let fall
> to disappear like an obedient chameleon in fifty shades of
> mauve and amethyst:
>
> (*Observations* 67–68)

Her male counterpart "towers" several lines above her, embodied by "Bluebeard's Tower above the coral reefs." Charles Perrault's Barbe Bleu was not only a womanizer but also a rapist and murderer of women. Though he is as distanced by legend as the lady herself, his "Tower" projects male economic and sexual potency as well as threats to nature ("coral reefs") and "acacia-like" femininity. The female body, Moore seems to suggest, remains a site in need of defense and protection rather than exposure. In comparison, Dickinson's metaphor of the body "bolt[ing] the Door" to the outside world ("Material Place") makes defensiveness originate from an internal, psychic strain. Significantly enough, Dickinson selected *corporeal* as a variant for *Material,* in this way aligning the materiality of the objective world with that of the human body. Nonetheless, she preserves the difference between these two "material" realities and insinuates that prospects of another, unified identity depend upon a double-faced negation that both escapes "Material Place" and cancels the body.

The foregrounding of discursive materiality, therefore, has to be read in relation to the particular metaphoric use Dickinson and Moore make of corpo-reality and the semantic function they assign to matters of the body. The tensions between these levels of representation, between "a personal, private style . . . as incomparable as your own body" (Jameson 114), a style that disrupts meaning and the body as a figure that assigns meanings, must not be evened out by an orthodox Kristevean reading. Interpretations that take modern aesthetics simply as a return of the repressed body necessarily evade the historical contexts and cultural and symbolic constraints of that body and fail to account for the ways in which gender feeds into subject constitution. A rereading of the relation between disruption, subjectivity, and gender should, instead, recontextualize transgressive cultural practices and reemphasize the symbolic. It needs to reconsider the function of disruption, as both a textual and a cultural strategy. It requires an analysis of the interrelations between Dickinson's and Moore's disruptive textual practice, the dominant cultural code of femininity, and the poets' marginal positions as female authors—that is, as both producers and reproducers of cultural images of femininity.

Whereas Kristeva stresses the force of preverbal physical desires as an origin of linguistic rupture, Dickinson and Moore employed unorthodox discourse to transgress the limits of language and stressed the intentionality of their idiosyncrasies. This does not mean that the poets' semiotic practice was simply a means for preconceived motives. In Moore's work, particularly, the poet's aesthetic principles conflict with textual practice. Despite her favor for clarity and concentration, the outcome, as Williams put it, was often "happily bewildering" (*Selected Letters* 159). And, even though Moore claimed her revisions to be "the result of impatience with unkempt diction and lapses in logic" and of "an awareness that for most defects to delete is the instantaneous cure" (*Prose* 507), they did not necessarily effect transparency and logical closure, as Moore's heavily revised version of "Poetry" (1924) exemplifies. And yet: much of

Moore's bewildering work was indeed meant to be wild. While enigmas should be avoided, she claimed, "we must have the courage of our own peculiarity" (*Prose* 398). Just as Dickinson for her "had the full COURAGE OF HER ODDITY,"[13] Moore herself had "a very special fondness for writing that is obscure, that does not quite succeed, because of the author's intuitive restraint. All that I can say," she wrote, "is that one must be as clear as one's natural reticence allows one to be. / / It is a commonplace that we are the most eloquent by reason of the not said" (*Prose* 435). Dickinson expresses similar preferences for restrained, reticent eloquence, for "Warbling Teller[s]" who "Tell all the Truth but tell it slant" (J 1545). Refusing to provide "explanation kind" (J 1129), Dickinson's poems succeed by circuit and dazzle the reader by deletions. By exploiting poetry's license to "quibble" (J 494), they enact what could not be "acted out" without consequences.

To both Dickinson and Moore transgression thus became a necessity of life. Both poets cultivated a curious kind of nonconformity. To both, indeed, applies what Randall Jarrell said about Moore: in spite of all their restraint, they are "excessive, and magnificent eccentric[s]" (163). Eccentricity served both poets as a refuge, a sacrosanct space, a kind of magic hat under which to hide, write, and handle life as well as a strategy for self-presentation by self-dramatization. Moore herself detected in her predecessor "a sense of drama with which we may not be quite at home," which she defended, nonetheless, as "part of that expansion of breath necessary to existence" (*Prose* 292). The problem is, however, that, as women, Dickinson and Moore were always already eccentrics in all senses of the word. With their acts of self-marginalization they do not only deviate from established patterns, as from the circular path of reproductive functions, for instance; they also reinforce their very positions off center. As a consequence, neither the deconstruction of "male discourse" nor the escape from conventions of femininity will guarantee women's subject position. This dilemma accounts for the most significant difference between their work and that of the French avant-garde writers, the fact that the female poets do not take their textual practice to Mallarméan extremes. Their texts suggest that, in contrast to Kristeva's view, women writers do not assume a wholly "negative function" that "reject[s] everything finite, definite, structured, loaded with meaning, in the existing state of society" ("Oscillation" 166). Instead, Dickinson's and Moore's poems, like their eccentric personal politics and public personae, reflect that their dedication to writing was a "precarious Gait" (J 875), an ongoing but double choice against conventional expectations and complete negation—that is, silence—alike: a "working (in) the in-between." Oscillating between deliberate disruptions and new forms of poetic authority, Dickinson and Moore do not destabilize subjectivity and meaning as radically as paradigmatic modern texts by male authors do, because, after all, women of their generation have not had a subject position to put at risk to begin with. Aware that neither conformity nor nonconformity grants female subjectivity, the poets tended to vacillate between an overfulfillment and exceeding of norms, on the one hand, and an exploitation of their marginal, eccentric, single-minded position, on the other.

This strategy of a "working (in) the in-between" can be most convincingly exemplified by an analysis of the poets' use of meter and prosody. From a reading of Dickinson's poems "She rose to His Requirement" (J 732) and "I rose—because He sank—" (J 616) and Moore's syllabic poem "The Fish" (1918) emerges a sense of (female) subjectivity that is built upon simultaneous deconstructions and reconstructions of authority.[14] Whereas, according to Kristeva, avant-garde texts displace subjectivity from the syntactical structures onto the level of language's rhythms and sounds and in this way let the passions enter into language, textual analysis shows that Dickinson and Moore's retention of flexible formal frames resists traditional associations of fragmentation and femininity and a desire to reestablish the (female) subject in a position of identity (Dickinson) and integrity (Moore). At the same time, a reading of Dickinson's and Moore's use of prosody foregrounds the particular functions that each poet's semiotic textual practice is assigned in representing the body.

Both Dickinson's and Moore's texts establish their sense of subjectivity on an awareness of lack that both fosters a capacity to deny, renunciate, do without, delete, and transforms negation into assertion, lack into wealth, disadvantage into privilege. Only Dickinson, however, takes this economy of scarcity, which accommodates gender conventions and Christian paradoxes alike, to an extreme. Lacking faith in orthodox religion and the roles that culture has assigned to women, she turned to writing as a means of surpassing her historical disposition. Focusing on threshold experiences—that is, experiences of excessive physical and emotional pain or joy, loss of consciousness and death—she attempted to extend the limits of life and consciousness by transgressing the limits of poetic discourse. In Moore's texts poetic disruption does not mediate a detour into culture but is directly related to her involvement in the contemporary cultural scene and to her critique of outmoded traditions and current trends alike. In contrast to Dickinson, Moore does not attempt to displace but, rather, disguises the female body, using the dazzling surfaces of her poems as a kind of "martial arts." This "battle-dressed" appearance of Moore's poetry has to be seen in the context of a cultural climate that partly welcomes the public presence of women yet continues to deny woman the position of subject by symbolically referring her to the place of the body. Reading Moore's early poems in conjunction with her first correspondence with Pound, I argue that the disruptive aesthetics of her poems not so much disguises a self or deflects sexuality, as New Criticism and feminist analysis alike have it; by drawing attention from textual body to surface structures, they instead deflect the male eye/I that turns to woman's writing in search of her body in order to confirm his own potency. In this way the formal "fiddle" and apparent "chasteness" of Moore's writing destabilizes the male subject. The "armor" in which Moore's poems are clad does not mean to transcend but to cope with the cultural constraints. These constraints Dickinson evaded, at least to a certain degree, by physical retreat, a retreat into a writing that insisted on desire.

## Dickinson's Threshold Glances; or, Putting the Subject on Edge

According to Kristeva, poetic language reclaims passion for signification by foregrounding features immanent in language itself. Unlike writing that conforms to metric and prosodic conventions, avant-garde texts such as Mallarmé's "Prose," for example, accumulate phonemes and sounds that both replace conventional metric patterns and compensate for elliptic syntax by what Kristeva calls rhythmic constraints. Like repetitions in dreams, Kristeva argues, repetitions of sounds produce effects foreign to the common usage of language, establish new structures of signification, and mark a core of resistance. Like Mallarmé's displacement of metric and syntactic structures by typographic patterns, they deconstruct the univocality of the word and displace the "unanimity of sense" by a "semantic polymorphism" (*La révolution* 219). This mixed function of language's sounds "opens the normative use of language partly in the direction of the body and the repressed semiotic *chora* underneath, partly in the direction of multiple displacements and condensations which produce a *deeply ambivalent, if not polymorph semantics*" (222).[15] In this way the genotext organizes a network of autonomous semantic values not given in the phenotext but dependent, instead, according to Kristeva, on the unique experience of the subject during the processes of signification. The sounds of language, it follows, are consequently more than phonemes: "they repossess the typography of the body through which they have been produced."[16]

Such interpretation of the prosodic features of language is driven by the notion that the passions were in dire need of being repossessed. This, however, as I have shown, has not been the most pressing problem of the female poet trying to claim authority and subjectivity. Thus, investigations of "the body in language" had better shift their focus. Dickinson's and Moore's particular use of prosody, therefore, reflects an in-between position that, as I will argue in this chapter, corresponds to a third sense of subjectivity. This sense of subjectivity mediates, in Dickinson's case, between this life and that and, in Moore's, between body and mind.

While both Dickinson and Moore experiment with form, neither abandons formal patterns completely. And yet Dickinson's choice of English hymnody, "ready to hand," in the form that Isaac Watts's *Church Psalmody* and *Psalms, Hymns, and Spiritual Songs,* available in the Dickinson library and part of popular rather than high culture, remains a rather single-minded selection. In fact, it makes her the "only canonical female poet before the turn of the century who resisted the authority of [standard blank verse]" (Finch 169). Appropriating the ballad measure, a common cultural code for those who sing in anonymity, Dickinson recruits namelessness as a basis for her individual voice and constructions of female subjectivity. Before many of her contemporaries did, Moore, in contrast, preferred the "absence of feet" (*CPMM* 85) and reverted to syllabic verse that characterizes most of her poems, except many of those written between 1920 and 1925. Like Dickinson's hymns, Moore's syllabics foreground the single word, cause tensions between syntax and form, and easily embed Moore's unobstrusive inner, or light, rhymes. In contrast to Dickinson's ballads, syllabics de-emphasize meaning intention by deleting stress count.

Like Dickinson, whose forms never were as radical as those of Whitman, Blake, or Hopkins, Moore never felt as comfortable with the rhymelessness and irregularity of "free verse" as some of her contemporaries did. Instead, both poets opted for a strategy of "both-and," for formal frames with paradoxical effects. Ballad meter and syllabic verse are flexible forms that foreground the materiality of language yet retain control and a sense of authority and take on distinct meanings, depending on whether they are orthodoxically fulfilled or violated. Rather than simply displacing syntax by sound, their texts employ several levels of signification and counterbalance deconstructive tendencies by reconstructive ones. At the same time, their specific prosodic idiosyncracies— Dickinson's use of a common measure, Moore's application of a particular one—take wholly distinct functions with regard to matters of the body. Stressing the physical features of language, both poets' texts tend to negate the body on the level of semantics and figuration. While both thus violate cultural conventions of femininity, the function that such disruption takes interrelates with each author's particular cultural context and her position in it. Engaging in the combats of culture, Moore turns disruption into a strategy of deflection that draws attention away from the materiality of the bodies she presents—be they objects or human bodies—to textual surfaces. Dickinson, by contrast, who neither accepts nor outspokenly rejects the social arrangements her culture offered to women, employs disruptive poetic patterns to retrieve in language the sense of identity and fulfillment usually deferred to a "beyond" of physical existence. As this sense of identity turns out to be much less desirable than expected, Dickinson comes to privilege the desire for desire.

Dickinson Working (in) the In-Between

Dickinson's poem "She rose to His Requirement" aligns orthodox fulfillment of the ballad measure with a seeming conformity to dominant codes of femininity. Her poem "I rose—because He sank—" links its extreme violation of meter with the transgression of that code. "She rose to His Requirement" lets conventional frames of meter and marriage clash with irregular syntax. Sound repetitions do not simply displace meter here but supplement the poem with another layer of nondiscursive signification. "I rose—because He sank—," in contrast, correlates a regular metric design with semantic trangressions of gender conventions. The text's comparatively clear syntax suggests, however, that this very transgression authorizes the subject.

"She rose to His Requirement" reads like a commentary on Elizabeth Barrett Browning's poem "A Man's Requirements" (1846). Browning's poem parodies the double standards of heterosexual love by listing a man's demands on woman's loving dedication ("Love me, Sweet, with all thou art," "Love me in full being," and so forth)—requirements that he himself would not fulfill ("I will love *thee*—half a year— / As a man is able."). Dickinson's text, in comparison, soberly critiques the institution of marriage and does so in part by a subtext of sound.

> She rose to His Requirement—dropt
> The Playthings of Her Life
> To take the honorable Work
> Of Woman, and of Wife—
>
> If ought She missed in Her new Day,
> Of Amplitude, or Awe—
> Or first Prospective—Or the Gold
> In using, wear away,
>
> It lay unmentioned—as the Sea
> Develop Pearl, and Weed,

But only to Himself—be known
The Fathoms they abide—

The limits marriage sets on woman's life corresponds to the regularity of the common meter here, which is significantly disrupted, however, in the poem's first line by an additional syllable and an archaic past tense ("dropt"). Semantically, the act of dropping indicates a decline from the playful "amplitudes" of premarital existence. By positioning this matter outside an otherwise regular formal frame, the poem associates marriage with loss (of pleasure) and suggests that the notion of marriage as eclipse of women's lives conceals the renunciations wedlock demands of women.

Within the formal frame the denied pleasures reassociate as rhetorical figures. Projecting passion, unbounded power, and infinity in Dickinson's poetry, the "Sea" symbolizes the undercurrent of women's conformity here. Grown in its darker regions, "Pearl and Weed" are manifestations of this potentially subversive surplus energy that resonate with the conventional association of femininity and nature simultaneously. Both pearl and weed develop from abnormal growth. A pearl is an anomalous excrescence within the shell of some mollusks with usually lustrous concretion formed of concentric layers of nacre. Precious and rare, pearls are status symbols and female accessories that Dickinson frequently employed as metaphors for poetry and its "business . . . Circumference" (L 268), thus aligning writing and femininity. *Weed,* in comparison, denotes an aquatic plant or a plant of rank growth, an organism that tends to overgrow and choke out more desirable vegetation. At the same time, it is everything that a gardener at a particular time considers rank growth. Repressions of pleasure thus produce both constructive and deconstructive energy, or, to put it differently: pressures to conform not only repress but also dislocate that which they mean to control.

The alliteration and repetition of the *w* sound in *Work, Woman, Wife, wear away,* and *Weed* underscore that woman's "honorable Work" and the growth of "Weed" are two sides of the same coin. Sound repetitions thus saturate meaning and counterbalance the conventional metric order that aligns *Life* and *Wife* as well as *Sea* and *Weed* but bypasses the conjunction of *Work, Wife,* and *Weed,* which is the subtext of repression and the potentially uncontrollable surplus energy generated by that repression ("the Fathoms they abide"). This subversive element is reinforced by the poem's unorthodox grammar, its ambiguous prepositions (*Of* in "Of Amplitude") and pronouns *(Himself),* as well as its irregular or disruptive verb forms *(dropt, be known).* In this way the poem suggests that the very (symbolic) order upon which the male subject depends suffocates female subjectivity. Accordingly, the woman who "rose to His Requirement" no longer speaks for herself.

Dickinson's poem "I rose—because He sank" reads like a counterpiece to "She rose to His Requirement." Its unconventional formal frame presents us with grammatically correct structures and a "stable" speaking subject or lyrical "I." Here meaning multiplies through disruptions of meter.

> I rose—because He sank—
> I thought it would be opposite—
> But when his power dropped—
> My Soul grew straight.
>
> I cheered my fainting Prince—
> I sang firm—even—Chants—
> I helped his Film—with Hymn—
>
> And when the Dews drew off
> That held his Forehead stiff—
> I met him—
> Balm to Balm—
>
> I told him Best—must pass
> Through this low Arch of Flesh—
> No Casque so brave
> It spurn the Grave—
>
> I told him Worlds I knew
> Where Emperors grew—
> Who recollected us
> If we were true—
>
> And so with Thews of Hymn—
> And Sinew from within—
> And ways I knew not that I knew—till then—
> I lifted Him—

The poem's metrical pattern is "even" only insofar as its central stanzas consist of six syllables or, as lines 3 and 4 of stanza 3, can be recomposed into a six-syllable line. The remaining parts of the poem alternate four-, six-, eight-, and ten-syllable lines. The line "I sang firm—even—Chants" itself is embedded in a stanza that has six-syllable lines only and is either short of one line or, if considered in conjunction with the following stanza, a split version of the extended common meter, which, however, lacks a regular rhyme scheme. With regard to metric convention the poem is thus extremely uneven.

This excessive formal disruption is counterbalanced by a fairly linear, predominantly paratactical syntax yet corresponds to radical semantic disruptions the level of semantics. The speaker recalls an instance of self-empowerment, based upon the conflation of gender and sexual roles. The decrease of male potency ("dropped") is echoed in the "castrated" common meter. The rise of power on her part "is manifested," as Cynthia Griffin Wolff puts it, "in attitudes of phallic rectitude" (455): "My Soul grew straight." Her strength to "erect" ("I lifted Him") and send him to kingdom come ("Worlds I knew / where Emperors grew") is not due to her femininity but, rather, to a force ascribed to the supposed (phallic) force of hymn poetry ("Thews of Hymn"). Echoed throughout the poem by assonance *(sinews, knew, grew, Dews, drew)*, this power ("thews") equals an unconscious knowledge ("ways I knew not that I knew") that, through puns and inner rhymes *(hymn/him/firm)*, gets associated with masculine firmness, not female fluidity. The transgressive act depicted here is consequently a female singer's attempt to appropriate male potency and subjectivity, which exemplifies Dickinson's "alienation from the female body" and her "technique of self-hermaphrodization" (Paglia 640). Such increase of female authority affords the decline, the death of the male, and a reversal of sexual hierarchies that, as the juxtaposition of a ten- and a four-syllable line in the final stanza suggests, severely affects established metric and, implicitly, symbolic and social structures. Attesting to the instability of the supposedly "firm" male position, Dickinson's poem delineates the limits of male powers.

In contrast to this gender-related "power play," the disruptive "evenness" of the central stanzas envisions an identity between female speaker and male other ("Balm to Balm"), a unity and indifference not to be achieved on this side of existence but beyond "the Grave." Only after the body is abolished ("this low Arch of Flesh"), differences of gender and power diminish. "Sloughing off her passive female body," Camille Paglia suggests, Dickinson makes "transsexual leaps into eternity" (641). Cutting the sequence "I met him Balm to Balm" in half, the text still decreases the distance between the two lines by doing without a dash after *him* and identifies "I" and "Him," subject and object, by parallelisms and end-rhyme. In contrast to Dickinson's chamber poem, in which repetition ("ourself behind ourself, concealed") suggests self-difference, sameness ("Balm to Balm") signals identity here. These glimpses beyond engendered power struggles into a realm of unmediated self-identity became the ultimate challenge of Dickinson's disruptive poetry.

The publication history of the two poems discussed here indicates what Dickinson's culture made of the sense of subjectivity they express. Compliant in both outer appearance and message, "She rose to His Requirement" was published in 1890 with several alterations, such as corrected verb forms and traditional punctuation, entitled "The Wife" and subsumed under the heading "Love." When Todd and Higginson suggested "I rose—because He sank—" for publication in the first series of Dickinson's poems, Arlo Bates cut the last two stanzas, even though their syntax is quite regular. Apparently, the emphasis on the equality of all people before God implied in the third stanza was a more acceptable conclusion than the announcement of female superiority embedded in (metric) disorder. Still, the poem was not published until 1929, when it appeared in the *Atlantic Monthly* with stanzas 2 and 3 omitted and some of Dickinson's variants adopted: *dropt* became *bent; stood* displaced *grew.*

What both textual analysis and early reception suggest is that Dickinson's feminist critique passed most easily when disguised in an apparent conformity or camouflage. The common hymn meter served as a mark of authority, outer pretense and protection, and disguise of subversive views, just as the poet's own appropriation of cultural conventions (such as the "angel in the house" figure) did. Instead of radically dismissing cultural as well as poetic constraints, and in this way reinforcing the notion of femininity as other, instead of "blow[ing] up the law" like Whitman did (Cixous, "Medusa" 292), Dickinson's poetry makes its own use of it. Most significant for an assessment of the relation between female subjectivity and the body in Dickinson's poems is that both "One need not be a Chamber" and "I rose— because He sank—" project identity not only beyond the "requirements" to which culture demands women to "rise" but also beyond physical existence. Unlike psychoanalysis, which locates identity in the dyadic unity of the preoedipal stage, Dickinson projected fantasies of fulfillment and completion into eternity and attempted to capture eternity in time, in the very act of writing, of "spreading wide [her] narrow Hands / To gather Paradise—" (J 657).

And yet, I will argue, Dickinson only seems to have "mastered life by rejecting it" (Tate 85). Renunciation was only half the trick. In fact, Dickinson's economy of desire does not so much, as Joan Burbick claims, "demand[] . . . as its price the total cancellation of the body" (372). Dickinson missed but also wanted "All" (J 985), and, despite her repeated deferrals, she wanted it *Here* and *Now.* Following the orthodox belief that the blindness and fragmentation of our physical existence would be compensated by the prospects of a "larger function" (J 745), by a "Compound Vision" (J 906) surpassing "that Covered Vision—Here" (J 745), she also insists that the beyond is no place to linger.

When she frames her "Covered Vision" by both *That* and *Here,* Dickinson underscores that her fragmented poetics attempts to retrieve the beyond ("That") for this life ("Here"). The fact that Dickinson's "larger function" lacks the monumentality resonating in the capitalized "Covered Vision" indicates, however, that the poet was rather disappointed by that which awaited her. That "Covered Vision," she concludes, is still more precious, more desirable, than an eternal transparancy.

Putting the Subject on Edge

Quite frequently, Dickinson situates her speakers at the threshold of existence and consciousness, at the edge of eternity, on the margins of subjectivity and representation. For the poet, who herself never traveled far, such excursions entailed more than the thrills of a tightrope walk over the abysses of being. The edges she ponders are not points in time but oftentimes painful processes of border crossings. This makes Dickinson's boundaries not limitations but possibilities that open vistas. As she transforms lines into wide-open views, her speakers peep into the unknown, into paradise.

Considering the cultural context in which Dickinson was immersed, such preoccupations with death and eternity come as no surprise. The author's treatment of such popular themes, however, is breathtakingly unique and insightful, motivated, as it was, by a "Love for the absent" (L 31). Therefore, it has little in common with the suicidal disposition Kristeva associated with the semiotic practice of Woolf, Tsvetayeva, and Plath in *Chinese Women.* Instead, Dickinson's texts underline that it is exactly the distance between death itself and the representation of death that makes all the difference. "To take the name of Gold— / And Gold to own—in solid Bars—," she wrote in a different context, "The Difference—made me bold—" (J 454). Knowing that any attempts to grasp eternity in time "Were hopeless, as the Rainbow's Raiment / To touch—" (J 680), Dickinson still found "The Impotence to Tell—" the "Ultimate of Talk" (J 407). The project to materialize bodiless states: Eden and eternity in language thus became a predilection that, not surprisingly, has preoccupied Dickinson scholarship from New Critical readings to poststructuralist analyses. Central to all of these inquiries has been the sense of self inhabiting Dickinson's disruptive dialectics of pain and paradise—a sense of self whose assessment has changed as the theoretical conceptions of self and, more recently, gendered subjectivity themselves have changed. Reading Dickinson's threshold glances through Kristeva, one finds not only parallels and fundamental differences in their sense of subject constitution. In addition, one discovers in Dickinson's texts what I, being highly indebted to the insightful work of Hagenbüchle, have come to call Dickinson's dialectics of "edgy" subjectivity—a dialectics that comes down on a subject in an in-between position, on a "third event" (J 1732) that reclaims eternity for life, thus also restores desire and despair to paradise.

Confronted with her own otherness, the speaker of Dickinson's poem "One need not be a Chamber—to be Haunted—" is situated at the edge of subjectivity and representation. Such threshold positions are crucial in Dickinson's poetry as well as in psychoanalysis, and Dickinson and Kristeva are similarly aware that subjectivity depends on acts of separation. Under psychoanalytic perspectives, Kristeva writes in *Powers of Horror: An Essay on Abjection* (1982), the speaking being is "always already haunted by the Other," from which he had to separate in order to speak (12). For her separation begins with the division of the infant (the subject that is not yet an ego) and the abject (that which is not yet an object) whose primary force is horror or abjection. "The paternal agency alone," Kristeva writes, "to the extent that it introduces the symbolic dimension between 'subject' (child) and 'object' (mother), can generate such a strict object relation" (44).

For the phobic subject, however, "the constituting barrier between subject and object" becomes "an insurmountable wall" (47), the "paternal function" fails "to establish a unitary bent between subject and object" (99), the ego becomes "barricaded and untouchable," and, "where objects are concerned he delegates phantoms, ghosts, 'false cards'" (47). As a consequence, the borderline subject turns into a "fortified castle" (46), a "strange configuration":

> an encompassment that is stifling (the container compressing the ego) and, at the same time, draining (the want of an other, qua object, produces nullity in the place of the subject). The ego then plunges into a pursuit of identifications that could repair narcissism—identifications that the subject will experience as in-significant, "empty," "null," "devitalized," "puppet-like." An empty castle, haunted by unappealing ghosts—"powerless" outside, "impossible" inside.

For Kristeva the impact of such rejection of paternal agency on subjectivity is a tendency toward abstraction and desemantization as well as physical effects: "the borderline patient," she explains, "speaks of a numbed body, of hands that hurt, of paralyzed legs" (49). Similarly, in Dickinson's verse the subject's connection to the objective world is frequently cut: paralysis and numbness are recurrent sensations; desemantization, abstraction, and scenelessness predominant modes of representation.

While such parallels between theoretical and poetic texts are noteworthy, their interpretation is yet another matter. Even though both Dickinson's poetry and Kristeva's theory push beyond the limits of the known and representable, the fundamental difference between their endeavors lies in the very boundaries they ponder, in the opposite direction of their errands. While Kristeva's phobic subject mourns the loss of the first love object and regresses to narcissism, "to a self-contemplative, conservative, self-sufficient haven" (14) that substitutes for the lost dyadic unity, Dickinson's borderline figures do not care for female origins. Whereas Rich's poems express a "homesickness for a woman, for ourselves" (*Dream* 75), Dickinson's speakers feel a "Homesickness / After Eternity" (J 900), thus long for a sense of subjectivity that transgresses life and the limits of gender. But more than that: with Dickinson it is not a "homesickness *for*" but a homesickness "*After* Eternity." Whereas Rich and Kristeva explore the primal processes located at the edge of subject constitution, Dickinson anticipates a realm "beyond" all oedipal constellations—"that odd Fork in Being's Road— / Eternity—by Term—" (J 615), "those great countries in the blue sky of which we don't know anything" (L 217)—in order to recreate this side of subjectivity. Intent on deconstructing the boundary between this and the other side of life, her poems parallel processes of pain, paralysis, parting, and paradise.

In Dickinson's poems the experience of pain parallels the transition from life to death, which the poet imagines as both an exchange and a continuity between this life and that.

> You left me—Sire—two Legacies—
> A Legacy of Love
> A Heavenly Father would suffice
> Had He the offer of—
>
> You left me Boundaries of Pain—
> Capacious as the Sea—
> Between Eternity and Time—
> Your Consciousness—and Me—
>
> (J 644)

Whereas paternal heritage entrusts the speaker with an economy of desire based on binary oppositions, her own account of this legacy transcends such binarisms. Love and pain as well as "Eternity and Time" are at best asymmetrical oppositions. Juxtaposing the "Legacy of Love" with "Boundaries of Pain / Capacious as the Sea," the speaker, moreover, dissolves their distance and proclaims the proximity of pain and eternity. By literally extending the concept of boundary, Dickinson tries to bridge the gap between time and eternity, to diminish the distance to Eden and love by stretching consciousness into the unknown and "Bodiless" (J 524).

Accordingly, Dickinson's sense of pain is distant from the "pain of sorrow in the modern world" that Kristeva finds reflected in Marguerite Duras's work, for instance, a pain "with neither cure nor God, without value or beauty other than the malady itself" ("Pain of Sorrow" 141). Likewise, Dickinson's sense of paralysis is distinct from Plath's notion of the "Paralytic" (1963), which comes closer to Kristeva's notion of borderline subjectivity. Plath, like Dickinson, associates paralysis with whiteness and monotony ("the white, tight / / Drum of my sleeping couch") and the loss of physical and mental functions. Subject-object relations no longer hold ("I lie / Whole / On a whole world I cannot touch"). With "No fingers to grip, no tongue," "[her] mind a rock," Plath's lyrical "I" is both out of touch and fused with the objects that surround her ("iron lung," "my sleeping couch") and regresses to a preoedipal-like state of utter confinement ("The still waters / Wrap my lips, / / Eyes, nose and ears, / A clear / Cellophane I cannot crack"). Like Dickinson, Plath discharges both body and subjectivity. Yet, unlike Dickinson's losses, Plath's remain uncompensated by gains and further prospects.

> I smile, a buddha, all
> Wants, desire
> Falling from me like rings
> Hugging their lights.
>
> The claw
> Of the magnolia,
> Drunk on its own scents,
> Asks nothing of life.
>
> (*Poems* 267)

Descriptions of paralytic states are recurrent in Dickinson's reflections on excessive psychic and physical despair. Moving from loss of physical function to loss of consciousness, her poem "After great pain, a formal feeling comes—" (J 341) is such a text on paralysis, as Moore noted in the margins of her handwritten copy of the poem.[17]

> After great pain, a formal feeling comes—
> The Nerves sit ceremonious, like Tombs—

The stiff Heart questions was it He, that bore,
And Yesterday, or Centuries before?

The Feet, mechanical, go round—
Of Ground, or Air, or Ought—
A Wooden way
Regardless grown,
A Quartz contentment, like a stone—

This is the Hour of Lead—
Remembered, if outlived,
As Freezing persons, recollect the Snow—
First—Chill—then Stupor—then the letting go—

Indifferent to causes, this poem recollects and "formalizes" the effect of extreme pain, depicts the body cut loose from nervous control and separated from its social contexts. The crisis of the subject is marked by the absense of an identifiable speaker, by synecdoches and other representations of a fragmented body, by nerves, heart, and (poetic) feet, by the monotonous movement of the iambic pentameter in the first and final lines, and by use of commas instead of dashes. Syntactically, Dickinson's depiction of paralysis tends toward disjunction and dismemberment, effected by parataxis and indeterminate prepositions as well as by deletion of conjunctions and adverbial endings ("mechanical"). The poem's first two lines, for instance, are paratactically and asyndetically linked, thus echoing the discontinuity of cause and effect. After the question ("was it He, that bore"), which aligns the speaker with Christ, Dickinson lists adverbs *(yesterday, centuries before)* instead of enumerating verbs. Rhyme connects ("before" / "bore"), where conjunction conflicts with content ("that bore, / And yesterday"). The metrical pattern gets dismissed; syntax further fragmented in the second stanza, about which Dickinson felt particularly ambivalent. In its variant the second and third line are inverted, thus effecting a syntactic doubling (see C. Miller, *Dickinson* 37–39). The deletion of the adverbial ending ("mechanical") "neutralizes" the word while creating a similar doubling effect; set between subject and predication, *mechanical* functions as both adjective and adverb. On the level of content paralysis corresponds to a confusion of disparate semantic categories and a propensity to abstract, represented in the second line by an alliance of increasingly dematerialized and metonymically connected elements ("Of ground, or Air, or Ought"). Syntactical discontinuity is partly counterbalanced phonetically *(ground/round; grown/stone; Air/way)* as well as by the deceptive clarity of the third stanza's opening statement. The

"Fight of the mind against letting go," Moore commented [on] the poem, "is a defense of the mind," yet eventually the speaker "can't suffer anymore."[18] The last line's paratactical structure, following upon the preceding hypotactic structures and the final nominalization ("the letting-go"), seal the dissolution of subjectivity semantically and syntactically.

Pain's "one acquaintance," Dickinson wrote, is death (J 1049). According to Moore, the experience depicted here "is itself like death." Yet death was not the end of the matter for Dickinson. It was "the final secret," "the overpowering sign of transcendence" (Hagenbüchle, "Precision" 43), as well as the vantage point from which to take threshold glances into a beyond.

> The Admirations—and Contempts—of time—
> Show justest—through an Open Tomb—
> The Dying—as it were a Hight—
> Reorganizes Estimate
> And what We saw not
> We distinguish clear—
> And mostly—see not
> What We saw before—
>
> 'Tis Compound Vision—
> Light—enabling Light—
> The Finite—furnished
> With the Infinite—
> Convex—and Concave Witness—
> Back—toward Time—
> And forward—
> Toward the God of Him—

(J 906)

Presenting "The Dying—as it were a Hight," a kind of observation tower, the poem takes a bird's-eye view on death, which alters perception and "Reorganizes Estimate." While the nominalized form of "The Dying" eliminates the grammatical subject, it underscores the process character of death, stretches out what is conventionally conceived as a finite moment, and strains toward a beyond. The "Compound Vision" achieved in the process enables the speaker to peep "Back—toward Time— / And forward—Toward the God of Him—," to attain glimpses of wholeness ("Convex—and Concave Witness"), to gain, as suggested by phrases like "Light enabling Light—," "The Finite—

furnished / With Infinite—" and "the God of Him," self-reflexivity and self-identity.

Curiously enough, Dickinson's sense of the beyond, however, compares to the preoedipal as it has been metaphorized by psychoanalytic theory. In a letter of March 1853 to Susan Gilbert, Dickinson herself compares eternity to an infinite embrace. "Bye and bye," she writes, "[eternity] will open it's [*sic*] everlasting arms, and gather us all" (L 103). "There is no first, or last, in Forever—," she put it in a later correspondance to Susan. "It is Centre, there, all the time—" (L 288). "To crumbling men," reads one of her poems, eternity looks "firm" and represents "The only Adamant Estate / In all Identity—" (J 1499). Viewed from the poet's privileged vantage point, "The Dying," eternity indeed presents itself as glimpses of identity, as the unmediated, mirroring gaze into the countenance of a beloved other (J 625). Somewhat paradoxically, by use of broken language, the poet figures the beyond as a limitless space, in which subjectivity dissolves, as a condition of nondifference, desirelessness, and fulfilled wholeness—a wholeness that, due to the split in which the subject is created, is unattainable on this side of subjectivity.

"I cannot tell how Eternity seems," Dickinson puts it in a letter to Louise and Frances Norcross, written after the death of her mother. "It sweeps around me like a sea" (L 785). Figured as "Miles on Miles of Nought" (J 443) or as a time of "Velocity or Pause/At Fundamental Signals/From Fundamental Laws" (J 1295), Dickinson's descriptions of eternity escape conventional measures of space and time while depending on them for representation. "Forever—is composed of Nows— / 'Tis not a different time"; "Eternity" is "omnipresence" (J 624). Dickinson's "Torrents of Eternity" (J 1380) trade history for a "leisure of the Future," boundaries and limitations for "[a] Wilderness of Size" (J 856) and for "Periods of Seas / Unvisited of Shores" (J 695), for a limitless oceanic space in which subjectivity dissolves. Such a sense of identity dominates this poem.

> Behind Me—dips Eternity—
> Before Me—Immortality—
> Myself—the Term between—
> Death but the Drift of Eastern Gray,
> Dissolving into Dawn away,
> Before the West begin—
>
> 'Tis Kingdoms—afterward—they say—
> In perfect—pauseless Monarchy—

Whose Prince—is Son of None—
Himself—His Dateless Dynasty—
Himself—Himself diversify—
In Duplicate divine—

'Tis Miracle before Me—then—
'Tis Miracle behind—between—
A Crescent in the Sea—
With Midnight to the North of Her—
And Midnight to the South of Her—
And Maelstrom—in the Sky—

(J 721)

Most striking about this text is its profileration of parallelisms, which permeate prosody, grammar, lexicon, and punctuation yet also compete with an element of trinity resonating in the repeated three-line structure and its threefold spatial dimension *(behind, before, between)*. Composed in an expanded version of common meter, the poem's form is unusually regular and abounds in alliteration *(Death, Drift, Dissolving, Dawn)*. The sound similarity in *Dateless Dynasty* and *Duplicate divine* allies death with divinity and counterbalances content, for death, after all, is described as drifting away.

Based on repetition, parallelism involves an element of circularity and ahistoricity, which gets underscored syntactically by a lack of verbs and semantically by an emphasis on timelessness ("pauseless," "Dateless"). Circumstances are primarily rendered in spatial terms ("behind," "between," "Eastern," "to the North," "in the sky," etc.). *Before* is used as a preposition, not as an adverb of time. As Dickinson's poem "Our journey had advanced—" (J 615) suggests, such shifts from temporal to spatial relations occur with the onset of eternity.

Before—were Cities—but Between—
The Forest of the Dead—

Retreat—was out of Hope—
Behind—a Sealed Route—
Eternity's White Flag—Before—
And God—at every Gate—

In the first four quoted lines, *before, between,* and *behind* still relate a chronological chain of events. When *before* is employed for a second time, however, it works as a preposition that marks a difference further underscored by the chiasmic position of the two uses of *before*. Dickinson's vision of eternity thus transforms temporality into spatial dimensions. But even spatial distances eventually diminish. Whereas the first stanza of "Behind Me—dips Eternity—" still distinguishes eternity and immortality, the last stanza discards this difference. There is miracle and midnight all over; eternity (or infinite time) and immortality (or never-ending existence) are one. In fact, distinctions of time and place ("Behind," "Before," "afterward," "into," etc.) have become obsolete. Down and above merge. The crescent drops into the sea. "Maelstrom," referring both to a whirlpool and a violently confused, turbulent, or dangerously agitated state of mind or affair, moves to the sky. Sea and sky reflect and mirror each other.

In such a universe hierarchies collapse, oppositions dissolve, and subjectivity turns into identity. While legend has it ("they say") that eternity is a kingdom and monarchy, the description of Christ as "Son of None," "Duplicate divine," "Himself—Himself diversify," trades family hierarchy for an all-inclusive self-reflexivity. Whereas on this side of life "opposites entice," "The Absolute—removed / The Relative away—" (J 765) in the beyond. Associated with the East and the rising sun, death marks not an end but a new beginning, a kind of rebirth that rapidly drifts into oblivion. The speaker evolves from death as both subject, "Myself," and object, "Me," but her self-portrait as "Term between" does not quite fit. For, where oppositions become self-reflections, notions of "betweenness" no longer apply. Instead, identity becomes all-pervasive, structurally as well as thematically. Presented as "Crescent in the Sea—/ . . . /And Maelstrom—in the Sky—," the subject has turned into a mirror image of utopian wholeness. In the hierarchically structured universe prior to eternity, contrastingly, "The Moon is distant from the Sea" (J 429). In the world projected by "Behind me—dips Eternity—," sky and sea reflecting each other envision identity regained.

Generally, the mirror is the "key metaphor of narcissism" (Wright 108). More specifically, the mirror stage marks the moment in ego constitution in which the child achieves its "first sense of a coherent identity, in which it can recognize itself" (Rose, "Introduction II" 30). Describing heaven as the meeting of "Fleshless Lovers," as a "Gaze" and the "Privilege / Of one another's Eyes—," Dickinson's poem "'Twas a long Parting" (J 625) similarly envisions eternity as a dematerialized state of unmediated identity, a place of indifference ("Heaven of Heavens"), in which a true marriage between self and other, of "Eyes" as well as "I's," materializes in an eternally prolonged gaze, in a recognition of oneself in the other. Similarly, the poem "One Year ago—jots what?" (J 296) projects the lovers as "each other's faces," whose mutual reidentification is figured as a nurturing gaze: "When farther Parted, than the Common Woe— / Look—feed upon each other's faces—so—." Such figures "stopped gauging—

satisfied— / For this enchanted size—" (J 756) and find themselves utterly desireless: "I knew no more of Want—or Cold / Phantasm both become."

In this imaginary state of identity between subject and object, gender differences tend to dissolve. God gets excluded from the "new Equation" (J 301) entailed in the lovers' circular gaze. He ceases to impersonate the unified father figure, which enforces division, and is himself decentered and multiplied. In eternity one finds "God—at every Gate—" (J 615) and love turned into a transcendent power and transcendental signifier.

> Love—is anterior to Life—
> Posterior—to Death—
> Initial of Creation, and
> The Exponent of Earth—
>
>                                              (J 917)

Love "assists" death (J 960), "reforms Vitality / Into Divinity" (J 809), is "the Fellow of the Resurrection" (J 491), prior and posterior to God and "coeval" with poetry (J 1247).

"*Heaven, Eden,* paradisical fantasies in general," Beverly Dahlen interprets the parallels between Dickinson's poetry and psychoanalysis, "replace th[e] loss [of the primal unity] and project a possible future restoration: Utopia" (19). Yet, while the metaphors of maternal haven and heavenly eternity may mirror each other, we should not ignore the differences disguised by such symbolic displacements. First of all, for Dickinson heaven is not a utopia to begin with, because, for her, lack of desire is by no means all that desirable; the poet's "paradisical fantasies" do not wholeheartedly embrace paradise but, rather, put its idealizations into perspective. And, second, intent to render in language a state that entails identity and presence, Dickinson has to materialize utopia as poetic practice, in a medium that, she knows, works through absence and difference and thus constantly reaffirms the economy of lack that it promises to transcend. I therefore resist reading Dickinson's threshold glances as longing for an ultimate reparation of the subject's sacrifices and sufferings. I instead take such figures as part of Dickinson's unorthodox dialectics of "edgy" subjectivity—a dialectics that, for various and partly gender-related reasons, is both deeply grounded in its cultural climate and aspiring not simply to transcend but to transform that climate. In its first step of negation Dickinson explores subjectivity as a "contract of sacrifice" (Kristeva). In what seems a negation of that negation, this "Covered Vision" of lack, loss, and pain is traded for a "Superior Spectre," for the vision of a realm "Nicknamed by God— / Eternity—" (J 453), a place in which the split between subject and object is supposedly repaired. "Suffering and vision," wrote Heinz Ickstadt with regard to Hart Crane's work, "form the Janus face of poetic experience" (18).[19] Yet "singing that Eternity possessed," as Crane put it in his dedication to Dickinson (170), the poet loses all certainty of that possession. With all the distance diminished, paradise proves too similar to pain, thus is no negation of negation at all. In a final move Dickinson therefore reclaims eternity for daily life by restoring desire—and despair—to paradise. Dickinson's paradise and the feminist preoedipal past therefore compare in function, not content. "Some feminists," Judith Butler puts it in *Gender Trouble* (1990), "have found in the prejuridical past traces of a utopian future, a potential resource for subversion or insurrection that promises to lead to the destruction of the law and the instatement of a new order" (36). Dickinson, by contrast, found in her culture's projection of a utopian future resources to reconstruct the present order, even if only in poetic practice. After we have seen how to get from this side to that, we may ask, however, why, of all things, "learn the Transport by the Pain" (J 167)?

Elaine Scarry's work on *The Body in Pain* (1985) explains why a pain-ridden, paralyzed subject serves perfectly as a pretext for explorations of the "Bodiless" and unrepresentable. "The first, the most essential, aspect of pain," she writes, "is its sheer aversiveness. While other sensations have content that may be positive, neutral, or negative, the very content of pain is itself negation" (52). As an internal sensation, pain turns against the subject by not taking an object. Unlike other emotional, perceptual, and somatic states that affirm "the human being's capacity to move out beyond the boundaries of his or her own body into the external, sharable world," writes Scarry, physical pain "is not *of* or *for* anything. It is precisely because it takes no object that it, more than any other phenomenon, resists objectification in language" (5). More than simply resisting language, she adds, physical pain "actively destroys it, bringing about an immediate reversion to a state anterior to language, to the sounds and cries a human being makes before language is learned" (4). The language of pain and paralysis thus once again suggests a regression to the preoedipal. With regard to subject position, however, the body in pain is at opposite ends with the subject that is not yet one yet is one with his or her first love object. In states of extreme pain or paralysis object relations are cut, completely estranging the subject. In the process Dickinson's speakers transgress boundaries of class and gender, turn into "Queen of Calvary" (J 348), and compare to Christ. They become crossdressers, gender benders, or disengendered beings, who strain from conventional femininity more than from the physical.

While pain and paradise are alike in that they are both inexpressible, unshareable, they are diametrically opposed, in that pain, on the one hand, lacks an object; paradise, on the other hand, belongs within the realm of the imagination, "the only state," Scarry points out, "that is wholly its objects. There is in imagining," she writes,

> no activity, no "state," no experienceable condition or felt-occurrence separate from the objects: the only evidence that one is "imagining" is that imaginary objects appear in the mind. Thus, while pain is like seeing or desiring but not like seeing $x$ or desiring $y$, the opposite but equally extraordinary characteristic belongs to imagining. It is like the $x$ or the $y$ that are the objects of vision or desire, but not like the felt-occurrences of seeing or desiring. (162)

Accordingly, pain and paradise, as pictured in Dickinson's poems, are part of a dialectics of a subjectivity-on-edge. Seemingly paradoxical, due to the very fact that physical pain takes no object, it reduces the subject to his or her own physical being, an object status represented, in poems such as "After great pain, a formal feeling comes" (J 341), by syntactical reduction and abstraction. Likewise apparently contradictory, though fantasies of bodiless paradise are a product of the imagination only and thus all object, they can project a subject that becomes whole through an identification with an other. In contrast to the physical oneness associated with the preoedipal, however, this wholeness has no material basis except the materiality of the discourse, which renders its expression.

This is exactly what makes paradise problematic. After all, Dickinson was all in doubt about states of disembodiment. "A letter always feels to me like immortality because it is the mind alone without corporeal friend" (L 330), Dickinson claimed in her correspondence with Higginson. The question how, in fact, the mind or soul could exist without a body occupied Dickinson throughout her life, in both letters and poetry.

> The Spirit lasts—but in what mode—
> Below, the Body speaks,
> But as the Spirit furnishes—
> Apart, it never talks—
> The Music in the Violin
> Does not emerge alone
> But Arm in Arm with Touch, yet Touch
> Alone—is not a Tune—
> The Spirit lurks within the Flesh

Like Tides within the Sea
That make the Water live, estranged
What would the Either be?
Does that know—now—or does it cease—
That which to this is done,
Resuming at a mutual date
With every future one?
Instinct pursues the Adamant,
Exacting this Reply—
Adversity if it may be, or
Wild Prosperity,
The Rumor's Gate was shut so tight
Before my Mind was sown,
Not even a Prognostic's Push
Could make a Dent thereon—

(J 1576)

The central question raised here concerns the form and status ("mode") of the spirit or soul after the death of the body. As music depends on both the player's touch on the instrument and the sounding board, the poem implies, existence is hard to be imagined apart from a physical body. The very difference between man and God is that the place of the former is in the body, whereas that of the latter is in voice (Scarry 192). Dickinson could imagine representation without meaning as body without soul: "How lonesome to be an Article!" she claimed, "I mean to have no Soul" (L 354). The notion of a soul "furnish[ing]— / Apart" (J 1576) from the body and presupposing meaning without representation seemed much less palpable to her.

Similarly, the notion of the body as a shelter for the spirit or soul ("The Spirit lurks within the Flesh / Like Tides within the Sea") is misleading. As the comparison between spirit and tide suggests, the soul is, rather, guided by an invisible, immaterial force, just as the tides depend on the sun and moon's force of attraction. At the same time, Dickinson sensed the belief "that the Body contains the Spirit" (L 643) to be as mistaken as the notion that meaning is inherent in the material sign or, as is suggested in "The Spirit lasts—but in what mode—," that truth depends on speech. Such metaphysics of presence and identity, which insinuates that meaning originates from the presence of the speaking subject and which privileges voice and speech over writing, is called into question each time the poet attempts to materialize eternity, immortality, and soul—that is, absence, lack of substance, and silence in language.

In part because of that, the images in which Dickinson's paradise is cast suggest as much pain as pleasure. Like pain, eternity lacks color, content, and history, is aligned with the silences of the white page, with perpetual presence, and with an ultimate "swerve from gender" (Paglia 640). "Pain . . . cannot recollect," writes Dickinson,

> When it begun—or if there were
> A time when it was not—
>
> It has no Future—but itself—
> It's infinite contain
> It's Past—enlightened to perceive
> New Periods—of Pain.
>
> (J 650)

The poet's infinite "Periods—of Pain parallel her depiction of eternity as an infinity of seas (J 695). Like pain, paradise constitutes a state of no distinction, in which "To stop—or perish—or advance" seem "[a]like indifferent" (J 761), in which "knowing" is finally "finished" (J 280). At the same time, it is paralysis, not vitality, as Hagenbüchle pointed out, that marks the very vantage point to knowledge.

>       'tis Paralysis
> Done perfecter on stone—
>
> Vitality is Carved and cool.
> My nerve in Marble lies—
> A Breathing Woman
> Yesterday—Endowed with Paradise.
>
> (J 1046)

Being "Endowed with Paradise," the paralyzed woman gains superiority over the breathing woman. As paradoxical as it may sound, paralysis and pain, in Dickinson's poetics, equal power and privilege, because they pave the way to paradise. Yet this very proximity of pain and paradise in turn endows eternity with a touch of paralysis.

The ultimate drive of Dickinson's poems, therefore, is not to dismiss this side of life, associated with lack of a utopian sense of self-identity, but to reassociate, in a "third event," eternity with desire and difference, to restore the sexual body and pleasure to identity. This she does, for instance, in her poem

"Come slowly—Eden!" (J 211), in which death is reclaimed as desire and ecstasy.

> Come slowly—Eden!
> Lips unused to Thee—
> Bashful—sip thy Jessamines—
> As the fainting Bee—
>
> Reaching late his flower,
> Round her chamber hums—
> Counts his nectars—
> Enters—and is lost in Balms.

Whereas Plath's magnolia is "Drunk on its own scents" and thus resonates self-infatuation, Dickinson's poem "Come slowly—Eden!" projects Eden as sexual encounter, aligning it with sexual consummation, nurture, fertility, and procreation.

Frequently, the passage into eternity described in Dickinson's poems bursts with sexual energy. Her poem "Wild Nights—Wild Nights!" (J 249), for instance, presents "Dying," that "wild Night and . . . New Road" (L 332), as a kind of *jouissance*.

> Wild Nights—Wild Nights!
> Were I with thee
> Wild Nights should be
> Our luxury!
>
> Futile—the Winds—
> To a Heart in port—
> Done with the Compass—
> Done with the Chart!
>
> Rowing in Eden—
> Ah, the Sea!
> Might I but moor—Tonight—
> In Thee!

Whereas sexuality is not explicit here, the simultaneity of rowing and mooring, of a loss of control, bearings, and ego boundaries ("Done with the Compass /

Done with the Chart"), conjoined with a feeling of security, intimacy, and love
("a Heart in Port"), parallels sexual consummation with eternal bliss. Dickin-
son's Eden is final defeat and ultimate gain at once, the proof of identity of self
and other.

> Dropped—my fate—a timid Pebble—
> In thy bolder Sea—
> Prove—me—Sweet—if I regret it—
> Prove Myself—of Thee—
>
> (J 966)

Therefore, if given their choice, Dickinson's speakers prefer unfulfilled
love affairs to the "indifferent" encounters of "Fleshless Lovers" (J 625). "I can-
not live with You," "die—with You—," "rise—with You—," Dickinson
writes in one of her love poems, "Because Your Face / Would put out Jesus'."

> Because You saturated Sight—
> And I had no more Eyes
> For sordid excellence
> As Paradise
>
> And were You lost, I would be—
> Though My Name
> Rang loudest
> On the Heavenly fame—
>
> And were You—saved—
> And I—condemned to be
> Where You were not—
> That self—were Hell to Me—
>
> So We must meet apart—
> You there—I—here—
> With just the Door ajar
> That Oceans are—and Prayer—
> And that White Sustenance—
> Despair—
>
> (J 640)

As Dickinson's speaker privileges her lover's countenance to that of Christ, she
opts for desire and despair—in fact: desire *as* despair in spite of "sordid" iden-

tity and indifference. For, let's face it, Dickinson suggests in another poem: To "Look—feed upon each other's faces" is a "doubtful meal, if it be possible" (J 296). Images of completion as represented, for instance, in Dickinson's gaze of identity are only an "illusion of autonomy" (Lacan 6), since identification always works through alienation and across a gap between self and other. "The image in which we first recognize ourselves," Jacqueline Rose explains, "is a misconception" and a myth ("Introduction II" 30).

Accordingly, Dickinson treasures "in-between" positions taken, for instance, by speakers who have returned from deathlike experiences. Those whose "life closed twice before its close" (J 1732), who "lost" when they expected to be "saved" (J 160), resemble sailors returned from foreign shores, "pale Reporter[s], from the awful doors / Before the Seal," with "Odd secrets of the line to tell."

> To this World she returned.
> But with a tinge of that—
> A Compound manner,
> As a Sod
> Espoused a Violet,
> That chiefer to the Skies
> Than to Himself, allied,
> Dwelt hesitating, half of Dust,
> And half of Day, the Bride.
>
> (J 830)

This identification of the borderline subject as bride is suggestive with regard to the sexual economy of eternity. The bride's transient status, heightened by the prospects, not the consummation, of marriage, have always especially attracted Dickinson. While the "real life" wife frequently becomes "the *wife forgotten*" (L 93), Dickinson's "new Marriage / Justified—through Calvaries of Love—" (J 322), her "New Accompanying" (J 966) implies the sexual and spiritual union of opposites, a dissolution of (gender) difference. Such foretastes of eternity, of the "Colossal substance/of Immortality," are the privilege of "a few" (J 306) and thus reassure the speaker.

Even more, however, Dickinson treasures in-between positions, which allow for "Convex—and Concave Witness," which "furnish" "The Finite . . . With the Infinite" (J 906), and let us see all of it "pile like Thunder to its close" in her poetry.

> To pile like Thunder to it's close
> Then crumble grand away
> While Everything created hid
> This—would be Poetry—
>
> Or Love—the two coeval come—
> We both and neither prove—
> Experience either and consume—
> For None see God and live—
>
> (J 1247)

For poetry, at its best, is a torment for Dickinson, a sexual exhilaration, an orgasmic discharge of deconstructive energy that blows up "Everything created," that is, everything that blocks the vision of "Heaven," creating its own possibilities, its own paradise, and its own subject on trial, at risk, on edge. It is this subject that both transcends the crisis of male subjectivity that Dickinson's culture was facing and precedes the emergence of a historical female subject. Most important: in its potential this subject-on-edge surpasses both male and female subjectivity—by far. At the same time, we need to keep in mind that the finality of the "final move" in Dickinson's dialectics is one of emphasis, amplitude, preference, and intensity, rather than linear temporality.[20] The very fact that Dickinson's most favorite subject position, by contrast, resists temporality and arrests the subject in an in-between state of affairs underscores the unorthodox yet purely poetic nature of her enterprise. Hers was indeed that "still—Volcano—Life," in which conventions were temporarily blown to pieces by "A quiet—Earthquake Style—" (J 601) and "crumble grand away," like the rushes of an orgasm, swallowed by "lips that never lie— / Whose hissing Corals part— and shut." A subject that keeps on desiring, however, is deprived of an ending, of death, of a history.

### Moore's "Martial Arts": Disruption as Deflection of the Male Eye / I

In August 1915 H.D. wrote her first letter to Moore, whom she remembered from college days at Bryn Mawr, concluding with the following remark: "I know, more or less, what you are up against, though I escaped some five years ago!"[21] Referring to her expatriate life in England as "escape," H.D. seems to suggest that the resistances that Moore's work met with were limited to a certain location and that Europe provided a particularly beneficial cultural climate for idiosyncratic art. The fact that both women were to attest to one another's "swordsmanship" and combative disposition implies, however, that gender more than cultural differences is at stake. One arena to observe such confrontations about gender matters is Moore's correspondence, among which the letters exchanged with Pound are most telling. They clearly reflect that part of Moore's "poetics of resistance" (Slatin 8) is provoked by conventions of both genre and gender and that Pound, in turn, is provoked by Moore's authority to reassign her to a position of otherness. When Moore responded to Pound's sexual/textual assaults by sending her poem "Those Various Scalpels," she reasserts her own notion of female subjectivity, which is inextricably intertwined with her modernist aesthetics and the "sense of privacy" she depicted in her poem "To Browning" (1915). Her idiosyncratic aesthetics, in particular, functions as a strategy that "deflects from [one's] estate / Offending eyes and will not tolerate / Effrontery." It diverts the gaze of the male critic, a gaze that tends to collapse the textuality of woman's writing with the textures of the female body.

H.D. sensed this element of defensive deflection in Moore's poetry from the very beginning. In her own defense of Moore's first publications, she insists that "the very screen [Moore] carves" combats "squalor and commercialism" (118, 119); that Moore's aesthetics displays an element reminiscent of the "laugh of the Medusa" (Cixous), a "laughter that catches us, that holds, fascinates and half-paralyses us, as light flashed from a very fine steel blade." "With all the assurance of the perfect swordsman, the perfect technician," Doolittle suggests, Moore "seems to say, half-pitying that the adversary is so dull—that we are so dull—'and I do not intend that you shall know—my sword is very much keener than your sword, my hand surer than your hand—but you shall not know that I know that you are beaten'" (118). Just like Amy Lowell in her poem "Sword Blades and Poppy Seeds," Dickinson and Moore associate pen, word, and sword, and Moore's view of H.D.'s *Hymen* applies just as well to her own poetics. In H.D.'s "talk of weapons" and "tendency to match one's intellectual and emotional vigor with the violence of nature," Moore detected "a connection between weapons and beauty," a "martial, an apparently masculine tone . . . the more so that women are regarded as belonging necessarily to either of two classes—that of the intellectual freelance and that of the eternally sleeping beauty" (82). Resisting such classifications, Moore, like H.D., turned writing into a kind of mental martial arts, cultural work into "combat cultural" (*CPMM* 199), and the female subject into an "intellectual freelance," indeed.

Framing my reading of Moore's early poems by a discussion of her correspondence with Pound, I will show that Moore's martial arts depend upon a cultural climate that kept denying women's subject position by referring them to the place of the body and the position of sexual object. Pound's letters display the very attitude that Moore's texts tried to counter by a sense of femininity that both parodies and equivocates what was commonly considered feminine. As a comparison to Moore's "Black Earth" shows, her poem "Those Various Scalpels" foregrounds the traditional identification of femininity with the fragmented female body. The text acknowledges that the use of discontinuous discourse for representations of female subjectivity necessarily reinforces woman's lack of subject position. At the same time, Moore's text reveals that parodies of such discourse as well as the appropriation of fictions of femininity from Renaissance literature serve not to deflect sexuality, as has been claimed,[22] but to protect the body by means of camouflage and deflect the male gaze, instead. In this way disrupted discourse functions as a kind of shield for the newly emerging female subject. The significant side effect of Moore's strategy of equivocating conventional marks of femininity is that it irritates the position of the male reader, whose stability depends on the very sexual/textual difference he expects to find reasserted in a woman's text.

My reading thus examines the much discussed "battle-dressed" protectiveness of Moore's poetics from a different vantage point, focusing not on her late poem "His Shield" (1944) but, rather, on its early feminine version. I will argue that, even though Moore's emphasis on surface structures and metaphors of armor has been central to the discussion of her work,[23] the common notion that Moore's defensive discourse primarily serves to protect a self supposedly hidden beyond the textual surface misses the mark. Instead, her imagery of armor, including the variously shielded skins of her armored animals and her deflective aesthetics, construct a subject by protecting its body. In "Those Various Scalpels" disruption creates a sense of female subjectivity by equivocating its "fleshy" presence. My reading of disruption and armor in Moore's work thus assesses its supposedly "chaste" quality. What was long considered a denial of "the bonds of the flesh" (Jarrell 184) and a pronounced prudishness to me looks more like an attempt to deconstruct the image of woman as an object of male desire and to reimagine a sense of female subjectivity, whose matrix is not merely physical. At the same time, Moore's poem foregrounds a dilemma of the modern woman poet: in poems that problematize female subjectivity a deconstructive aesthetics necessarily reinscribes femininity as fragmentation. Before turning to the correspondance and aforementioned poems, I will therefore explore the particular motives of Moore's martial arts by looking at her syllabic practice.

## Moore Working (in) the In-Between

Compared with Dickinson's hymns, Moore's syllabic patterns mark a major cultural shift within modernism. As it seems to flow with the voice, handwriting has traditionally suggested a continuity between body, being, and language. Documenting the different strokes, strengths, and sizes of her hand, Dickinson's manuscripts suggest an interrelatedness between body and being in line with a desire to keep her poetry close to her body, to prevent its reproduction, its being outdistanced in print. Though drafted by hand, Moore's typographically arranged poems, by contrast, refer "less to the voice than to the click of the keys and the ratcheting of the carriage" (Kenner 98). Reflecting the increasing mechanization of writing, syllabics are not merely a different poetic form but also the sign of "a completely new order of things" (Burghagen; qtd. in Kittler 278).[24] Writing as an attack on the keys displaced the "continuous-coherent flow of ink, this material base of all bourgeois individuals or indivisibilities" (Kittler 287).[25] Moreover, according to Marshall McLuhan, the typewriter effected "a whole new attitude vis-à-vis the written or printed word," because it "associates poetic creation and publication" (qtd. in Kittler 295). According to Kittler, the increasing circulation of the typewriter furthermore deprived written discourse of its "intimacy" and the writer of "a core item of occidental symbolic systems"—the pen (277).[26] The consequence, Kittler argues, was a rupture of the traditional sexual economy of writing, the confrontation of male mind and pen/penis with the virgin page. In a move from man's hand to woman's machine, he concludes, the gender of writing got reversed (273).

Needless to say, the increasing number of women who achieved access to the typewriter has not affected women's position in discourse. Throughout her formative years Moore herself vascillated between authorship and stereotypically female professional occupations. Having worked as a secretary and teacher of typewriting, she was well aware that technology can turn into a new kind of imprisonment, particularly for women. In a 1926 review of two exhibitions—the Grolier's Club displayed items on the art of printing and typography; the New York Public Library, woodcuts and a facsimile of the pictorial edition of "The Letter of Columbus on the Discovery of America"—Moore comments on the latter document:

> [Columbus] found the natives "timid and full of fear" and says that "the women appear to work more than men," prompting perhaps no inevitable comparison with the present. Assisted by the typewriter, the sewing-

machine, and the telephone, the American white woman—and with her, every other—seems as time goes on, more serviceable and less servile and the "natives" are, one likes to think, becoming more at home. (*Prose* 174)

Full of suggestive ambivalences and bitter ironies, this passage somewhat hesitatingly ("no inevitable comparison") compares the situation of Native American women in the late fifteenth century to that of modern American white women. Even though Moore emphasizes women's development from "servile" to "serviceable," the implied pun closely connects women's usefulness with her submission. By use of parallel structure ("more serviceable," "more at home") and metaphor ("becoming more at home"), Moore furthermore associates this submission ("serviceable," "servile") with colonization and proselytization.

While colonization turned the natives into strangers in their own home, women have remained strangers to all but the home, Moore subtly suggests. Women, she explicitly claims in her 1923 review of H.D.'s *Hymen,* are still "regarded as necessarily belonging to either of two classes—that of the intellectual freelance and that of the eternally sleeping beauty, effortless yet effective in the indestructible limestone keep of domesticity" (*Prose* 82). The particular use Moore made of the typewriter, however, counters such conventional notions of femininity and reflects decisive gender differences. As I will show in my reading of "The Fish," her idiosyncratic syllabic verse forms mark subjectivity as an in-between position that reject an established authority for an unorthodox one and mediate body and mind, beauty and intellect. At the same time, the poem displays what I consider a major principle of Moore's poetics: the use of deflection as a device of physical protection.

Using syllabic patterns, Moore takes a clearly radical position within the contemporaneous discussion of poetic form, even if she never theorized and advertised her practice the way her male contemporaries did. Her first essay, "The Accented Syllable" (1916), rejects both "rhymed" and "free" verse. In "rhymed verse," Moore argues, "a distinctive tone of voice is dependent on naturalistic effects, and naturalistic effects are so rare in rhyme as almost not to exist." Likewise, she opposes free verse's tendency toward mimesis: "So far as free verse is concerned," she writes, "it is the easiest thing in the world to create one intonation in the image of another" (*Prose* 34). Providing a variable and arbitrary structural device that cannot be transferred from one poem to another, syllabics neither create poetic conventions nor completely "avoid . . . the auras . . . of authority" (Holley, *Moore* 85). They assert, as Kenner puts it, an "authority of number . . . and typography" (99).

Syllabics are thus freed from traditional metric constraints while retaining measure, principle, and pattern—even though their measure is inaudible, their principle is hidden, and their (visual) pattern disappears when read out loud. For a poet who described her passion for writing as "too much in line with my natural excesses for me to experiment with it ad libitum" and who claimed that her "observations cannot be regularized" (*Prose* 436), they supplied a flexible frame. This frame incorporated what Moore called her "prime objective": rhythm. "If I succeeded in embodying a rhythm that preoccupied me, I was satisfied" (587). Rhythm, Moore repeatedly claimed, "is the person" (396). Just as Dickinson neglected the pentameter line for the functionally more appropriate hymns, Moore rejected meter for music, a music that is "by no means mimetic" but, rather, contrapuntual (Costello, "Wild Decorum" 52). In various ways syllabics assume their own particular authority by remaining "between the lines" of tradition and unconventionality. Notwithstanding his gender bias, Jarrell thus aptly called Moore "Miss-Facing-Both-Ways" (182).

Like the texts of Apollinaire, Mallarmé, or cummings, Moore's syllabics employ the page's white space for signification. One effect of such *espacement* is, as Mallarmé explained, in his preface to "Un coup de dés," that every time the paper "intervenes . . . an image, of itself," it prismatically subdivides ideas, has fiction even out and scatter. Narrative is avoided and displaced by an "unadorned use of thought with doublings back, goings on, runnings away," making the poem a "musical score" rather than a medium for verbal signification. Displaying a greater proportion of the "whiteness" that has traditionally symbolized the image of the flawless, mute female body "shaped and appropriated by the male creative pen" (Johnson, *World* 125) or, to use Mallarmé's own words, "controlled by his little manly reason," such *espacement,* moreover, as Johnson suggests, reclaims that body as voice.

Like Mallarmé's texts, Moore's syllabic patterns disrupt linearity, isolate subject, predicate, and object ("The Fish / / wade / through black jade") and underscore that "the meaning has very little to do with the pleasure the words give us" (Moore, *Prose* 31). Yet, apart from a few inversions, "The Fish" remains syntactically fully intact. And, just as Moore's reading of Mallarmé focused not on the page/body underlying his poems but on the verbal figures suggesting the movement of the mind, her own syllabic stanza patterns deconstruct the association of femininity and body by reassociating body and mind. Accordingly, typography for Moore "is not something superimposed on the meaning," as she writes in her review of cummings's *Eimi,* "but the author's mental handwriting" (301)—a strategy that, by realigning body and intellect, silence and speech, reconstitutes subjectivity. Likewise cummings's "line drawings" (562) represent to Moore "one who knew how 'in an epoque of Unself of noneself 'to be ONEself'" (563). Though by no means original, the desire for such balance of body and mind is highly significant in a female author's text. Whereas Whitman's celebrations of the body claim for the male subject what conventional constructions of manhood exclude, Moore usurps a supposedly male territory to reconceptualize femininity. Her depiction of H.D. as "intellectual, social woman, non-public and 'feminine'" (82) reflects an awareness that intellectuality in women's writing refashions femininity.

My claim that Moore's syllabics function in part to realign body and mind and to deconstruct this traditionally gendered binarism in the process is supported by the development of Moore's poem "The Fish." The early nonsyllabic version explicitly thematizes such union.

> The turquoise sea
> Of bodies.
> Sincerity of edge, in
> Such recesses of the mind, we
> Find flowers entwined
> With bodies there.
>
> (Qtd. in Holley, *Moore* 61)

The later syllabic version, by contrast, embodies such an alliance by inserting a third level of signification and subjectivity. This third level eases the tension between the poem's orderly physical appearance, its "neatness of finish" and the sense of wholeness and timelessness it evokes, and the elements of disorder, fragility, and violence inherent in its fragmented discourse and imagery, both of which undercut the poem's pretense of formal unity. This is the version reprinted in *Poems:*

THE FISH

> wade
> through black jade.
>   Of the crow-blue musselshells, one
>     keeps
>     adjusting the ash heaps;
>   opening and shutting itself like
>
> an
> injured fan.

The barnacles which encrust the
  side
    of the wave, cannot hide
  there for the submerged shafts of the

sun,
split like spun
  glass, move themselves with spotlight swift-
    ness
    into the crevices—
  in and out, illuminating

the
turquoise sea
  of bodies. The water drives a
    wedge
    of iron through the iron edge
  of the cliff, whereupon the stars,

pink
rice grains, ink
  bespattered jelly-fish, crabs like
    green
    lilies and submarine
  toadstools, slide each on the other.

All
external
  marks of abuse are present on
    this
    defiant edifice—
  all the physical features of

ac-
cident—lack
  of cornice, dynamite grooves, burns
    and
    hatchet strokes, these things stand
  out on it; the chasm side is

dead.
Repeated

   evidence has proved that it can
    live
   on what cannot revive
   its youth. The sea grows old in it.

Discussing this poem in the context of World War I, Slatin emphasized its vio-
lent nature and concern with the political climate in Europe, which preoccu-
pied so many writers at the time. "It is impossible for any one writing to-day,"
Lowell opened her 1917 publication *Tendencies in American Modern Poetry*, "not
to be affected by the war. It has overwhelmed us like a tidal wave" (v). Yet
Moore's poem does not merely relocate the armed conflict between nations in
a submarine scenery, in a "turquoise / sea of bodies." Instead, she appropriates
such violence to dramatize the interdependence of cultural forces, subject con-
stitution, and the body. In this way "The Fish" compares to Dickinson's "She
rose to His Requirement." Dickinson's text suggests that conformity to cultural
constraints represses fundamental aspects of female subjectivity, generating sub-
versive energy in the process. Moore's poem, conversely, exposes its patterned
surface structures as a protective device and resistance against the destabilizing
forces that endanger otherness—an otherness that "The Fish" as well as earlier
poems such as "To a Steam Roller" (1915) and "Diligence Is to Magic as
Progress Is to Flight" (1915) associate with corporeality, flexibility, and femi-
ninity.

  While the early texts juxtapose conformity with freewheeling otherness
and femininity, culture with nature, "The Fish" equivocates this binarism by
foregrounding its own physical features. Motivated by a compassion for the sea's
"bodies," the text transforms their materiality and projects it onto its textual
surface. The first four stanzas of "The Fish" depict an underwater wasteland,
where nature and otherness are invaded by culture or, more precisely, by nat-
ural energies rewritten as cultural forces. The fish "wade" through waters of
jade, the "opening and closing" shell resembles "an / injured fan," and the bar-
nacles cannot hide from the "enlightening" forces of the sun ("the submerged
shafts of the sun, / split like spun / glass"), which penetrate and usurp the sub-
merged, dark spaces of their existence. As light eliminates darkness, culture
comes to dominate nature. Comparing the "crow-blue musselshell" to "an /
injured fan" and the sun to "spun glass," taking water as "a wedge / of iron"
and the cliff as an "iron edge," the poem in fact draws the reader's attention
from the submerged physical entities to another scene, from nature to culture,
from depth to surface.

  The subjection of the fragile aquatic fauna and flora to powers of darkness and light, solids and fluids, to forces that touch, cut, penetrate, and reflect upon one another, finds its correspondence in the "external / marks of abuse" that the syllabic pattern inflicts upon the poem itself. Setting the spotlight on these edges of signification, the text "suppresses" and in this way also protects supposedly "deeper" meanings, preserves the poem's body and the sea animals alike, and reinstalls materiality on another level of the poem. By use of metaphor—the poem parallels the moving surfaces of the water ("wedge of iron") with the vertical "iron edge / of the cliff"—and the obsolete conjunction *whereupon* whose reference remains indefinite, the poem collapses the opposition of flexibility and resistance that characterizes the earlier poems. Using *whereupon* in a spatial instead of a causal sense, linearity is suspended. The surface becomes the place where high ("stars") and low ("crabs"), transcendence and immanence, timelessness ("stars") and transitoriness ("crabs," submarine toadstools"), meet and turn into something else ("pink / rice grains," "green / lilies"). Thus, the poem also draws a line between the materiality of language and the metaphorical value of corporeality and the body.

At stake in Moore's poem is, consequently, not the return of the body but its protection by means of projection and deflection. The foregrounding of dazzling surfaces is part of the predominantly defensive disposition of Moore's poetry, which also shows in her early "poetics of resistance," in the figures of her much discussed armored animals, and in the self-protective pose of the "acacia-like lady" featured in "People's Surroundings." This focus on defense—defined by psychoanalysis as a set of operations that limit or suppress whatever is apt to endanger the integrity and constancy of the biopsychological individual—is a fundamental element of Moore's designs of subjectivity. It serves as a shield against the various pressures of cultural conformity, "conventional opinion" (*CPMM* 51), and current literary trends, against conventions of ideal womanhood as well as against new ideals of femininity, which promoted freer attitudes toward sexuality and the body. The emphasis on poetic surfaces works as a device of deflection, which by the very means of fragmentation fashions subjectivity and protects the female body.

Many of Moore's readers have been irritated—in fact, frustrated—by her "battle-dressed" forms and figures, which are deemed responsible for the absence of erotic flavor in her work. Taking textual representation as an expression of actual experience, critics have tended to identify the poet herself with the aloof acacia-like lady, have taken her as an "archetype of the quaint literary spinster" (Kramer 7). Eliot's famous alliance of Moore with Christina Rossetti, for instance ("Moore" 51), builds on parallels between the poets' single lives more than on literary criteria. Moore's editing politics at the *Dial* elicited Hart

Crane's notion that "American poetry was in the hands of two hysterical virgins" (Molesworth 220). Williams's depiction of Moore as "saint" in the scene of contemporary poetry (*Autobiography* 146) has a comparable undertone, particularly in contrast to his remark "God knows, I am no saint or virgin" (*Letters* 156). Pound came to consider Moore as the exemplar of the "dispassionate" observer. "Marianne is scarce an exuberance," he wrote to Eliot in 1937, "rather protagonist for the rights of vitrification and petrifaxis" (*Letters* 387, 377).

The New Critics put all this even more bluntly. R. P. Blackmur, for example, claimed that "there is no sex anywhere in her poetry. No poet has been so chaste; but it is not the chastity that arises from an awareness—healthy or morbid—of the flesh, it is a special chastity aside from the flesh—a purity by birth and from the void" ("Method" 85). In a similar vein Jarrell generalizes:

> We are uncomfortable—or else too comfortable—in a world in which feeling, affection, charity, are so entirely divorced from sexuality and power, the bonds of the flesh. In this world of [Moore's] poems there are many thoughts, things, animals, sentiments, moral insights; but money and passion and power, the brute fact that *works,* whether or not correctly, whether or not precisely—the whole Medusa-face of the world: these are gone. (184)

Why, however, should there be "sex" and "flesh" in women's writing? What does this "fleshy" component consist of in a female author's text? Why does Moore prefer to draw the reader's attention from body to surface? And how does this bracketing of the body feed into her designs of female subjectivity?

To investigate these questions I will turn to Moore's poems "Those Various Scalpels" (1917) and "Black Earth" (1918). Embedding my analysis in a reading of Moore's early correspondence with Pound, I will show that the battle-dressed disposition of Moore's poetry depends on a cultural climate that denied women their own (subject) position by verbally referring them to the place of the body and the position of sexual object. In this context the body is not simply a metaphor for the self; it turns into a figure for women's cultural disposition. "Those Various Scalpels" delineates Moore's idiosyncratic aesthetics as a device that signals subjectivity, protects the female body, and reclaims Renaissance fictions of femininity for the modern female subject, thus recreating her in another scenario.

## Reading for the Body

Eight months after Pound's essay "Marianne Moore and Mina Loy" (1918) appeared in the *Little Review,* Moore sent its author a letter accompanied by two

poems and a prose note. Pound's reply was not restricted to professional mat-
ters; it also commented on the textures of Moore's life and looks, thus inter-
mingled what Dickinson and Moore themselves tried to keep apart. Dickinson's
first unsigned correspondence to Higginson included a card with her name in a
separate envelope, separating her own person from the "supposed person[s]" of
her poems (L 268). When Higginson inquired about her looks, she remained
elusive and drew the critic's gaze from her physical features toward the figures
of language, instead. "I had no portrait, now, but am small, like the Wren, and
my Hair is bold, like the Chestnut Bur—and my eyes, like the Sherry in the
Glass, that the Guest leaves." Moore's worry "that the bare facts that [she has]
to offer, may not cause work that [she] may do from time to time, utterly to fail
in interest," takes a similar function ("Letter" 16). The word *bare* projects her
inclination to conceal her private life as an attempt to cover and protect the
body. Pound's reading of Moore's poems, in contrast, attempts to put her in
place—that is, to project the female writer as other, body, and silence.

This becomes evident when Pound intertwines poetry with biography: "I
want to know, relatively," he wrote, "your age, and whether you are working
on Greek quantitive measures or on René Ghil or simply by ear (if so a very
good ear)" (203). "O what about your age," he inquired, "how much more
youngness is there to go into the work, and how much closening can be
expected?" (204). By measuring age in the context of meter, Pound aligns the
rhythms of language with those of woman's body, the originality of her text
with her sexual innocence, lack of closure with youth, closure with the circu-
larity of women's existence. Referring Moore's metric practice to the senses
("simply by ear") and male influences, be they "Greek quantitive measures,"
"Renè Ghil," or his own work,[27] Pound diminishes her own achievements.
Aware that her syllabics had covered new ground in American poetry, Moore,
however, was by no means ready to retreat from her territory.

Pound's inquiry about Moore's looks comes along squeezed in between
matters of publication and payment. Having just suggested places of publication
for Moore's poems, he launches the following question: "And are you a jet
black Ethiopian Othello-hued, or was that line in one of your *Egoist* poems but
part of your general elaboration and allegory and designed to differentiate your
colour from that of the surrounding menagerie?" (204–5). As a response, Moore
offers the following data:

> I was born in 1887 and brought up in the home of my grandfather, a cler-
> gyman of the Presbyterian church. I am Irish by descent, possibly Scotch
> also, but purely Celtic. . . . Black Earth, the poem to which I think you
> refer, was written about an elephant that I have, [*sic*] named Melancthon;

and contrary to your impression, I am altogether a blond and have red hair. ("Letter" 16)

Eliding the father from her lifeline, Moore outbalanced this gap by emphasizing the religious faiths of her grandfather and the maternal, Irish line of her heritage. Most suggestive, though, is Moore's misreading of Pound's reference to the "Dark King" as connoting "Black Earth"[28] and her insistence on her blondness and Presbytarian, Celtic background, which interferes with Pound's fantasies concerning her possibly dark and exotic ("Ethopian") appearance and ancestry, just as her poem "Those Various Scalpels" does. Pound's hysterical response to Moore's letter and poem, to which I will return at a later point, shows that the poem's sense of subjectivity frustrates the desire for sexual/textual contentment with which male readers approach women's writing. As a consequence, Pound's complaints not only demonstrate that the male critic judges women's cultural work by reading through her body. They also attest that Moore's poetry destabilizes the position of her reader.

"Those Various Scalpels": Femininity as Fragmentation

First published in Bryn Mawr's magazine *Lantern* in 1917, "Those Various Scalpels" has been reprinted without severe changes in all of Moore's collected volumes as well as in *Contact* (1921) and Pound's anthology *Profiles* (1932). This is the 1921 version from *Poems*:

THOSE VARIOUS SCALPELS

Those
various sounds consistently indistinct, like intermingled
          echoes
     struck from thin glass successively at random—the
     inflection disguised: your hair, the tails of two
          fighting-cocks head to head in stone—like sculptured
          scimitars re-
       peating the curve of your ears in reverse order: your eyes,
          flowers of ice

and
snow sown by tearing winds on the cordage of disabled
          ships: your raised hand

an ambiguous signature: your cheeks, those rosettes
of blood on the stone floors of French châteaux, with
        regard to which guides are so affirmative:
    your other hand

a
bundle of lances all alike, partly hid by emeralds from
        Persia
    and the fractional magnificence of Florentine
    goldwork—a collection of half a dozen little objects
        made fine
        with enamel in gray, yellow, and dragonfly blue: a lemon, a

pear
and three bunches of grapes, tied with silver: your dress, a
        magnificent square
    cathedral of uniform
    and at the same time, diverse appearance—a species of
        vertical vineyard rustling in the storm
        of conventional opinion. Are they weapons or scalpels?
        Whetted

to
brilliance by the hard majesty of that sophistication which
        is su-
    perior to opportunity, these things are rich
    instruments with which to experiment but surgery is
        not tentative: why dissect destiny with instruments
        which
        are more highly specialized than the tissues of destiny
        itself?

                                                                (7)

This poem is significant here not simply because it focuses on the repre-
sentation of femininity. More than any other of Moore's poems, it foregrounds
the part disruptive discourse plays in the construction of female subjectivity.
Interrelating the portrait of a female figure with a debate on the function of lan-
guage as scalpel and weapon, it recreates female subjectivity as an ambivalent
bidirectional stance, geared both to explore and analyze the material world's
otherness and to protect the otherness of the female body and being. The text's

idiosyncracies work in a way comparable to the striking garment in which the female figure is clad. They distract attention away from the woman's body to that of the poem.

"Those Various Scalpels" displays the many idiosyncracies of Moore's poetics. The poem's visual pattern alternates short and long lines and symmetrically indents the left-hand margin, though the number of syllables in lines and stanzas varies throughout the poem and the number of lines in the stanzas decreases and increases. Presenting an array of "details in one long, syntactically dismembered sentence" (Schulman 31), the text compares with "People's Surroundings." With a few exceptions *(and, like)*, conjunctions are replaced by punctuation, sound repetitions, and inner rhyme. The colons keep the interrelation between clauses indefinite. The reader finds "rains of nouns" and adjectives (Kenner 101), yet most inflections are "disguised." Verbs frequently appear in their present or past participle forms and are used as adjectives ("sculptured / scimitars," "tearing winds," "disabled / ships"), in participial clauses ("scimitars re- / peating"), or as passive constructions ("snow sown by," "partly hid by"). As in Moore's more explicitly philosophical poems, forms of *to be* suggest stability. The catalogue part of the poem, moreover, deletes copulas, thus turning subject and complement into appositions ("your eyes / flowers of ice"). The dash—trademark of Dickinson's aesthetics—is used thrice in place of a copula, thereby equivocating the alliances it creates, such as the association of woman's hair and "sculptured / scimitars." In the last stanza syntactic overdetermination and the final question counterbalance closure. And, like most of Moore's early poems, "Those Various Scalpels" addresses an other. Here, however, the addressee is a female whom the speaker neither rejects nor allies with but feels rather ambivalent about ("ambiguous signature"). In any case, "Those Various Scalpels" is not a "parody of [Moore] herself" (Koch 164). It is the portrait of a woman put in a frame that reflects on the poem's very processes of picture taking. Before turning to the self-referential frame, let us take a look at the portrait.

As Moore's "portrait of a lady," "Those Various Scalpels" stands in the tradition of the blazon, a Renaissance convention, which represents woman by cataloguing her physical attributes and describing the various parts of her body from tip to toe. The blazon thus contains two kinds of figures that cut, condense, and finally displace woman: on the one hand, the poem's addressee, not a "you" but, rather, a female figure in fragments, objectified and represented by her bodily parts and dress; on the other, the rhetorical figures, metaphors, similes, and images that substitute for an already compartmentalized figure. Moore's poem has been read in relation to Sidney's blazon as well as to modern versions such as Pound's "Portrait d'une Femme" (1912), Eliot's "Portrait of a

Lady" (1917), and Williams's poem of the same title (1934). Like these texts, Moore paints her picture through catalogue rhetoric, an extended simile, which reinforces the association of woman with objects from nature and art in elaborate detail. Unlike the speakers in her contemporaries' poems who "experience their own entirety at the expense of their femmes and ladies" (Heuving, "Gender" 121), Moore's speaker, preoccupied with "these rich instruments with which to experiment," is herself as "pulverized" as the female figure she depicts. By employing the convention of the blazon more faithfully than her contemporaries, Moore parodies a genre that has served to (mis)represent women. And yet her choice of the blazon is not merely ironic. Williams's "Portrait of a Lady" employs the blazon for a critique of metaphor as a means to capture immediacy. Moore more likely chose the genre because it reflects both women's culturally inscribed disposition and the cultural operation that refers woman to that position by fragmenting her body and being alike.

Fragmentation dominates the first part of the poem's frame ("Those Various Scalpels . . . inflection disguised"), whose apposition of *scalpels* and *sounds* presents Moore's poetic practice as an instrument for analysis and dissection. Here sense and subjectivity are governed by the succession of "intermingled echoes struck from" the various "consistently indistinct" s sounds that gradually decrease in number toward the third stanza, only to increase again toward the fifth and last stanza. For Kristeva such accumulation of phonemes compensates for the poem's lack of syntax. Associating sounds with scalpels, Moore, in contrast, functionalizes them as tools for analysis and dissection and redefines writing as surgery.

Such analogies between writing and surgery are not foreign to Dickinson either, occurring both in her sense of criticism as "surgery"[29] and in poems that depict the female writer as surgeon, such as "She dealt her pretty words like Blades—" (J 479). They can be illuminated by Walter Benjamin's essay "The Work of Art in the Age of Mechanical Reproduction" (1936), which compares cameraman and painter to surgeon and magician.

> The surgeon represents the polar opposite of the magician. The magician heals a sick person by the laying on of hands; the surgeon cuts into the patient's body. The magician maintains the natural distance between the patient and himself; though he reduces it very slightly by the laying on of hands, he greatly increases it by virtue of his authority. The surgeon does exactly the reverse; he greatly diminishes the distance between himself and the patient by penetrating into the patient's body, and increases it but little by the caution with which his hand moves among the organs. In short,

in contrast to the magician—who is still hidden in the medical practitioner—the surgeon at the decisive moment abstains from facing the patient man to man; rather, it is through the operation that he penetrates into him.

Magician and surgeon compare to painter and cameraman. The painter maintains in his work a natural distance from reality, the cameraman penetrates deeply into its web. There is a tremendous difference between the pictures they obtain. That of the painter is a total one, that of the cameraman consists of multiple fragments which are assembled under a new law. (*Illuminations* 233–34)

Like Benjamin, Moore's volume *Poems* juxtaposes surgeon and magician, as "Those Various Scalpels" is placed right next to "Diligence Is to Magic as Progress Is to Flight." Only the writer as surgeon, however, dissects subjectivity and reassembles the fragments under the law of sounds and other nonreferential functions of language. Apposing *scalpels* and *sounds*, "Those Various Scalpels" reassociates the text's heading and body—an alliance further strengthened in a later version, which adds a comma to the title and deletes the capitalization at the beginning of the first line. Likewise, the poem's colons function as joints: facing both ways, they reconnect the poem's frame with the dismembered parts of its centerpiece like a permeable membrane.

The gypsy featured in Moore's poem "Diligence Is to Magic," in contrast, "ride[s] upon" but does not interfere with the physical integrity symbolized by the elephant's trunk. Such sense of unity characteristic of "enlightened" concepts of (male) subjectivity gets interrogated in Moore's poem "Black Earth," which compares to "Those Various Scalpels" on the grounds of formal pattern, topic, and historical context. Both poems negotiate dangers of disintegration and the need for protection. Both are, by reference or generic convention, set in the Renaissance. They differ, however, with regard to gender: whereas "Those Various Scalpels" figures the female subject as a fragmented body whose defensive disposition destabilizes the (male) reader, "Black Earth" presents the self-centered position of the enlightened male subject whose "airy" rationality is destabilized by "earthen" unreason.

"The Beautiful Element of Unreason": Disseminating
the Self-Centered Subject

Applying the device of the persona, the mask of an elephant-skinned animal, and the lyrical "I" to ponder the Gnostic concern with the dualism of matter

and spirit, body and soul, "Black Earth" remains an exceptional piece in
Moore's oeuvre. Opening with a sense of wholeness and integrity, symbolized
by the trunk of the elephant, the poem's persona and voice come apart at the
seams in the second half of the poem, due to a foregrounding of what is pre-
sented as the "Beautiful element of unreason." Here is the text's first version, of
April 1918.

Openly, yes,
With the naturalness
    Of the hippopotamus or the alligator
    When it climbs out on the bank to experience the

Sun, I do these
Things which I do, which please
    No one but myself. Now I breathe and now I am sub-
    Merged; the blemishes stand up and shout when the object

In view was a
Renaissance; shall I say
    The contrary? The sediment of the river which
    Encrusts my joints, makes me very gray but I am used

To it, it may
Remain there; do away
    With it and I am myself done away with, for the
    Patina of circumstance can but enrich what was

There to begin
With. This elephant skin
    Which I inhabit, fibred over like the shell of
    The coco-nut, this piece of black glass through which no light

Can filter—cut
Into checkers by rut
    Upon rut of unpreventable experience—
    It is a manual for the peanut-tongued and the

Hairy toed. Black
But beautiful, my back

Is full of the history of power. Of power? What
Is powerful and what is not? My soul shall never

Be cut into
By a wooden spear; through-
　　Out childhood to the present time, the unity of
　　Life and death has been expressed by the circumference

Described by my
Trunk; nevertheless, I
　　Perceive feats of strength to be inexplicable after
　　All; and I am on my guard; external poise, it

Has its centre
Well nurtured—we know
　　Where—in pride, but spiritual poise, it has its centre where?
　　My ears are sensitized to more than the sound of

The wind. I see
And I hear, unlike the
　　Wandlike body of which one hears so much, which was made
　　To see and not to see; to hear and not to hear,

That tree trunk without
Roots, accustomed to shout
　　Its own thoughts to itself like a shell, maintained intact
　　By who knows what strange pressure of the atmosphere; that

Spiritual
Brother to the coral
　　Plant, absorbed into which, the equable sapphire light
　　Becomes a nebulous green. The I of each is to

The I of each,
A kind of fretful speech
　　Which sets a limit on itself; the elephant is?
　　Black earth preceded by a tendril? It is to that

Phenomenon
The above formation
　　Translucent like the atmosphere—a cortex merely—
　　That on which darts cannot strike decisively the first

Time, a substance
Needful as an instance
    Of the indestructibility of matter; it
    Has looked at the electricity and at the earth-

Quake and is still
Here; the name means thick. Will
    Depth be depth, thick skin be thick, to one who can see no
    Beautiful element of unreason under it?

The poem opens with a somewhat narcissistic celebration of the speaker's physical and hedonistic existence. Visualized by the contractions and expansions of the syllabic pattern, the animal's oscillation between exposure and retreat is a movement that recurs throughout Moore's poetry, including the poems "Ennui," "O to Be a Dragon," "Those Various Scalpels," and "The Fish." The immersion suggests dyadic unity, protection, and baptism, emergence a kind of (re)birth ("the object / In view was a / Renaissance"). As in "The Fish" images of light and dark mark these moves, though with a difference. Whereas the "black jade" waters in "The Fish" are being penetrated, the water in "Black Earth" is impeccable, a "piece of black glass through which no light can filter." In contrast to "Those Various Scalpels" and "The Fish," which project subjectivity as fragmentation, the speaker of "Black Earth" insists on his unity and wholeness of being: "My soul shall never / Be cut into / By a wooden spear."

This notion of unity is supported by the image of the river, whose waters are both a protective, nurturing place and a symbol of "time, a substance," which leave their traces on the animal's skin. Like "The Fish" and "Those Various Scalpels," "Black Earth" thus assigns surface structures two fundamental functions. The physical marks of "unpreventable experience" both signify ("manual") the animal's "history of power" and serve as a shield, a kind of camouflage that protects the speaker's desired integrity against outer attacks. Since the elephant's "trunk" is a polyvalent image, suggesting ego, globe, and universal soul ("Spiritual / Brother to the coral / Plant"), its patina embodies the crust of the earth as well as the ego boundary upon which the speaker deems his existence to depend ("do away / With it and I am myself done away with"). Thus protected, "the unity of/Life and death" seems to remain unaffected by the circumstances of history.

First insisting on his integrated identity, the speaker's doubt-ridden reflections on the origin of power—that is, on the relation between self and other—mark a turning point. Unable to locate the center of "spiritual poise," the speaker acknowledges forces that resist unity and remain "inexplicable after / All." As the lyrical "I" opens toward otherness ("I see / And I hear, unlike the / Wandlike body . . . / That tree trunk without / Roots, accustomed to shout / Its own thoughts to itself like a shell"), his self-centeredness is dispersed. Interestingly enough, the shell—here a figure of narcicism and a place of echoes in which "the I of each is to / / The I of each, / A kind of fretful speech"—is reimagined as a place of maternal nurture and protection in Moore's later poem "The Paper Nautilus" (1941). In the last half of the poem, the lyrical "I" gradually dissolves, displaced by a communal "we," a third-person speaker, and synecdoches. This destabilization is reinforced by an increase of interrogative constructions and, throughout the last third of the text, ambiguous articles and pronoun references. It corresponds to an impairment of the poem's syntactical structure and syllabic pattern. As the "Beautiful element of unreason" comes to dominate the poem, it adds a third dimension and thus deconstructs both the supposed unity and the binarism of body and soul.

Moore's poem interrogates this dichotomy between body and spirit within a religious context. Attributing "Black Earth" to "an elephant . . . named Melancthon," it refers the reader to the Reformation and the beginning of the modern age. In Moore's text Melancthon, the reformist theologian and Martin Luther's closest collaborator (whose Christian name, Philipp Schwarzert, literally translates into "black earth,") embodies these eras, which destroyed the central authority of the Church of Rome, led to the establishment of various Reformed and Protestant churches in northwestern and central Europe, and fostered the emergence of the concept of the individual. The "object in view" in Moore's poem was thus, indeed, "a Renaissance," which, as the indefinite article suggests, refers to both the beginning of the modern age and to "the American Renaissance of 1912" (*Prose* 675).

Situating its critique of unity and centricity in a context that aligns the emergence of modern man with modernist discourse, Moore's poem opposes the Ptolemaic worldview, the concept of the rounded Renaissance person, the Cartesian sense of self, as well as the self-centeredness of her own age. As she dismantles the binarism between the "indestructability of matter" and a transcendent sense of wholeness by foregrounding the "unreason" of destabilized discourse, Moore underscores that "speech . . . sets a limit on itself," that concepts of unity and identity always already exclude the speaker. As "Those Various Scalpels" suggests, they have always excluded woman. When the "object in view was [the] Renaissance" of the female subject, fragmentation reigned. Presenting a female figure, Moore consequently comes to doubt the value of her deconstructive aesthetics and questions the adequacy of her sophisticated "surgery": "why dissect destiny," "Those Various Scalpels" asks, "with instruments which are more highly specialized than the tissues of destiny itself?" Yet, even though the poem's turn to the philosophical is underscored by use of complete sentence structures, unreason prevails. While the opening frame produces sense and subjectivity by sound rather than syntax, the poem's final part loses sense and subject to an overdose of correct yet confusing syntax, to a hyperbole of subordinate clauses and indefinite conjunctions, to pronouns, determiners, prepositions, and articles with ambivalent references.

Most significant, however, is the question "Are they weapons or scalpels?" as it reconnects the frame's two parts and emphasizes the twofold function that sounds may take. The answer is: both, because the difference between weapon and tool is, as Scarry explains, only slight, depending not so much on the object used but on the object operated upon (such as the presence of a sentient or insentient surface). Just as a knife can be both tool and arm, language may be both scalpel and weapon. In any case the user is magnified because the change effected objectifies his or her presence in the world (Scarry 172–74). Moreover, though the use of tool or weapon substitutes the work of the muscles, it always extends the human body (67). The battle-dressed disposition of Moore's female figure, of her poems, thus serves two functions: it dissects conventional femininity and defends an emerging female subject.

Fragmentation as a Shield of Female Subjectivity

Accordingly, even though the images presenting woman's multifarious otherness compare to Renaissance poems, Moore's figure has come a long way from "the piece-meal female of the Renaissance catalogue" (Carruthers 297). Moore parodies traditional images of femininity and generic conventions alike. Describing the female's "eyes" as "flowers of ice and snow," she clearly distinguishes this woman from Spenser's lady whose "modest eyes" were "abashed to behold / So many gazers, as on her do stare, / Upon the lowly ground affixed are" ("Epithalamion" 159–61). Resonating with traditional connotations of innocence, purity, and death, Moore's metaphor creates the image of a crystal cool beauty, appropriating Milton's depiction of winds, "arm'd with ice / And snow and stormy gust and flaw" (PL 10:697–98). Whereas Moore's later poem "Poetry" (1919) presents hands able to "grasp, eyes / that can dilate, hair that can rise," the fragmented female figure seems frozen stiff. Comparing her hair to "the tails of two / fighting-cocks head to head in stone," her hand to "a / bundle of lances," her cheeks to "rosettes / of blood on the stone floors of French châteaux," and her dress to "a magnificent square / cathedral of uniform," Moore rewrites "woman's nature" as culture, using the very strategy applied in "The Fish." Employing images of combat and cultural production such as sculpture, stonemasonry, architecture, and gold work to represent femininity, the poet, moreover, reassociates culture and nature in significant ways. While the female body has traditionally served as model for men's cultural practice, Moore reappropriates their products as female armor. This implies that (mis)representations of femininity also protect women and subvert their makers' intentions. And, finally, Moore's portrait aligns women's cultural work with violence and warring, thus redefines it as cultural combat.

Instead of being adorned in fairness, Moore's female figure—exposed to the "storm of conventional opinion," the "tearing winds on the cordage of disabled / ships"—resembles a battle-dressed fortress clad in a coat of arms. In this way Moore's poem is a blazon in more than one sense. The poem, in fact, plays upon the ambiguity of the word's original literal meaning and its meaning as a literary term. As a verb, *blazon* means to describe in proper heraldic language, to paint or depict in colors, to illuminate; to inscribe (anything) with arms, paintings, names of distinction; to adorn or give luster to, and to proclaim and make public. The noun *blazon* is defined as armorial bearing, coat of arms, escutcheon; as the description or representation of heraldic or armorial bearings; and as ostentious display, show, or publication. Its original meaning, however, is shield. "Those Various Scalpels" thus is a pretext of "His Shield," indeed.

A shield is a device that protects the body in combat, known since prehistoric times. Made of wood, wickerwork, or metal, circular, square, or tricornered, flat or vaulted, it may cover the whole body or the breast only. Heraldic shields or bearings use ornamentation to identify the knights in their armor or later to signify their master's position within the feudal hierarchy. By the end of the thirteenth century heraldic bearings became hereditary; nowadays anyone can wear his or her own coat of arms.[30] With the rise of firearms the shield lost its significance. Not so in the animal kingdom, where, as Moore's poems remind us, arthropodes and reptiles keep using shields, the ossified and horny skins of their carapaces, the "sting-proof-scales," and "artichoke set leg-and body plates" for protection (*CPMM* 118). And neither does this apply to Moore's poetics: "A suit of armor," she wrote in 1925, "is impressively poetic. The moveable plates suggest the wearer" (qtd. in Molesworth xxi). Like a heraldic shield that protects, signifies, and covers and also identifies its owner, Moore's "sting-proof" poetic practice does not efface a self, as has been claimed. Reproducing the conventional sense of femininity as fragmentation, it appropriates fragmentation as a shield for a newly emerging female subject and, like the ornamentation on a shield, functions as her *carte d'identité* and means of subject constitution. Poetic disruptions are, like Moore's striking eccentric dress code, not only a kind of camouflage but also an ostentatious sign, an inscription on the body suggesting the subject.

As mere sensual object, [the body] in itself has no meaning;
clothes ensure the transition from the sensual to
signification.[31]
                                                    —Roland Barthes

## Styles and Fashions

"It is not so much that clothes make the man," Moore copied from a review of J. Hügel's book *The Psychology of Clothes,* "as that they stand for him. They are like writing on his body, explaining what he is, for the world to decipher if it has the key."[32] Moore herself took fashion as a kind of discourse and frequently interrelated poetic style with dress code. Not only was Moore's portrait of a lady, according to Molesworth, partly inspired by a cover design from a 1915 issue of *Vogue,* showing a woman in an extraordinary costume (106). Its question, "Are they weapons or scalpels?" refers to the poem's sounds just as to the lady's apparel, suggesting that she is indeed "dressed to kill" as well as to signify. Somewhat analogously, both Dickinson's and Moore's self-dramatization strategically play with dress codes, and—like the unorthodox attire of their poems—respond, in the words Moore copied from Frank Parson, to "the human requirement for shelter" as well as expression.[33] Both poets employed a somewhat "showy" outer appearance to create a room of their own, walk behind a veil, while also staging and disrupting gender conventions. Unlike Dickinson's white dress, the polysemic material sign of her "White Election" (J 528), Moore's suits and hats cultivated a battle-dressed appearance. Like the female figure in "Those Various Scalpels," she favored a kind of "uniform" and what Parson called the "'male style' for women," thus employing elements of cross-dressing and camouflage in order to wrap herself in an aura of distance.[34] What Moore said about Dickinson also applies to herself: "To free and to protect was her necessity" (*Prose* 291).

Moore's favorite fashions parallel her inclinations in writing. Just as her essays on style emphasize the necessity of clarity without denying the circuitousness of her own poetics, Moore's articles on fashion privilege the functional and plain without dismissing "jewelry of intricate detail with no thought of time wasted in the making" (*Prose* 597). Just as her poems' eye-catching irregularities, elaborate accessories can deflect the observer's gaze. "If a wide expanse of skin is favored," Moore writes in "Dress and Kindred Subjects" (1965), "there could be a tulle, marabou, lace or fur border to divert the eye from banal skin and bone" (*Prose* 597). Whereas "males merely 'show of their muscularity, like a coat of armor made by their own flesh,'" Judith Gaines comments on the recent proliferation of male bodies on display, "undressed females typically reveal their weakness, openness and vulnerability" (12). Accordingly, when deprived of the opportunity to polish her early texts before they were published as poems, Moore felt exposed. In a letter addressed to Bryher on the very day she had received her first copy of *Poems,* Moore wrote:

> Now that I am a pterodactyl, it is perhaps well that you even with your hardened gaze, cannot see what it is to be a pterodactyl with no rock in which to hide. In "Variations of Plants and Animals under Domestication," Darwin speaks of a variety of pigeon that is born naked without any down whatsoever. I feel like that Darwinian gosling.[35]

Potential changes, omissions, and gaps would have served as rocks under which to hide, as down in which to dress. They would have created a surface "whetted to brilliance" that deflects the reader's "hardened gaze" from the poem's body ("ptero*dactyl*"). But, more than that, as Jarrell's aforementioned complaint implies, the brilliant surfaces of Moore's poems also undermine her reader's position, whose potency depends upon the (sexual) difference he detects in the text.

Disruption as Deflection of the Male Eye / I

Let's hear it again:

> We are uncomfortable—or else too comfortable—in a world in which feeling, affection, charity, are so entirely divorced from sexuality and power, the bonds of the flesh. In this world of [Moore's] poems there are many thoughts, things, animals, sentiments, moral insights; but money and passion and power, the brute fact that works, whether or not correctly, whether or not precisely—the whole Medusa-face of the world: these are gone. (Jarrell 184)

For an analysis of the desire expressed here let us turn to Freud's reading of the myth of the Medusa. In "Medusa's Head" (1922) Freud associates Medusa's serpent hair and her decapitated head with the horrors of castration. The viewer's paralysis effected by Medusa's own gaze, by contrast, symbolizes erection to Freud and thus "offers consolation to the spectator: he is still in possession of a penis, and the stiffening reassures him of the fact" (212). Highlighting Medusa's lack instead of her possessions, such an interpretation disempowers female authority. While, historically, Medusa's serpent hairs have been read as an image of menstrual secrets and female wisdom, as a figure of force and inspiration, or, as in Cixous's essay "The Laugh of the Medusa," of the dissolution of phallic unity, Freud denied Medusa's potency. Whether alive and castrating or decapitated and castrated, the male spectator / reader scores the ego boost.[36]

In view of Freud's claim that man overcomes his fear of castration and is reassured in his identity by witnessing woman's lack, Jarrell's discomfort with Moore's writing reflects his dissatisfaction with a body of texts that fails to confirm his potency. Lacking conventional marks of femininity, Moore's writing refuses to "erect" her reader and, instead, questions masculinity by appropriating male authority. Jarrell's critique thus implicitly acknowledges the very power of Moore's (phallic) female figures, dressed in "a magnificent square cathedral of uniform" or explicitly modeled after Medusa, "stiff with jewels / her dress embroidered all over slightly with snakes of . . . gold and silver."[37]

My claim that the battle-dressed, "chaste" appearance of Moore's poetry irritates the male reader's position finds support in Pound's early reading of Moore. In his first letter to Moore, Pound still announced that her texts attract and "hold" his eye / I:

> Your stuff holds my eye. Most verse I merely slide off of (God I do ye thank for this automatic self-protection), BUT my held eye goes forward very slowly, and I know how simple many things appear to me which people of supposed intelligence come to me to have explained. (*Letters* 204)

After reading Moore's poetic portrait "Those Various Scalpels" and her brief biographical sketch, Pound loses his erect, self-congratulatory posture. While his letter refrains from explicitly sexist remarks, the mock poem that supplemented his correspondence launches a blunt attack. The poem, which was reprinted in its unexpurgated form for the first time in Bonnie Kime Scott's anthology *The Gender of Modernism* (1990), clearly ridicules Moore's poetry, self-presentation, and Christian morality. Self-described as blond and Celtic, Moore turns into the archetype of monotheistic Protestantism that Pound rejected in favor of his belief in anti-Christian, "ecstatic," and life-asserting forces (Sieburth, *Instigations* 130), symbolized by elements of sexual, ethnic, and cultural otherness featured in his text. Assuming that his addressee cannot "stand for [his] temple to Pallas Athene and for [his] cult of / other ancient and less prohibitive deities: for [his] preference of Omar to Melancthon" and objecting to her "Nathaniel Hawthorne frigidities" (*Gender* 364), Pound dismisses Moore both as muse and as object of sexual longing. At the same time, he projects the desire that would have occurred had she been more "other"—that is, "dark, nubian, ethiopian." In the given context questions such as "could I have risen to it," "could I have transcended into Ethopia," "could I / have stood Ethiopia," suggest potency and penetration (363). Bursting with suggestiveness, Pound's letter reads like a symbolic sexual assault; the male figure with "varied contacts" transforms into a "polygamous" "cockleshell [that] calls at so many ports," turns "intruder." At the same time, when Pound decides to "leave [Moore] to Mr Kreymborg and Bill Williams / and leave off meddling in American matters" (364), his "poem" merely refigures the relation between female author and male critic/editor/author(ity) as a sexual affair. Only a reader devoid of humor and literary understanding, Pound seems to suggest, would take the slipperiness of his text seriously. "You, my dear correspondent, / are a stabilized female" (363), who knows better, he seems to imply.

The sexual aggression inherent in Pound's text throws yet a different light on the battle-dressed and chaste disposition of Moore's work. It urges us to reconsider the seemingly ironic representation of the "acacia-like lady, shivering at the touch of a hand." Seen in this context, the rejection of touch and "the raised hand" of Moore's blazoned female figure indeed become "ambiguous signature[s]," signaling precautions against physical violence. Fear of physical contact is not simply motivated by what is commonly considered prudishness, armor not only a matter of virtuousness here but a shield against (male) aggression. The aesthetic and semantic "armor" of Moore's poetry thus deflects in order to react to and cope with gender and sexual difference. And so does her recourse to the Renaissance.

Female figures of Renaissance literature such as Sidney's Pamela, Spenser's Britomart, and Milton's Sabrina compare by their virtuous chastity. Celebrating this chastity as a superiority of reason and wisdom over passion and as a protective device against male physical assaults, Renaissance literature rediscovered Greek notions of chastity. While Christianity, according to Foucault, promoted the sexual abstinence of both men and women as a way to salvation and eternal life, ancient Greek culture understood chastity as an exercise of self-mastery, fundamental to freedom and the exercise of political power—that is, the power over others. "To be free in relation to pleasures was to be free of their authority; it was not to be their slave," writes Foucault (*Use of Pleasure* 79). "[T]he power of relinquishing / what one would keep," Moore puts it in "His Shield," "that is freedom" (*CPMM* 144). Likewise, for Spenser chastity signifies "not repression but a noble and disciplined life" (Kendrick 62). In Milton's *Comus* sexual purity and "the sage / And serious doctrine of virginity" (ll. 786–87) are celebrated as women's "hidden strengths" (l. 414), as the following passage— marked in Moore's copy of *The Poetical Works of John Milton* (1913)—suggests:

'Tis chastity, my brother, chastity:
She that has that, is clad in complete steel,
And like a quiver'd Nymph with Arrows keen
May trace huge Forests and unharbor'd Heaths,
Infamous Hills and sandy perilous wilds,
Where through the sacred rays of Chastity,
No savage fierce, Bandit or mountaineer
Will dare to soil her Virgin purity:

(ll. 420–27)

*Comus* is of interest here not only because of the interest Moore herself took in it but also because it is a text about ravishment, or rape—that is, about "a touch of a hand" that woman has every right to fear.[38] At the same time, by associating woman's physical mobility with silence, her eloquence with paralysis, Milton's masque declares intellect, speech, and femininity incompatible and defines the female body as the site of constraints and confinements.

Dickinson and Moore, each in her own way, appropriated these culturally ascribed dispositions of femininity to camouflage a cultural practice that designed its own sense of female subjectivity—a subjectivity that, by equivocating conventional marks of gender, surpasses the limits they set. Moore revives and appropriates fictions of femininity from Renaissance literature as battle dress for a female subject, who is both mobile and eloquent, who moves within yet also confronts cultural constraints. Her poetic displays of virgin strength are thus wholly different from what Charles Altieri considers "Mallarmé's fascination with virginity." "What was for Mallarmé largely speculation about the resources of virginity become for her absolutely fundamental questions of poetic identity" (*Painterly Abstraction* 259)—and of female subjectivity, I would add.

Overlayed by a high degree of ironization and parody, Moore's destabilized poetic discourse suggests that the emergence of the historical female subject is accompanied by strategies of travesty. Moore's "martial" (female) figures and mimic voices are in fact different configurations of that subject, fighting her way into cultural combat, equipped with an array of camouflage. Appropriating generic conventions such as the Renaissance blazon, Moore dresses her females in traditional apparal while at the same time appropriating that apparel as a shield, which both protects and signifies the emerging subject. In this way Moore's poetic disruptions function both as camouflage and as ostentatious signs suggesting the emerging female subject. Moore's writing thus confirms Irigaray's claim that mimicry and camouflage serve women as interim strategies on the way to female subjectivity. More than that, by proving these terms apt to conceptualize women's access to the symbolic order, Dickinson's and especially Moore's cultural practice, in turn, historicize Irigaray's theory. For Dickinson mimicry (of the mid-nineteenth-century "angel in the house" image, e.g.) still worked as a kind of magic hat, allowing her to retreat into private space and the production of unorthodox poetry. Moore, by contrast, used camouflage to protect her public appearance. For Rich, finally, mimicry of established aesthetic modes meant recognition but became a straitjacket once her poetry accommodated new political agendas.

In a response of July 1921 to a letter from H.D., Moore calls her *Poems* "my Cretan twilight baby or . . . veiled Mohammedan woman."[39] The "veiled Mohammedan woman," an image suggested by Moore's mother Mary Warner Moore, captures the poet's sense of female subjectivity, as other and female, as observing, yet veiled and hidden from the viewer's eye by a "uniform," though still capable of destabilizing, paralyzing that very eye / I. Unlike Mohammedan women, Moore could choose her own kind of camouflage; neither in dress codes nor in fictions of femininity, however, has such choice ever been free. Echoing both H.D.'s own phrase "my baby 'Hymen'" and invoking the Cretan pottery pattern on the cover design of her *Poems,* Moore's phrase "my Cretan twilight baby," in contrast, mediates a sense of the female origin and power of her work.[40] Minoan Crete, Paglia points out, was "the last major Western society to worship female powers." Moore thus locates her work in the "twilight" zone, on the edge between a female earth cult with elements of unreasonable beauty and a "sky-cult" of Apollonian and Judeo-Christian traditions (8), in a historically in-between position. Aligning creativity and reproduction, Moore's baby metaphor anticipates her later focus on the maternal, which parallels her poetry with that of Adrienne Rich—to a certain degree, that is.

I want to close by turning to Rich, who repeatedly rejected Moore's poetics and sense of subjectivity. In her review of Hayden Carruth's volumes *For You* and *The Clay Hill Anthology,* entitled "A Tool or a Weapon" (1971), however, she shares part of Moore's perspective on the function of poetry while also insisting on the significant differences between modernist and political post-modern verse. Carruth's title *For You*, Rich wrote,

> goes to the root of what this kind of poetry is really about: a man who uses language as a tool or weapon for his own survival, picks up that tool, honed and tempered by him, its handle stained with his sweat, and offers it to us, as if it might be of use to us, too. There is no brilliance of craft or aesthetic surface that can do this for us of itself; this is a quality of poetry that the poet conceives as functional, as a way of existing—first for oneself, then perhaps for others. (409)

Like Moore and Dickinson, Rich takes language as a tool and a weapon for survival, though it is no longer the "brilliance of craft" nor the "aesthetic surface" that fulfills these functions. It is not the "personal, private style, as unmistakable as your fingerprint, as incomparable as your own body" (Jameson 114) that poetry is all about but, rather, the communal and communicative aspect of poems that "embody a very inward world" (Rich, "A Tool" 408).

Accordingly, Rich could detect neither poetry nor a sense of female subjectivity in "a suit of armor." While for Moore the "moveable plates suggest the wearer," for Rich a "great breastplate" merely serves to hide and cover up the fighter's wounds. And, whereas Moore's female figures engage in cultural combat protected by camouflage, Rich's poem "The Knight" (1957) wants the freelancing fighter "free from protection."

> Who will unhorse this rider
> and free h[er] from between
> the walls of iron, the emblems
> crushing h[er] chest with their weight?
> Will they defeat h[er] gently,
> or leave [her] hurled on the green,
> h[er] rags and wounds still hidden
> under the great breastplate?
>
> > (*Snapshots* 14)

Whereas Dickinson and Moore deleted verbs and pronouns in order to evade, Rich retrospectively "altered a verb or a prounoun" in her earlier poems, because she felt that "it had served as an evasion in the original poem" (*Poems* xv). In reproducing this poem, I have changed the pronouns (in a text in which such alterations would not have occurred to Rich) to suggest that the development of female subjectivity from Moore's to Rich's writing encompassed the claim to a female body previously equivocated by camouflage and travesty. Instead of disrupting surfaces to protect the body, Rich came to insist on "the need to begin with the female body and on locating the grounds from which to speak with authority *as* women" in the female body itself (*Blood* 213). Before such reappropriation was possible, however, Rich's dismissal of martial arts evolved the female body as a cultural battlefield.

## Chapter 2

# Marianne Moore and Adrienne Rich: Daughters-in-Law or Outlaws?

Marianne Moore and Adrienne Rich seem to make an odd couple. The modern "writing master" (Moore, *CPMM* 119) has apparently little in common with the radical feminist. Whereas Moore's poems are "whetted to brilliance" and tend to destabilize and distance the speaking subject, Rich's texts came to distrust aesthetic surfaces and poetic distance and have, instead, attempted to close the gap between life and literature, between author and text, between enunciation and enounced. While Rich's early volumes earned a fair amount of applause from some of Moore's acquaintants, such as W. H. Auden, Moore herself never mentioned the young poet in her writing. Rich, by comparison, acknowledges Moore, though merely as a model not to be followed. In her critical essays of the 1970s Moore functions primarily as an example of tokenism, representing the commonly respected poet-critic within an "old boys' network" as one "who was maidenly, elegant, intellectual, discreet" (*On Lies* 39), who "kept sexuality at a measured and chiseled distance in her poems" (36), and who "fled into a universe of forms" ("Voices" 3)—"two minds, two messages," so it seems (Rich, *Snapshots* 46).

Rich's critique of Moore's supposed mimicry of male standards, formalistic pedantry, and her suppression of sexuality and "female experience" anticipated what came to be the standard feminist perspective for a while. Echoing the critique of both Moore's contemporaries and the New Critics concerning the supposedly chaste quality of Moore's work, such views seem all but original in content, though their political motivation was quite distinct. Starting from their own bias concerning women's experience and their appropriate means of expression, many feminist literary critics have complained that Moore's, Bishop's, and Louise Bogan's verse as well as Rich's early volumes offer too little of woman's life and fiddle too much with lifeless forms—forms that supposedly efface the self rather than effect subjectivity and were therefore considered an inadequate tool for a "female voice."[1] While such a view tended to dismiss the fact that Moore's defensive poetics does not deflect but, rather, bespeaks her particular gendered disposition, there is little sense in simply insisting upon present-day feminist sophistication. Early feminist critiques of modernist writing have to be seen within their own political and historical contexts. Likewise, Rich's neglect of Moore has its own motives. It needs to be understood as part of her own identity practice, of a wholesale rejection of modernism meant to reconstruct her own (poetic) past. Rich crystallized this past into a style "formed first by male poets: by the men I was reading as an undergraduate—Frost, Dylan Thomas, Donne, Auden, MacNiece [*sic*], Stevens, Yeats," into a formalism that "was part of a strategy—like asbestos gloves, it allowed me to handle the materials I couldn't pick up bare-handed" (*On Lies* 39, 40–41).

Put in terms of family structure, Rich's repudiation of modernist poetics resembles a rejection of the predominant male parent, of the father as much as his figures. In this dismissal Rich did not stand alone. Modernism's innovations had turned into constraints under postmodern conditions. Most poets, whether they belonged with the "confessionals," the political, the feminist, or the postmodern authors, distanced themselves from this tradition, in one way or another. John Ashbery's 1966 reviews of Moore's *Tell Me, Tell Me: Granite, Steel, and Other Topics* (1966) and Rich's *Necessities of Life* (1966), for instance, show that the author's dislike of Rich as well as his admiration for Moore were partly motivated by a dislike of Eliot. Unlike Rich, who retrospectively repudiated modernism in total, Ashbery underscored the distinct quality of Moore's work within modernist discourse, thus anticipating recent revisionary perspectives on her work. Moore's poetry, Ashbery admitted in a letter to her brother John Warner Moore, has always been "deeply a part of my life" and "means more to me than I could ever say in a book review."[2] Considering Moore, "with the possible exception of Pound and Auden, the greatest living poet in English," Ashbery admires her talent to make any subject of interest to her interesting and urgent to us, to render "the feeling that life is softly exploding around us, within easy reach." Reading Moore, he closes,

> one has the illusion that one could somehow manage without the other great modern poets if one had to. Suddenly Eliot seems heavy after all, Stevens unprofitably moony, Auden too close to the issues, Pound rhetorical, William Carlos Williams' grasp of modern idiom and life somehow superfluous. These illusions are, to be sure, always dispelled by one's next reading of these poets. But no poet ever lets us feel that we could do without Marianne Moore. ("Jerboas" 8)

While Ashbery aligns Rich with Eliot, he clearly distinguishes Moore from other modern innovators. Singling her out as a (maternal) precursor, he distances himself from his paternal heritage. Rich's dismissal of Moore marks the relationship among women writers of these succeeding generations or, metaphorically spoken, mother-daughter relations as similarly troublesome affiliations, troublesome in a different way, though. Considering modern women writers inapt precursors of contemporary women's poetry and recovering her "grandmother" Dickinson as "a source and a foremother," instead (*On Lies* 167), Rich not only "represses" a maternal generation of women authors. By discarding Woolf, Bishop, and Moore as obedient daughters who supposedly adapted to dominant literary discourse and addressed a male audience primarily, Rich revises her own past as an obedient daughter, reconsiders those parts of her oeuvre that do not, as Auden put it, "conceal their family tree" ("Foreword" 10). The fact that Rich herself arranged for the publication of her first two volumes, *A Change of World* (1951) and *The Diamond Cutters and Other Poems* (1956), to be stopped speaks for itself.

Rich's self-censorship, however, was not primarily a fiddle about form. In fact, Rich herself never was as much of a formalist as she made herself look in retrospect. Robert Lowell was quite right when he detected in her earlier writing a "tingling harmony of an older more severe training" (31).

> It's as though the writer had begun as a 19th-century imitator and ended up as a 19th-century original. No, a 20th-century original, a strange, belated one, developed by the last century's standards, idealism and education, and then tossed into our own unforeseen and embattled contradictions. ("Modesty" 30)

Rich's rejection of modernism is first of all a rebellion against the conservative gender politics that modernist writing entailed.[3] Rich herself became a radical  in matters of politics and gender whose poetics desired to break the strangleholds that modernist forms had turned out to be. During her process of politicization she also realized, however, that a radically feminist poetics and its constructions of identity politics depend upon a somewhat stable, if not established, rhetoric, a rhetoric that, as Lowell suggests, has been part of her poetry all along. In this way Rich takes Dickinson's and Moore's sense of authority into completely new directions. It is in this sense that Rich has been a real innovator whose crucial impact on other (women) poets still waits to be explored more systematically.

This chapter retraces Rich's troubled relation to modernism's gender politics and aesthetics by retracing her affiliation with Moore. This affiliation can be based on two aspects of Moore's and Rich's texts—their use of citation and their interrogation of the maternal—both of which can be subsumed under the term *reproduction*. Both negotiate the relation of poetic form and feminism and will be discussed, at least to a certain extent, in the framework of Irigaray's writings. The first aspect concerns matters of voice: by use of quotation, repetition, and translation both poets' earlier texts fragment the traditional lyrical voice, problematize women's exclusion from language, and hint that, even though there is no common voice in women's verse, there is a common problem, which is voice. This problem confronts male as well as female authors but does so in different ways. Whereas the inclusion of fragments from other literary texts characterizes modern literature in general, citation in women's texts, Irigaray claims, turns into mimicry and exposes women's very position in the symbolic order. This correlation between woman's destabilized voice and her lack of subject position becomes particularly significant in Moore's poem "Marriage" (1923) and Rich's "Snapshots of a Daughter-in-Law" (1958–62), texts that question the very cultural institution that has inscribed women's silent position.

These texts compare in several ways. Like Moore's poem, Rich's had been a "work-in-progress" during an early formative period. Like the publication of "Marriage" one year after Eliot's *The Waste Land* (1922), the appearance of Rich's volume *Snapshots of a Daughter-in-Law* (1963) succeeded Lowell's similarly controversial and influential *Life Studies* (1959). Both poems are quite long poems. Most important, however, is that both "Marriage" and "Snapshots of a Daughter-in-Law" foreground voice as a primary and highly engendered issue and do so in a similar semantic scenario: within the confines of marriage. Both texts portray matrimony as modern paradise lost, highlighting the absence of communication in an institution that supposedly marshals interaction and dialogue between the sexes. Giving voice to a variety of other texts from which they quote, these poems turn into verbal patchworks. They replace intersubjectivity with intertextuality and thus claim, or better disclaim, voice through literary reference, quotation, and allusion. In this way Moore's "Marriage" and Rich's "Snapshots" similarly embody and associate the absence of conjugal union and unified voice. Suggesting that marriage "requir[es] all one's criminal ingenuity to avoid" (Moore, *CPMM* 62) or, as Rich wrote, that it provokes the desire to "smash the mould straight off" (Rich, *Snapshots* 24), both poems at the same time display a disloyal desire for a significant space "outside" the law.

For poststructuralist and Lacanian psychoanalytic theory, however, woman as speaking subject cannot be anything but a daughter-in-law. Based on the repression of the maternal, the constitution of the (male and female) subject is preceded by language, the symbolic order in which the name of the father (*le nom du père*), his laws and his prohibitions (*le non du père*), and thereby all rules that structure human relations are always already inscribed. According to Claude Lévi-Strauss, the most basic social norms and necessities within this symbolic order are the incest taboo; "the supreme rule of the gift," which, "universal like language," imposes the exchange of women; and the institutionalization of marriage, a "dramatic encounter between nature and culture, between alliance and kinship." Marriage thus operates as a communication device between groups, in which the woman takes the double function of being both sign and value (478–97). As object of exchange, however, woman is, as Lacan maintains, "excluded by the nature of things, which is the nature of words" (*Feminine Sexuality* 144). Her position as speaking subject is characterized by lack, absence, and silence.[4]

The question how and from which position woman speaks, writes, and creates consequently preoccupies feminist criticism and theory, and Irigaray offers a preliminary answer. She sees woman, caught in patriarchal linguistics and logic, facing two alternatives: she can either choose to remain silent or else, as an interim strategy, mime, parody, paraphrase, and quote male discourse. Deliberately acting out the role that is historically assigned to women, reproduction, the female writer exposes what she mimics and undermines and thus subverts the symbolic order and its representations of women.

> To play with mimesis is thus, for a woman, to try to recover the place of her exploitation by discourse, without allowing herself to be simply reduced to it. It means to resubmit herself—inasmuch as she is on the side of the "perceptible," of "matter"—to "ideas," in particular to ideas about herself, that are elaborated in/by a masculine logic, but so as to make "visible," by an effect of playful repetition, what was supposed to remain invisible: the cover-up of a possible operation of the feminine in language. It also means "to unveil" the fact that, if women are such good mimics, it is because they are not simply resorbed in this function. *They also remain elsewhere:* another case of the persistence of "matter," but also of "sexual pleasure." (Irigaray, *This Sex* 76)

Such playful repetition, exemplified in Irigaray's *Speculum de l'autre femme* (1974), characterizes Moore's and Rich's poetry as well. Both "Marriage" and "Snapshots of a Daughter-in-Law" read like rehearsals of other texts that challenge the privileged position of their originals while simultaneously dividing and multiplying voice. At the same time, they display the difference within such mimetic practices and split utterances. Moore uses quotation, in Irigaray's sense of playful repetition that exposes, without necessarily opposing, mimicry as the very operation that imposes silence upon women. Accordingly, she does not reject the institution of marriage but, rather, acknowledges its fundamental function for "civilization." Rich, by contrast, uses mimicry in the context of marriage and mother-daughter relations. Intending to counter misconceptions of femininity, she eventually echoes and reinforces the very voices she set out to oppose. Mimicry, parody, and travesty of male discourse thus stage, perform, and implicitly reproach women's exclusion from the symbolic order, without providing for new (speaking) positions.

As they involve a negation of the mother, Rich's practice of mimicry and her projections of another female voice reflect the Freudian view that subject constitution depends upon the taming of the maternal economy. The increasing interest feminist criticism and theory, by contrast, have developed in mother-daughter relations and matters of motherhood, as well as their various attempts to account for the—psychological and historical—maternal lineage of female subjectivity, symbolize the daughter's return to the mother.[5] This focus on the maternal is by no means a new theoretical enterprise. Motherhood and related matters have been a concern of American women's writing since the days of Anne Bradstreet; this includes the work of Dickinson, Moore, and Rich.[6] Unlike Dickinson's texts, which reject mother figures and maternal fantasies, Moore's and Rich's poems revalue an ethics and aesthetics of mothering and maternal nurture. This is done by clearly distinguishing this ethics and aesthetics from motherhood as an experience and institution as well as from lived mother-daughter relations. Whereas both poets' writing salvages the maternal as a realm of a potentially other discourse and economy of exchange, the issue of motherhood more often conflicts with, rather than inspires, creativity. In what ways, then, do Moore's and Rich's texts engage in the ongoing debate about mothering and maternal? And what does the maternal entail for female subjectivity?

In feminist theory strong interest in maternal origins and mother-daughter relations arose within revisions of psychoanalysis and its concern with the insufficient answers it had provided to the question of "how, when and why [the female infant] detaches herself from her mother" (Freud, *Sexuality* 194). Freud himself had first assumed that male and female sexual development ran parallel and was equally based upon the separation from the first love object, the mother. For both male and female infant the dyadic unity of preoedipal relations is ruptured by an intervening father/phallus at the age of eighteen months. This onset of the oedipal phase initiates language acquisition and the recognition of sexual difference. Due to a likeness in sexual anatomy, Freud claimed, the male infant identifies with the father, accepts the imposed incest taboo, and, experiencing the loss of the mother as a lack, learns to desire. From this time on the male subject seeks to substitute the mother by language and by means of the (female) love objects he chooses. The female infant, by contrast, rejects the mother for both not having and not having provided the phallus for her. By becoming a mother herself, Freud assumed, woman repossesses the desired phallus in the child she bears.[7]

In his later work, most notably in "Female Sexuality" (1931), Freud admits that the preoedipal phase plays a much more significant function in female development than it had hitherto been granted by psychoanalysis and that so far "the duration of this attachment to the mother had been greatly underestimated." Freud concedes that "everything connected with this first-mother-attachment has in analysis seemed to me so elusive, lost in a past so dim and shadowy, so hard to resuscitate, that it seemed as if it had undergone some specially inexorable repression." Comparing the discovery of the preoedipal with that of "the Minoan-Mycenaean civilization behind that of Greece" (195), Freud acknowledges that this repression is not simply a process in the psychogenesis of the female subject but a culturally inscribed and reinforced exclusion of the maternal. Projecting the origin of human culture onto the murder of the father by his sons, Freud himself, of course, engages in such exclusionary practices. Even after he realized, "first, that the great dependence on the father in women merely takes over the heritage of an equally great attachment to the mother and secondly, that this earlier phase lasts longer than we should have anticipated" (196), Freud focuses not on how women continue being affiliated with their mothers but, rather, on how they manage to displace them.

Feminist revisions of psychoanalysis, by contrast, have emphasized that patriarchy is erected upon the destruction of matriarchal societies and—whether based on object relations theory, such as Nancy Chodorow's work, or on Freud and Lacan, such as Irigaray's—have foregrounded the continuous attachment of mother and daughter. Arguing that women's sense of self is highly dependent on affiliation, this revisionary psychoanalysis sees the synchronicity of separation and attachment, of a double-minded desire for identification and differentiation, as a particular mark of female subjectivity. Therefore, unlike Lacanian psychoanalysis, which assumes that only the rupture of preoedipal roots, the "separation from a presumed state of nature . . . may constitute meaning" and subjectivity (Kristeva, "Women's Time" 23), revisionary psychoanalysis seeks to recover woman's voice and female subjectivity from what was prior to power structures, laws, and signification.

Irigaray's essay "When Our Lips Speak Together" (1977), a daugher's address to her mother, is one such attempt to explore, or rather reinvent, mother-daughter relations and their particular economy of desire and discourse. According to Irigaray, the language of sameness, which originates in the absence of the maternal and the separation between subject and object, fails to account for an affiliation grounded in indifference and difference alike. For her the recovery of this affiliation consequently entails the deconstruction of "their language." The strategy Irigaray proposes in order to escape male categories is to "find our body's language," which in practice means to "invent a language" (*This Sex* 214). The discourse suited to delineate the dyadic relation of mother and daughter, she suggests, should be fluid, multidimensional, abundant, expanding, unlimited. Structured by another "syntax," another "grammar" of culture, it would dissolve truth, unity, and exchange, disintegrate ego boundaries, and relocate mother and daughter in a space of endless embraces.

The central metaphor for an alliance of body and speech, Irigaray's "lips speaking together," was introduced in Irigaray's essay "The Sex Which Is Not One" and provoked much controversy.[8] Connoting the plurality of women's discourse and female sexuality, the image counters phallic unity and, as Jane Gallop emphasized, creates "a point of unusually suggestive tension about the referent" ("Quand nos lèvres" 83). It visualizes a discourse without dualisms and a sense of female subjectivity that entails indifference as well as difference. The fact that Irigaray reverts to metaphor indicates, however, that there is no escaping the language of the same. Conventional in syntax and figuration, Irigaray's depictions of the return to pre-symbolic conditions reflect that "speaking the body" is less a practice of writing than a poetic-political program. Or, as Kristeva puts it, "this motherhood is the fantasy that is nurtured by the adult, man or woman, of a lost territory; what is more, it involves less an idealized archaic mother than the idealization of the *relationship* that binds us to her, one that cannot be localized—an idealization of primary narcissism" ("Stabat Mater" 161). The very fact that motherhood and the maternal are not merely biological, psychological, and social functions but also serve as fantasies that materialize fundamental desires, that these fantasies "touch" upon and perhaps partially retrieve, that is recreate, the unnameable and the body in language, makes it equally attractive for feminist theory and women's writing.

Representations of the maternal and motherhood in Moore's and Rich's work are the second focus of each of the following two sections. Moore closely aligns creativity with reproduction in her poetry yet avoids direct references to woman's body. Imagining figures of maternal heroes and heroic mothers, her poems dissociate gender from bodies and equivocate sexual difference. Instead, her writings on the maternal produce images of mirroring and specularization as well as a discourse that signifies through difference and indifference alike. Moore thus reproduces, in poetry, revisionary psychoanalysis's very projections of the preoedipal phase and the economy of mother-daughter relations as well as its ambivalence toward the silence of both.

Rich, in comparison, sees in motherhood clear limitations to cultural practice and self-realization. This is partly due to what she considers to be the "radicaliz[ing]" experience of being a mother to three sons (*Blood* 117). It is mostly informed, though, by her critique of heterosexuality and its institutions—a critique that strongly aligns Rich with Moore. Rich's attempts, from the mid-1970s on, to revaluate motherhood and the maternal retain this position. Her book *Of Woman Born: Motherhood as Experience and Institution* (1976) desires to reclaim a mythical matrilineage yet clearly rejects reproduction as an institutionalized suppression of women. Her collection *The Dream of a Common Language* (1978), which reinvents the maternal as the historical, psychological, and physical "ground-note" (74) of female subjectivity and "lesbian existence," as the matrix of what Rich termed the "lesbian continuum" of female experience (*Blood* 51), likewise insists on this difference. Reappropriating the female body as the matrix of female subjectivity, Rich attemps to remake this body into an element that constitutes, rather than subverts, the symbolic order. This implies that she has to accept language "as it is" and give up the search for a unified female voice, "the dream of a common language." At the same time, she comes to insist on an ethically responsible use of that language, a reconstructive, rather than deconstructive, identity practice in the 1980s.

The separate approaches that Moore and Rich take to matters of motherhood and the maternal require that their texts be read in different contexts. As indicated by the circumstances from which Moore's poem "The Paper Nautilus" developed, her poetics of mothering involves her personal relations to other women (writers), relations based on mutual emotional and professional support. In this way Moore was in fact much closer to Rich than feminist literary criticism, for a long time, has been willing to admit. In this context, however, the focus on Moore's female friendships serves yet another function. Her affiliation with Elizabeth Bishop calls upon a third female figure who may function as missing link and mediator between Moore and Rich. It is Bishop, not Moore, through whom Rich reconsiders her relation to modernism; it is Bishop's work and life that more closely compare to Rich's own. Unlike Bishop's and Rich's writing, Moore's poetry is politically conservative, and this is made unmistakably clear in her texts on marriage and motherhood. Exemplifying what has come to be known as feminine discourse, ultimately, Moore's sense of mothering and the maternal keeps the symbolic order intact. Rich's poetics of the maternal and the body, by contrast, is eager to change that order while also accepting the limitations of such an agenda, set by language itself. The ambivalence that infused both authors' negotiation of the maternal, mothering, and motherhood indicates how equally inspiring and confining the representation of reproduction and the maternal as a space of female subjectivity has been.

## Marriage, Mimicry, and the Maternal: Evolving the Politics of Moore's Poetics

For Rich quotation, imitation, and mimicry has primarily had negative implications. In her essay on Bishop she considers the poet's "coy use of quoted phrases" as "traces of Miss Moore" and "a mannerism Bishop soon discarded" (*Blood* 125). Bishop herself saw Moore's imitative manners in a much more positive light, reading it as a capacity for observation and accurate description, a "gift of being able to give herself up almost entirely to the object under contemplation" ("As We Like It" 131). On various occasions Moore has pictured herself as a mimic or chameleon, associating no defect or self-denial with the practice of mimicry, of adjusting to one's circumstances like a lizard that changes its skin color for protection or the "sand-brown jumping-rat," which "honors the sand by assuming its color" (*CPMM* 13, 14). Unlike Keats, who considered the chameleon poet an author without a sense of self and authority, Moore took such nonopportunist ability to adapt as a precondition of independence. In addition, mimicry had a particular American ring for her. Asked, in 1938, whether she belonged with an American tradition or, rather, dissociated herself from national identity, Moore declared herself "an American chameleon on an American leaf" (*Prose* 675). Considering imitation and parody as distinctively American (see Slatin 227–29), Moore aligned herself with Stein, whose aesthetics thrives on repetition. "There are no nightingales . . . ," Moore paraphrased Stein in her 1936 review of *Geographical History of America,* "and the eagle is not the characteristic bird it once was; whereas 'the mocking-birds . . . have spread . . . and perhaps they will be all over, the national bird of the United States'" (*Prose* 339).

   Many of Moore's male contemporaries, by comparison, declared originality one of the chief assets of modern poetry. Echoing Emerson, Williams preferred novelty to imitation: "Nothing is good," he claimed, "save the new" (*Selected Essays* 21). Closer to Eliot's insistence on tradition and "historical sense" (*Sacred Wood* 49) than to Williams's faith in innovation, Moore believed that, when it comes to classic literature, "ignorance of originals is suicide" (*Prose* 688). Skeptical about the actual newness of the "'New' Poetry since 1912" (120), Moore found Dickinson "later than she actually was . . . and G. Hopkins," she observed, "might in certain respects be writing today."[9] Aware that the imagination is incapable of creating novelties, Moore redefined originality as "a byproduct of sincerity" (421).

While Dickinson insisted that she would never "consciously touch a paint, mixed by another person" (L 271)—a principle Moore acknowledged as "lack of predatory spirit"[10]—Moore's excessive use of quotations proves that poetry that relies heavily upon other authorities can still be highly original. To Moore quotation became a trademark, an integral part of her lyrical stance, a speaking position showing even in her private letters (see Molesworth 92). Her prose is packed with fragments from the pieces under consideration, be they other critics' comments or parts of literary texts. In this way Moore's "appreciative imitation" (Goodridge 19) abolishes genre distinctions and, as H.D. suggested in a comment on Moore's review of her *Collected Poems* (1925), uses one text or author to highlight another: "I come across my own prose quotation enshrined in your exquisite prose. What a more than doubly distilled subtlety. I stand glowing from the reflected splendour of Marianne and Sappho."[11] In Moore's poetry quotation dominates the free verse texts composed between 1921 and 1925, which thus transform the early resistant voice into polyvocality (Slatin 3, 88–89). In "Marriage" this polylogue sounds at full blow.

## Moore's "Marriage": Mimicry as Deconstruction?

> This institution,
> perhaps one should say enterprise
> out of respect for which
> one says one need not change one's mind
> about a thing one has believed in,
> requiring public promises
> of one's intention
> to fulfil a private obligation:
> I wonder what Adam and Eve
> think of it by this time,
> this fire-gilt steel
> alive with goldenness;
> how bright it shows—
> "of circular traditions and impostures,

committing many spoils,"
requiring all one's criminal ingenuity
to avoid!
Psychology which explains everything
explains nothing,
and we are still in doubt.

(*CPMM* 62)

In the course of these first lines the speaker turns from indeterminate "one" to universal "we" and introduces Adam and Eve, "Patriarch" and the "Mother of Mankind" (Milton, *PL* 5:506, 388), prototypical man and woman, as the main characters of the drama that develops over eight pages. Gradually, the speaker gives up the center stage to the impersonation of multiple, indeterminate speaking positions. "Robbed of speech by speech which has delighted" (*CPMM* 91), the speaker turns into the masterful manipulator of her model discourse, juxtaposes ironies and illusions, appearances, stereotypes, and myths, indeed "playfully repeating" and thus attempting to deconstruct the conventional structures of poetic authority and voice as well as of marriage. Making mimicry and the multiplication of voice go hand in hand, "Marriage" seems to enact the very paradox inherent in Irigaray's notion of a *parler femme,* her contradictory claim that woman is both exluded from language and escapes signification, "remain[s] elsewhere," and that her voice is nonetheless unlimited, indefinite, and multiple.

In her idiosyncratic manner of understatement Moore herself once described "Marriage" as "a little anthology of statements that took my fancy—phrasings that I liked" (*Reader* xv). A similar phrase in the *Complete Poems* elides the term *anthology,* thus acknowledging that the poem bears little resemblance to what was once considered an anthology. Instead, it loosely connects a variety of sources, including texts from Francis Bacon and Richard Baxter, Anatole France and William Godwin, Edmund Burke and Pound; from La Fontaine's *Fables,* Edward Thomas's *Feminine Influence on the Poets,* and a review of Santayana's *Poems.* Like Eliot's *The Waste Land,* Moore's text refers to Ecclesiastes, Milton's *Paradise Lost,* and Shakespeare's *The Tempest.* Unlike Eliot, Moore neither shuns citation from the noncanonical, such as the *Scientific American,* the French magazine *Femina,* or a parody by Mary Frances Nearing "with suggestions from M. Moore" (*CPMM* 272). Nor does it refer exclusively to printed texts but invokes conversations and inscriptions on cultural artifacts as well. Employing the motto from Daniel Webster's statue in Central Park, Moore connects historical with rhetorical figures and "gives body" to rhetoric and its postures.

Moore's manner of quotation obviously differs from her contemporaries' poetic practices.[12] Moore choses her fragments as much for their "raw" materiality as for their meaning; Eliot and Pound intend to re-collect and conserve lines of tradition. While Eliot appropriates texts from an established poetic tradition into his texts—and thus, as Lloyd Frankenberg points out, has his style pulled in the direction of the past—Moore transforms prose fragments into poetry without "subjugat[ing] them to her own idiom" ("Imaginary Garden" 214). Yet, as Moore juxtaposes voices from various genres, from high and popular culture, she does so without dissolving their distinctiveness. For her quotation does not allude to literary authority; it represents other (speaking) positions manipulated by, yet separated from, her own text through the space provided by the quotation mark. Therein Moore's texts do not "discriminate against business documents and schoolbooks"; they hold little prejudice against readers unfamiliar with the great traditions. Rereading *Paradise Lost* from a liberal feminist position, Moore's "Marriage" not only "democratize[s] 'tradition'" (Kenner 111). It challenges tradition, canonicity, and John Milton, the "patron saint of companionate marriage" himself (Nyquist 99), some time before literary criticism did. Referring, in 1925, to Eliot's regard of masterminds from Aristotle to Emerson as "our foremost educators during the last 2300 years," Moore concedes that "one's predilection for these justly celebrated persons has in some measure been instructed" (*Prose* 154) and, in this way, anticipates contemporary debates around canonicity.

Attracted to statements that "took [her] fancy" (*CPMM* 271), Moore privileges the accidental. Recalling Coleridge's distinction between fancy and imagination, she also belittles her own creativity and associates herself with the prototype of femininity starring in her poem. "Mimic Fancy," Adam tells fanciful Eve in *Paradise Lost,* is one of the "lesser Faculties that serve / Reason." "[O]f all external things . . . ," Eve learns, "She forms Imaginations, Aery Shapes," and in reasons's absence "wakes / To imitate her; but misjoining shapes / Wild work produces oft" (5:101–12). Moore's poem rephrases this association of fancy and female ("there is in woman / a quality of mind / which as an instinctive manifestation / is unsafe" [64]), reminding us of the playful unreliability of her own poetic practice. Her manipulation of citation, erratic manner of annotation, and other idiosyncratic inconsistencies have provoked, as Moore admits, various, often "contradictory objections."[13] Refusing to turn her work "into the donkey that finally found itself being carried by its masters" (*CPMM* 262), she nonetheless continues to parody the apparatus of poetic authority playfully and to exploit it for her own purposes.

Therefore, fancy and inconsistency in Moore's poetic practice should not be mistaken as randomness. Her choice of quoted material is highly selective and operates both on the surface and in the subtext of her poems. When Moore's modern Eve relies not on Adam's order but on the authority of Martha Carey Thomas's speech, various intertextual threads are woven between Moore's poem, the issues and bias of liberal feminism, and Milton's epic. After all, Carey Thomas strongly opposed marriage as a hindrance to women's intellectual "growth" and remembered "weeping over [Milton's] account of Adam and Eve because it seemed to me that the curse pronounced on Eve might impair girls going to college" (qtd. in Schneider 427).[14] For Eve there was indeed no need for higher education, because Adam acted as educator, guide, and voice all at once: "God is thy Law, thou mine: to know no more / Is woman's happiest knowledge and her praise" (*PL* 4:637–38). When Moore's Eve, by contrast, choses Carey Thomas as teacher and preacher, the gender of authority changes, if only for the instance of the utterance.

To Moore herself Milton has always been within the range of vision yet distant, "a kind of poetic Mt. Everest," whose "greatness has in certain instances, been less to us than the great simplicity of Isaac Watts" (*Prose* 155). She accepts his authority within the world's literary history but redesigns the topography of the geopolitical literary landscape. Eliot, by contrast, first considers Milton a strong, devastating precursor, whose dead rhetoric meant "bad influence" on the history of poetry and "damage" done to the English language (*On Poetry* 138, 145). Correcting his earlier, "erroneous" view, he retains his prejudice "towards Milton the man," whose work is, more than any other poet's texts, "so difficult to consider . . . simply as poetry, without our theological and political dispositions, conscious and unconscious, inherited or acquired, making an unlawful entry" (148). Just these "theological and political dispositions" entered women's rereadings of Milton's *Paradise Lost,* from Wollstonecraft's *Vindication of the Rights of Women* (1792) to Moore's "Marriage."

Moore may have shared, as Vivienne Koch suggested, Milton's kind of Protestantism "without any orthodox theological anchorage" (166). Undoubtedly, she lacked the faith in marriage that *Paradise Lost* seemed to contrast. According to book 8, marriage and conjugal love result from Adam's strong attraction to his "likeness," his "fit help," his "other self," his "wish, exactly to [his] heart's desire" (8:450–51), are remedy to "His single imperfection" (8:423). For, although Adam was created in his Maker's likeness, unlike his Maker, he was not made perfect himself. Like ordinary man, who is in need of communication, original man did not lack material goods and power but, rather, fit company and conversation. Adam desires fellowship, community, and camaraderie with one who is "Like of his like, his Image multiplied"; being "in unity defective," he "requires / Colateral love, and dearest amity" (8:424–26). Happy marriage consequently becomes synonymous with harmonious conversation and communication; argumentation, dispute, and difference a threat to the marital bond(age).

Until Eve was created, Adam did not know desire. With woman herself such longing was born. Her difference, however, is not merely a matter of outer appearances but entails a dissimilar development, which shows in Eve's unorthodoxy and supposed narcissism. "She loves herself so much," Moore puts it, "she cannot see herself enough— / a statuette of ivory on ivory" (*CPMM* 68). Milton goes into greater detail. Before meeting Adam, Eve was in love with her own likeness. In the very scene in which she "consigns her authority to Adam" (Froula 327), by addressing him as

> O thou for whom
> And from whom I was form'd flesh of thy flesh,
> And without whom am to no end, my Guide
> And Head
>
> (4:440–44)

she also remembers the first days of her life. She recalls the "murmering sound / Of waters issu'd from a Cave" which formed a "clear / Smooth Lake, that to me seem'd another Sky" and the reflection of her face, "A Shape . . . with answering looks / Of sympathy and love." Adam clearly seemed "less fair,"

> Less winning soft, less amiably mild,
> Than that smooth wat'ry image; back I turn'd,
> Thou following cri'd'st aloud, Return fair *Eve*,
> Whom fli'st thou? whom thou fli'st, of him thou art.
>
> (4:453–82)

Eve's early resistance and return to the pool's mirroring surface—according to Milton, an "immature," narcissistic self-infatuation inferior to Adam's true love for his "other self"—metaphorizes the drama that precedes the constitution of male subjectivity and female otherness. Eve's conversion to matrimony, Froula points out, requires her to abandon her own self-image. Whereas "domestic Adam" strongly desires the bonds of "Matrimonial Love" (9:319), the unity with his "other self," Eve remains torn between her own likeness and male difference and much "Less attributed to Faith sincere" (9:320) and her role as "Mother of Mankind" (5:388).

Moore's "Marriage" recalls illusions of conjugal love and marital equality, reminding the reader how the Renaissance, and Milton's epic particularly, celebrated marriage as an institution that unites two incomplete halves. At the same time, Moore secularizes Milton's version of the biblical myth, revises Eve's conversion to orthodoxy, and glances at the flip side of the coin. For, after all, early capitalist times transformed matrimony into a contract, a "match" (*CPMM* 112), an economic necessity and exclusive social norm, which left few alternatives for women's lives. Despite attempts, on the part of social and literary historians, to recover the English Renaissance as the origin of Anglo-American feminism, there is, according to Fitz, "no escaping the fact that the English Renaissance institutionalized, where it did not invent, the restrictive marriage-oriented attitude toward women that feminists have been struggling against ever since" (11).

Milton himself calls for legal separation of the sexes in case of "indisposition, unfitness, or contrariety of mind" (705). Unhappy marriages, he claims, affect family, state, church, and even God; the denial of divorce devalues "true" marriage. According to John Halkett, there is no suggestion in Milton's tracts, however, "that a wife may divorce her husband for not fulfilling her with the needs of her nature, for not fulfilling the ideal matrimonial conversation, or for not being a 'meet help.' Her position does not give her the right to plead these causes" (90). Moore blames not the "unfit" individual, therefore, but the institution itself. Her speaker finds "ways out but no way in[to]" marriage, considering it an "amalgamation, which can never be more / than an interesting impossibility" (*CPMM* 63). Referring to both interracial unions and the chemical process that unites different solid elements by a supply of heat and a process of melting, the term *amalgamation* suggests that marriage unites two separate, if not incompatible, creatures. This to the speaker of Moore's poem constitutes a "crystal-fine experiment" bound to fail.[15] Moore's marriage is hardly a privileged place for interaction, neither a "blissful coming together of equal voices speaking in unison" nor an "ongoing dialogue between individuals affirming in turn their difference" (Furman 59). Juxtaposing unconnected quotations, Moore's poem both foregrounds the deficiency of human chemistry and carries out another experiment. The poem's voices remain "opposed to each other, not in unity," or, in accordance with the racial—if not racist—overtones, separate but equal.[16] Accordingly, marriage is like a collage of clashing materials, a song of dissonance resonant with divorce.

The communication gap between Adam and Eve is due to the fact that sexual difference translates into a difference in discourse. While Milton's Adam wonders "who can enjoy alone" (8:365), Moore's poem fashions marriage as shared loneliness:

> *"I* should like to be alone";
> to which the visitor replies,
> "I should like to be alone;
> why not be alone together?"
>
> (CPMM 62)

Having Adam repeat Eve's phrase, Moore ironically underscores that speaking the same language does not necessarily foster communication, understanding, and "fitness," if the speakers occupy distinct positions in language. Woman, Moore copied from Ralph Hodgson's poem "Eve" into her reading notebook, is "mute as a mouse."[17] Accordingly, her poem distinguishes its major figures by their rhetoric. Offering Adam more occasion to speak than Eve, Moore remains true to the sources. Reciting, with some poetic license, Carey Thomas's rhetoric, Moore's Eve reminds us that Adam "is not merely a well-preserved memory." Men in general tend to behave like "monopolists of oration and debate." Moore's poem, in fact, identifies Adam with (Milton's) Eve's apostrophe to her "Guide / And Head," her "Author and Disposer" (4:442–43, 635). "Alive with words," Adam is turned into the embodiment of a rhetorical device, "the O thou / to whom from whom / without whom nothing." Present and univocal, prophetic and devoid of doubt, he speaks in a formal customary strain,

> of "past states, the present state,
> seals, promises
> the evil one suffered,
> the good one enjoys
> hell, heaven,
> everything convenient
> to promote one's joy."
>
> (CPMM 64)

While Adam's insistent "oneness" advances a supposedly unified voice, Eve and woman are throughout the poem associated with either silence or a slippery polyvocality. Depicting Eve as "the nightingale / in the new leaves / with its silence— / not its silence but its silences" (*CPMM* 64), Moore echoes Romantic traditions. The curious emphasis on the plural ("not its silence but its silences") reminds us that the voice of the male Romantic speaker emerges as the nightingale's song and silence alternate, as he fears losing, so Keats's "Ode to a Nightingale" has it, "The voice [he] hear[s] this passing night." Accordingly, Moore's note to a citation from A. Mitram Rhibany's *The Syrian Christ*

("The fact of woman / is 'not the sound of the flute / but very poison'")
testifies that women's silence is not a natural fact. It is produced by male domi-
nance, instead—a dominance as universal as women's resistance to it.

> Silence on the part of women—"to an Oriental, this is as poetry set to
> music" although "in the Orient as here, husbands have difficulty in enforc-
> ing their authority"; "it is a common saying that not all the angels in
> heaven could subdue a woman." (*Observations* 104)

If woman escapes her subjection, it is for her ability to shift position in dis-
course. Accordingly, making reference to an article about "multiple conscious-
ness" published in *Scientific American* in 1922 the poem aligns woman with its
own fragmented structure, its shifting tones and dissonances.

> Eve: beautiful woman—
> I have seen her
> when she was so handsome
> she gave me a start,
> able to write simultaneously
> in three languages—
> English, German and French—
> and talk in the meantime;
> equally positive in demanding a commotion
> and in stipulating quiet:
>
> (*CPMM* 62)

Unlike Eve, who shuns matrimony, Adam idealizes and describes it

> as that "strange paradise
> unlike flesh, stones,
> gold or stately buildings,
> the choicest piece of my life:
> the heart rising
> in its estate of peace
> as a boat rises
> with the rising of the water";
>
> (*CPMM* 63)

*Paradise Lost* promotes marriage as companionship, as a rational love, subjugating passion to reason. Similarly, these lines, appropriated from Baxter's *The Saint's Everlasting Rest* (1650), picture marriage as a metaphysical ideal apart from concrete matter ("unlike flesh, stone") and material reality ("gold or stately buildings"). Not the partner but marriage itself becomes the supreme object of desire ("the choicest piece of my life"), a state of mind in "everlasting rest," an "estate of peace."

Ironically enough, the poem calls upon Baxter once again to expose the false appearances of marriage. Impelled by an illusion, Adam is tempted by what turns out to be a "voluntarily sprung . . . trap,"[18] pure convention or pompous ritual, a mixture of "servitude and flutter" (*CPMM* 194).

Unnerved by the nightingale
and dazzled by the apple,
impelled by "the illusion of a fire
effectual to extinguish fire,"
compared with which
the shining of the earth
is but deformity—a fire
"as high as deep
as bright as broad
as long as life itself,"
he stumbles over marriage,
"a very trivial object indeed"
to have destroyed the attitude
in which he stood—
the ease of the philosopher
unfathered by a women.
Unhelpful Hymen!
a kind of overgrown cupid
reduced to insignificance
by the mechanical advertising
parading as involuntary comment
by that experiment of Adam's
with ways out but no way in—
the ritual of marriage,
augmenting all its lavishness;
its fiddle-head ferns,

lotus flowers, opuntias, white dromedaries,
its hippopotamus—
nose and mouth combined
in one magnificent hopper—
its snake and the potent apple.

(*CPMM* 65–66)

Moore's quotation from Godwin ("a very trivial object indeed") bears a particular irony. While the fragments from Baxter represent juxtaposed views on matrimony, Godwin himself changed his mind about an institution for which he once had no respect whatsoever. Convinced that men acted according to reason, he advocated liberal relations between the sexes outside of matrimony. Marriage, he argues in *Enquiries Concerning Political Justice* (1793), belongs with the "evils" of cooperation and cohabitation, which undo individuality and intellect, and "melt our opinions into a common mould" (506). Changing habits, preferences, and perspectives frequently, people are not made for "eternal attachments," particularly when these are decided on by "circumstances full of delusion" (507). In sum, he claims, marriage is

> a monopoly, and the worst of monopolies. So long as two human beings are forbidden, by positive institution, to follow the dictates of their own mind, prejudice will be alive and vigorous. So long as I seek by despotic and artificial means, to maintain my possession of a woman, I am guilty of the most odious selfishness. (508)

Demanding "the abolition of the present system of marriage," Godwin envisions a promiscuous society or one in which partners adhere to each other temporarily. In a culture that dismisses the marital contract, he projects, intellectual friendship and engaged conversation will counterbalance "sexual commerce" (511): "Friendship therefore may be expected to come in aid of sexual intercourse, to refine its grossness, and increase its delight" (508) and "to determine our judgment in favor of marriage as a salutary and respectable institution, but not of that species of marriage, in which there is no room for repentance, and to which liberty and hope are equally strangers" (509–10).

Despite these convictions, Godwin himself "stumbled" over that "trivial object" marriage at the age of forty. Hitherto an "unfathered" philosopher, he married Wollstonecraft—much to the surprise of both parties' friends and acquaintances—and was, as Moore put down in her notes, "within a few months a husband, a widower, a stepfather and a father."[19] But there is more to

Moore's quotation from Godwin. The note that she offered to render her source ("Marriage is a law, and the worst of all laws . . . a very trivial object indeed" [*CPMM* 271]) deletes part of Godwin's text, thus effecting a significant change of reference in her poem. This omission can be partly restored through her reading note, which offers the following paraphrase of Godwin's text: "marriage is a law and the worst of all laws . . . If men happen to feel a preference for the same woman, let them both enjoy her conversation and be wise enough to consider sexual intercourse (marriage) 'a very trivial object indeed'" (cf. Goodwin 511). Evidently, the "trivial object" Moore's poem refers to is not marriage but, rather, sexual intercourse. By omitting this reference, Moore identifies marriage with (the silences of) sexuality and opposes it to conversation and speech. Her poem's distance to marriage and its rituals entails a distance to (hetero)sexuality as well.

This resentment is underlined by the exclamation "Unhelpful Hymen!" which trails Moore's reference to the unfathered philosopher. Denoting membrane and matrimony, maidenhead and marriage god, Johnson explains in her introduction to Derrida's *Dissemination,* hymen "designates both the virginal intactness of the distinction, between the inside and the outside and the erasing of that distinction through the commingling of self and other" (xxvii–xxviii). Presenting the hymen as an "overgrown cupid / reduced to insignificance / by the mechanical advertising," Moore attests to this ambiguity but also objects to reducing marriage and eros to sexuality and to courtship being dominated by the dynamics of the marriage market economy ("mechanical advertising"). At the same time, the phrase "Unhelpful Hymen!" bears reference to H.D.'s collection *Hymen* (1921), which Moore reviewed in January 1923. Its title poem explores a defloration ritual and oscillates, as Gary Burnett puts it, between "celebrating the impending marriage and lamenting the loss of the bride to the male world of the groom" (34). In H.D.'s poem this loss entails the end of pleasure and lets silence emerge. After the sexual act is consummated, "Love passes out with a crash of cymbals"; "music dies away and is finally cut short with a few deep, muted chords" (*Poems* 109, 110).

As in H.D.'s poem and Milton's epic, paradise is lost in Moore's "Marriage." Adam and Eve eventually leave the stage to a central figure of American myth, to the paradox of liberty and union, and to an image of stability and uniformity. "'I have encountered it [that striking grasp of opposites]," the poem reads,

> among those unpretentious
> protégés of wisdom

where seeming to parade
as the debater and the Roman,
the statesmanship
of an archaic Daniel Webster
persists to their simplicity of temper
as the essence of the matter:
  'Liberty and union
  now and forever';
the Book on the writing-table;
the hand in the breast-pocket."

(CPMM 69–70)

Webster—statesman, orator, and dedicated defender of the Union—has replaced Adam, "that orator reminding you, / 'I am yours to command,'" with whom he shares the "solemn joy / in seeing that he has become an idol." Presenting Webster's words as the essence of the subject marriage, the poem widens its scope to questions of national identity. At the same time, it circles back to its initial notion of marriage as a political institution.

For Moore the fundament of this institution is not "liberty and union" but law: "Independence as an argument for marriage," she put down in her notes, "does not occur to one."[20] Concluding on Webster's enthusiastic claim, Moore presents the Constitution of the United States—which unites the single and, to a certain degree, independent states under a federal government—as a model of the marriage ideal. Accordingly, the alternatives Moore contemplated for the poem's next to last line include "the constitution of the United States upon the writing table," "the book of common law," "the lawbook on the writing table." From this final scene woman is excluded; in fact, she disappears before the subject America is brought up. Leaving the last word to the orator, the Constitution, the law of God, and legal law, marriage is diminished to its structural function as a contract between men.

In a letter to Bryher of August 1921 Moore defined marriage as "our attempt to solve a problem."[21] Her poem certainly offers "no solution . . . and no attempt at a solution" (Williams, "Moore" 57). Nor does it dismiss marriage; to Moore the matter was simply "deaf to argument": "there are 3 things wh[ich] one cannot advise upon one way or the other," she copied from a 1919 Bulletin of the Metropolitan Museum—"marriage, war and the pilgrimage to the Holy Land." And from Chesterton she took down in her notes that "there is no such thing as a prudent marriage—Marriage is like an adventure, like going to war there's always tragedy in it as in anything in wh[ich] men and women are concerned jointly."[22]

Though Moore had claimed that her poem "Marriage" "is no philosophical precipate; nor does it veil anything personal in the way of, triumphs, entrapments, or dangerous colloquies" (*Moore Reader* xv), we are tempted to read her poems on matrimony as a kind of creed or defense of her own single life. Marriage did concern Moore personally insofar as it was a matter of much debate among her New York friends. Interrogated with regard to her personal perspective, the poet usually offered a modern woman's reply that, out of context, would place her alongside feminists as radical (for the time, i.e.) as Emma Goldman. Goldman considered love the "defier of all laws, of all conventions" and wondered how "such an all-compelling force [can] be synonymous with that poor little State-and Church-begotten weed, marriage?" (165). Likewise, Moore insisted that "each's devotion to the other is all that matters—conventions are incidental" (qtd. in Stapleton 195). Moore called marriage "the proper thing for everyone but *me*" (qtd. in Phillips 52) and simply denied being "matrimonially ambitious" (qtd. in Juhasz 39).

Like Goldman's views, Moore's attitude toward marriage was ambivalent, though. Her comments on women's issues reflect the same gender bias that has dominated liberal feminism throughout. "Marriage" is not, as was claimed, the work of "a convinced feminist" (Stapleton 38), and it is misleading to overemphasize Moore's commitment to the woman's suffrage movement, which Bryn Mawr encouraged yet which her brother highly disapproved of. Despite her objection to stereotyping women, Moore herself held her own prejudices. Her notion that "women are no longer debarred from the professions that are open to men," coupled with the aside that, "if one cares to be femininely lazy, traditions of the past still afford shelter" (*Prose* 61) resonates with Carey Thomas's boast: "Our failures only marry" (qtd. in Schneider 491). Attracted by feminine fancy and intellectual freelancing, Moore resented, but nonetheless accepted, that women were still facing an either-or choice between marriage and silence, on the one hand, and single life and voice, on the other.

Disapproving of particular matches among her friends and acquaintances, Moore nevertheless believed in marriage's indispensible function for society and civilization. In her August 1921 letter to Bryher she elaborated:

> I don't like divorce and marriage is difficult but marriage is our attempt to solve a problem and I can't think of anything better. I think if people have a feeling for being married, they ought to be married and if they have

made a mistake, or if one of them is not on a marriage level, there may have to be a separation. Any intentional matrimonial grand right and left has no point whatever so far as I can see; in Turkey, monogamy is gaining as it is everywhere else and there is confusion of thought I think in advocating anything different in a place where there is any kind of civil contract. If we do away with the marriage contract, the case is different but nobody seems to wish to do that since if we do, we get back to cave life. The canker in the whole situation, I think, is that people who have no respect for marriage, insist on the respectability of the marriage contract.[23]

Respecting the marriage contract as a basis of "civilization," this passage reconfirms both the conclusion of "Marriage" and the implications of its mimicking strategies. Taking various discursive positions and perspectives, mimicry does not affect the structures of discourse, the symbolic order itself. Even though Moore's multivoiced poetics deconstructs (male) authority, it leaves its fundaments—one of them being marriage—intact. And, even more so: it aligns the ideals of marriage, like the practice of mimicry, with the Constitution of the United States, with the construction of an American identity.

In closing, I want to turn to Moore's poem "Is Your Town Nineveh?" (1916), an earlier, more personal statement on the conflict of union and liberty.

> Why so desolate?
>   And why multiply
>     in phantasmagoria about fishes,
>       what disgusts you? Could
>         not all personal upheaval in
>           the name of freedom, be tabood?
>
> Is it Nineveh
>   and are you Jonah
>     in the sweltering east wind of your wishes?
>       I, myself have stood
>         there by the aquarium, looking
>           at the Statue of Liberty.

(Poems 24)

According to Slatin, this poem relates to Warner Moore's gradual retreat from the family triangle, which, as Moore and her mother agreed, should have been his first responsibility. Such reading aligns Warner with Jonah, who was torn between his personal desires and his obligation to obey God's orders first to rise against and then to repent Nineveh. The poem's speaker, by contrast, seems to content herself with a safe position ("by the aquarium") and a vision of liberty. With or without biographical references the text's central tension negotiates between the speaker's and the addressee's conflicting sense of obligation.

By placing the debate about the limits of liberty into biblical, national, and interpersonal contexts—and in this way anticipating the cultural complexities of "Marriage"—the image of the "phantasmagoria of fishes" indeed multiplies. In the Book of Jonah the fish's belly is both a place of utter silence, the exile of one who fled God's voice, and a place of repentance, in which Jonah regains his voice, prays for forgiveness, and takes on his obligation toward God. With regard to interpersonal relations the "phantasmagoria of fishes," like the aquarium, stands for the safety of close attachments and for self-annihilating forces, as a location of both maternal protection and confinement, contrasted with the Statue of Liberty, the American symbol of freedom and separation from the mother country. Whereas the addressee seeks to break away, the speaker is ambivalently located, close to the maternal space and facing this icon of independence. In this way the speaker's position resembles that of the female subject, who oscillates between a close attachment to the mother and the desire to break free from that attachment. The poem's juxtaposed notions of obligation thus correspond to the distinct loyalties of male and female subject vis-à-vis paternal law.

As the male subject separates from the mother through marriage, however, he turns, as Anne Sexton's poem "Housewife" suggests, toward another "phantasmagorium of fishes."

> Some women marry houses.
> It's another kind of skin; it has a heart,
> a mouth, a liver and bowel movements.
> The walls are permanent and pink.
> See how she sits on her knees all day,
> faithfully washing herself down.
> Men enter by force, drawn back like Jonah
> into their fleshy mothers.
> A woman *is* her mother.
> That's the main thing.

(77)

Marriage, for Moore "universally associated with the fear of loss,"[24] compensates men for the loss of their first love object and turns women into mothers, into housewives—that is, literally speaking, wives of houses, into physical matter, to which their husbands turn as to a place of primordial bliss, security, and silence. Like Moore, Sexton thus locates matrimony / sexuality and discourse / dialogue at opposite ends.

Liberty, Moore suggests in the reading diary she kept during the composition of "Marriage," means language and dialogue.

> one cannot marry a man one
> cannot talk to
> It is a big consideration
> but one can talk to a girl one
> cannot marry how satisfactory
> overwhelming thoughts. Conversation
> is not taxable
> talk is free.[25]

This passage appropriates Godwin's notion that friendship and conversation compensate "sexual commerce" and constitute an alternative to marriage. Juxtaposing the lack of communication between men and women with a "satisfactory" and significant conversation among women, Moore projects another kind of connection, a different kind of discourse and understanding. Women-to-women relations could achieve "liberty and union, now and forever," apart from contracts and constitutions. One of the "girls" Moore talked to intensively throughout her later life was the poet Elizabeth Bishop. Recalling Moore's eloquence during their first encounter in 1934, Bishop wrote in her "Memoir of Marianne Moore": "It seems to me that Marianne talked to me steadily for the next thirty-five years, but of course," she adds, "that is nonsensical," reminding us of the two women's physical distance and their very distinct lifes (*Prose* 124).

## Heroism at Home: Moore's Economy of the Maternal

Moore's personal decision against marriage was one in favor of a life with her own mother, of a relationship that, as myth has it, made people "think of the two women as a single personality" (Sargeant 55). Since, during the 1930s and 1940s, Moore became more of a caretaker than a companion to her mother, it comes as no surprise that mothering and the maternal turned into central issues in Moore's writing of that time. Focusing on "The Paper Nautilus" (1940) as well as "The Hero" (1932), "Bird-Witted" (1936), "He 'Digesteth Harde Yron,'" (1941), and "A Face" (1947), the following pages investigate Moore's sense of the maternal. They explore the ways it relates to conventional views of motherhood and how it ties in with her personal and professional affiliation with other women.

Interestingly enough, even though Moore's discourse on the maternal figures predominantly in descriptions of animal behavior, her sense of mothering and the maternal parallels the conceptions developed by revisionary psychoanalysis. In "The Paper Nautilus" mothering is a process moving from a state of symbiotic or dyadic unity to separation and involving both care and a kind of heroism on the part of mother and offspring. After separation attachment persists, pictured by a prolonged emphasis on the maternal embrace and on the marks the nautilus' eggs have imprinted onto the surface of its protective shell. In this way not the bodily bond but, rather, the traces of close attachment are most highly priced. Underlying this sense of mothering is a strong ambivalence toward maternal powers and a conservatism that aligns motherhood with the values of the home.

Suggested by the genesis of "The Paper Nautilus," a reading of Moore's poems on the maternal needs to involve Moore's female friendships, most notably that with Bishop and Louise Crane. From 1934 on Bishop and Moore engaged in lifelong contacts, based less upon personal and political like-mindedness than on a mutual enthusiasm for literature and writing and, later in their lives, translation. Through Bishop, Moore was also introduced to Crane, with whom she developed a wholly different relation. As wealthy heiress to the Crane Paper Company, Crane was a generous sponsor of the arts and culture who offered Moore monetary support and legal assistance, introduced her to affluent social circles, and provided emotional support in times of personal crisis.[26]

For someone living "without the benefit of a father," Molesworth suggested, those affiliations "could be imagined as a kind of family relationship" (364). Female friendships differ from family life, of course, by the very absence of the father, and, unlike Dickinson and Rich, Bishop and Moore each grew up without a father. Bishop, whose mother was hospitalized when she was five and died the same year she met Moore, was practically raised without parents. Still, most critics have preferred reading Bishop and Moore's affiliation as one of mentor and protegé to likening it to mother-daughter bonds.[27] While Bishop's posthumously published essay "Efforts of Affection: A Memoir of Marianne Moore" (ca. 1969) presents Moore as "mentor" (*Prose* 145), its final paragraph subtly hints at another quality of their relation. "I find it impossible," Bishop writes,

to draw conclusions or even to summarize. When I try to, I become fool-
ishly bemused: I have a sort of subliminal glimpse of the capital letter *M*
multiplying. I am turning the pages of an illuminated manuscript and see-
ing that initial letter again and again: Marianne's monogram; mother,
manners; morals; and I catch myself murmuring, "Manners and morals;
manners *as* morals? Or morals *as* manners?" (*Prose* 156)

In her musings on Moore, between *monogram* and *manners,* Bishop includes
"mother" only to exclude her once again from her final murmurings on morals
and manners. But "omissions are not accidents," and this passage, like Moore's
poems, shows both how desirable and how combatted a matter the maternal
may be.

### *"Flaws of White on White": Representing the Maternal*

Contemplating titles such as "Second Hercules," "Her Marine Cradle," "A
Mermaid," and "A Nest," Moore first published her nautilus poem as "The
Glass-Ribbed Nest" in the *Kenyon Review* in 1940. The text's moral overtones
resonate with its political context, World War II. Like Moore's antiwar poem
"In Distrust of Merits" (1943), "The Paper Nautilus" has been considered an
exception in Moore's work. Its treatment of birth and maternal love—in fact,
the very use of the term love—has made readers extremely uncomfortable and
raised objections to the poem's "depend[ence] on intuition more than observa-
tion" (Stapleton 121), its "hauntingly emotional" quality (Taffy Martin 99), and
its "sentimental treatment of maternity" (Slatin 256). Such critique, though,
testifies less to the poem's deficiency than to readers' difficulties in dealing with
what Susan Schweik calls "too much . . . pressure of gender" (536) and in con-
ceiving Moore as a woman-identified and politically opinionated, though con-
servative, person. "The Paper Nautilus" delineates the maternal economy in
terms of reproduction as well as production yet clearly avoids reference to the
female body. Instead, the maternal materializes as a discourse sensitive to differ-
ences within apparent indifference, to the "flaws of white on white" that bor-
der on silence. This is the poem's final version:

> For authorities whose hopes
> are shaped by mercenaries?
>     Writers entrapped by
>     teatime fame and by
> commuters' comforts? Not for these

the paper nautilus
constructs her thin glass shell.

Giving her perishable
souvenir of hope, a dull
     white outside and smooth-
     edged inner surface
glossy as the sea, the watchful
     maker of it guards it
     day and night; she scarcely

     eats until the eggs are hatched.
Buried eight-fold in her eight
     arms, for she is in
     a sense a devil-
fish, her glass ram'shorn-cradled freight
     is hid but is not crushed;
     as Hercules, bitten

     by the crab loyal to the hydra
was hindered to succeed,
     the intensively
     watched eggs coming from
the shell free it when they are freed,—
     leaving its wasp-nest flaws
     of white on white, and close-

     laid Ionic chiton-folds
like the lines of the mane of
     a Parthenon horse.
     round which the arms had
wound themselves as if they knew love
     is the only fortress
     strong enough to trust to.

                                             (*CPMM* 121–22)

"The Paper Nautilus" is one among several of Moore's texts that take a
bifocal view on animal behavior and make nature resonate culture and vice
versa. Like the fable, Moore's animal poems anthropomorphize nature and
allow animals to display "certain postures of a man" (*CPMM* 119). Like La
Fontaine's texts, they are primarily "vehicles for [her] philosophy, not studies in

natural history" (Moore, *Prose* 595). Unlike fables, they guide willing readers into strange worlds. Framed by a critique of conventional authority and aphoristic closure, "The Paper Nautilus" presents a rare species whose precious shell serves as a vehicle of representation, a metaphor for metaphor.

Nevertheless, the animal's biology is in itself suggestive. The nautilus, or argonaut, is a mollusk and belongs to the only living species of a group of cephalopods, which includes squids, cuttlefish, and octopuses. Since it was assumed that the nautilus glides over the sea, using the folds of the skin on its arms as sails, its name was derived from the Greek *argonautes*. It thus refers to the ship in which the Argonauts sailed, the heroes who accompanied Jason in his quest for the golden fleece, and, more generally, to any adventurer engaged in a quest. The animal's habitat is the surface waters of tropical and subtropical seas. Resembling the octopus, the female is twenty times the size of the male, who was consequently considered its parasite for a long time. Characteristic of the female is that its entrails and mantle are covered entirely by a shell that develops from the membranes of its dorsally located arms. Reduced during the phylogeny of other cephalopods and lacking in the male counterpart, this fragile, unchambered shell in which the eggs develop can measure up to sixteen inches in diameter. By employing an animal that reproduces by eggs, Moore avoids metaphorizing the female reproductive organs. Unlike the womb, or Kristeva's chora even, the nautilus' shell relates only metonymically to woman's body. At the same time, the shell is transformed into a place of discourse and a metaphor for protection and shelter, for house and home alike.

Unlike Oliver Wendell Holmes's "The Chambered Nautilus" (1858) which takes the chambered nautilus as a figure for fragmentation, movement, and progress, Moore's poem juxtaposes historical with ontogenetic development (see Costello, "Wild Decorum" 48) and affirms wholeness, stability, and maternal nurture. At the same time, its mythological connotations make mothering a quest and reproduction part of a history of seafaring that has conventionally excluded female figures. This double context brings to mind Roland Barthes's piece on Jules Verne, "The Nautilus and the Drunken Boat." "The ship," writes Barthes,

> may well be a symbol for departure; it is, at a deeper level, the emblem of closure. An inclination for ships always means the joy of perfectly enclosing oneself, of having at hand the greatest possible number of objects, and having at one's disposal an absolutely finite space. To like ships is first and foremost to like a house, a superlative one since it is unremittingly closed,

and not at all vague sailings into the unknown: a ship is a habitat before being a means of transport. (*Mythologies* 66–67)

Reading Verne's Nautilus "as the most desirable of all cages," Barthes reverberates a traditional symbolism that associates ships and vessels with women and wombs.[28] Like Barthes's ship, Moore's shell is habitat before it is transport. Unlike both the nautilus and Barthes's vessel, it is, however, made of paper.

## *The Gift and the Proper*

"The Paper Nautilus" juxtaposes two different economies of discourse, distinguishing writing as alienated labor from writing as an activity comparable to the labors of reproduction. The poem puts off writers who work merely for pay or sordid advantage ("mercenaries") and sympathizes with a creature that labors apart from the economy of exchange. At the same time, it aligns reproduction with production ("constructs"), thereby dissolving a binarism that is conventionally conceived as analogous to male and female. In this way the text composes an alternative economy of exchange apart from entrapments in property, an economy of "Giving," liberty, and love.

Moore's poem thus distinguishes between the realm of the proper and the realm of the gift. According to Cixous, the proper connotes property and appropriation, is associated with proximity and self-identity, the fear of separation and castration, and, as Moi points out, "leads to the masculine obsession with classification, systematization and hierarchization" (111). The gift, by comparison, is an offer not meant to be returned and aligned with femininity. "If there is a 'propriety of woman,'" Cixous claims, "it is paradoxically her capacity to depropriate unselfishly" ("Medusa" 293). While Moore would not define property and gift as distinctive marks of male and female libidinal economy, she herself subscribed to an ethics of nonpossessiveness, to "the power of relinquishing / what one would keep" (*CPMM* 144). Phrases such as "possession is the grave of bliss" or "nothing is worth anything unless it is priceless" adorn her notebooks.[29] "Modesty is a good system," runs a line from Moore's fragments of La Fontaine's *Fables,* "and mercenariness, a bad one" (*Prose* 627).

At the same time, the gift takes several functions in Moore's life. Gifts in the sense of presents served as means of communication. "All of [Moore's] friends," claimed Bishop, "seemed to share the desire of giving her presents" (*Prose* 134). Gift giving, of course, involves objects as well as intellectual abilities, which Moore encouraged in others: "I have always been observant,"

Bishop admitted, "but I might not have put this gift to use as much if it hadn't been for Marianne" (qtd. in L. Keller, "Words" 413). Referring to Moore's later poetry of occasion, Molesworth speaks of an "aesthetic of gift-giving" (44). The genesis of "The Paper Nautilus" exemplifies perfectly her particular knack for "convert[ing] a gift given her into gifts for others" (368). While occasioned in part by a present from Crane, the poem turned into a gift for Crane, who passed it on to Bishop as a souvenir from New York. Finally, "Dedications imply giving" to Moore (*Selected Poems* 122). Dedicating her *Complete Poems* to Crane, Moore offered a gift to someone who had, for decades, generously given to her. Interrelating in this way, women establish their own economy of exchange, seemingly apart from the cultural commerce in which women serve as gifts and communication between men.

In February 1937 Crane sent Moore the shell of a paper nautilus "as a form of 'interest.'"[30] The word *interest* echos Moore's poem "Poetry," acknowledging her preference for curious objects as subject matter. It also relates to a paper clip from *Town and Country* that Crane had included. The article contains a list of forty-six women, among them Malvina Hoffman, Laura Harding, and Moore, who are described as follows:

> Here is a classification that includes blue-stockings, women belonging to a vaguely Bohemian group, women either active in or allied with the arts, and women with INTERESTS. . . . In any event these are the girls to ask in to dinner at your own house. Most of them like the theatre, few of them go to night clubs very much, one group goes in for all games from sniff to hearts to twenty questions, and all can hold their own with either intellectuals or Bohemians.

As a "classification," this list is part of the realm of the proper and at opposite ends from the realm of the gift represented by the shell.

In her reply to Crane's correspondence Moore first of all admired the nautilus—the right kind of curio to stimulate her interest, indeed.

> It is well I did not know when I received the mysterious box, that a nautilus was inside as my hand might have shaken so as to injure it. A nautilus has always seemed to me something supernatural. The more I look at it the less I can credit it,—this large, yet weightless thing, with a glaze like ivory on the entrance and even on the sides. How curious the sudden change of direction in the corrugations, and the transparent oyster white dullness of the "paper." The wings are so symmetrical I should not know any part had been broken if you had not said so.

> The clipping you enclose makes me need a house by no means transparent. But I protect myself by a ruse. There is another Marianne Moore, I have heard,—the daughter of a professor in the West, and there are two other Marianne Moores in Brooklyn. Nevertheless I am dismayed.[31]

This passage highlights the nautilus' very features Moore's poem was going to celebrate: the shell's lack of weight, glaze of whiteness, and dull "protectiveness"; its function as a metaphor for house and home; and even the "sudden change of direction" occurring at the end of the poem. At the same time, Moore's "ruse" issues a warning of definite interpretations. One name, she insists, can have more than one reference. Unable to "credit" the nautilus' shell, Moore resists translating its value into monetary terms and refers it to another kind of economy instead ("supernatural"). In this way she discriminates her own manner of appreciation from that of author(itie)s who judge people by capitalized/capitalist "INTERESTS," by the degree to which their investments pay off. Preferring the "dullness" of the nautilus over the flamboyance of the financially more advantageous, Moore subtly critiques Crane herself, who both entertained and attended Bohemian parties. Crane's letter accompanying the nautilus closed with an invitation for tea, which Moore's poem belatedly rejects with its rebuke of "teatime fame." Moore's text thus expresses an ambivalence toward the financial "nurture" provided by Crane and blurs its own distinction between disinterested mothering and interested mercenaries, between the realm of the gift and the realm of the proper.

## The Economy of the Maternal

"The Paper Nautilus" privileges an economy of discourse balanced by (maternal) power and restraint over one that reacts to the pressures of the marketplace. At the same time, the poem's various manuscript versions reflect Moore's reluctance to identify the writer's "efforts of affection" (*CPMM* 147) explicitly with the maternal. In fact, the last lines of the second stanza ("the watchful / maker of it guards it / day and night / she scarcely / eats until the eggs are hatched") caused Moore considerable trouble. These are two of the versions she contemplated yet finally abandoned:

> the watchful
> the tense mother, clutches
> it, scarcely leaving or
>
> eating till the eggs are hatched.

                    the watchful
          animal takes charge of
          it herself and scarcely

          leaves it till the eggs are hatched.[32]


The poem's final version eliminates the sense of overprotectiveness these pas-
sages entail ("tense," "clutches") in favor of "a process of reciprocal protection
and freedom" (Schulman 67) and displaces *mother* and *animal* with *maker*. Like
*mother,* the term *maker* converges subject and predication, agent and activity.
Derived from the function of kneading and pressing, the word *maker* in the
sense of manufacturer aligns mothering and writing with other kinds of pro-
duction. It also bears reference to God, the first maker, thus, like *mother,* res-
onates a sense of origin. Being, in addition, an archaic word for *poet,* the term
*maker* strengthens the poem's alliance of creation and procreation. All of these
connotations reflect cultural values rather than natural instincts; replacing *mother*
or *animal* with *maker,* immanence gives way to transcendence. Denoting a per-
son who borrows money on a promissory basis, the *maker* moreover drags eco-
nomic matters back into view. Still, the poem creates its own economy of
mutual and unmediated exchange. As the nautilus/writer borrows from her
own resources ("she scarcely eats") to feed her offspring, active ("Giving,"
"guards") and passive constructions alternate ("are hatched," "Buried," "is hid
but is not crushed"), having both nautilus and shell function as subject and mak-
ing subject and object position seemingly interchangeable.

     This maternal economy of exchange fully unfolds toward the end of the
poem, with its surplus of indefinite pronouns and spatial imagery. While syn-
tactical linearity is equivocated, image and simile, the "close- / laid Ionic chi-
ton-folds / like the lines in the mane / of a Parthenon horse," give prominence
to the visual and tactile over the temporal. The term *chiton* denotes both an
ancient Greek garment and an order of marine mollusks comparable, yet dis-
tinct from, the nautilus. Like the "Parthenon horse," the term thus blends
nature and culture and suggests a similar sense of difference within indifference
already expressed in the phrase "white on white." Comparing nautilus and
devilfish (which denotes a group of rays as well as the octopus or any other large
eight-armed cephalopod like and unlike the nautilus), Moore had already pre-
pared the reader for this redundant yet remarkable doubleness, this indifferent
difference of meaning. Like the destabilization of referentiality, the
remetaphorization of the maternal advances difference within indifference or
indifference within difference. In this way the "flaws of white on white" left by

the nautilus' egg read as symbols of the maternal matrix, "original" birthmarks of a dynamics of exchange distinct from the ordinary economy of discourse and voice—an economy that tends to know white because it knows black and that means by *différance*. The graft left by the nautilus' eggs, those "wasp-nest flaws / of white on white," by comparison, signify difference within sameness, separation within connectiveness, and inscribe a slight though significant difference into the economy of gain for loss.

Conventionally, a flaw denotes a hidden defect, a faulty part, a crack. Eve, as Moore put it in "Marriage," was the "flaw" in Adam's experiment. In "The Paper Nautilus," in contrast, the "flaws of white on white" are both a "trace of . . . contact" (Costello, *Imaginary Possessions* 119) and a sign of minimal difference. In this way they constitute meaning and subjectivity—a subjectivity that, based upon a synchronicity of difference and indifference, counters Adam's sense of self built across the gap of self and other. Echoing both H.D.'s depiction of the bride in "Hymen" and Moore's own image of Eve's self-love in "Marriage," the "flaws of white on white" recontextualize images of female narcissism and the economy of voice that goes along with them—the complicity of silence and echo. More specifically, they recall a scene from "Hymen" in which the maidens debase the bride's self-reflective virginal posture as a lack of beauty and involvement:

Who can say if she is fair?
For her head is covered over
With her mantle
White on white,
Snow on whiter amaranth,
Snow on hoar-frost,
Snow on snow,
Snow on whitest buds of myrrh.

(106)

Similarly, "Marriage" portrayed Eve as "a statuette of ivory on ivory," caught and immobilized in the seductive processes of mirroring. Moore's "Paper Nautilus," in contrast, reappropriates such "white on whiteness" as a figure for another discursive economy.

And yet Moore's "Paper Nautilus" ends on a highly ambivalent note. Whereas the poem celebrates the security provided by the enclosed maternal space, as well as the sense of release evoked by the liberation of the eggs, its final stanzas drag the confining moments of maternal affection back in. The speaker remembers how the animals's arms "had / wound themselves" around the shell's "wasp-nest flaws / of white on white, and close- / / laid Ionic chiton folds"

> as if they knew love
> is the only fortress
> strong enough to trust to.

These lines preserve the memory of nurturance and protection of the maternal embrace. Dominated by the metaphor of the "fortress," they also object to the possessiveness, the desire for appropriation and self-identity, inherent in maternal care. By reverting to metaphor at this particular moment, Moore's final ambivalence about mothering entails a critique of metaphor as well. "The Paper Nautilus" does not, as Kalstone suggested, "locate[ ] and enact[ ] a powerful source of creative energy in . . . the discharge of the ego in love" (77). Instead, maternal love is depicted as an affection that cannot let go of its object. As the figure of the the fortress, which itself is a symbol of "the formation of the I" (Lacan 5), a metaphor of identity, displaces the preceding image of difference and identity, the maternal embrace of identity, like marriage, becomes a "strongly binding . . . love [that] cannot be gay,"[33] a stranglehold.

Like Verne's "Nautilus," the nautilus' shell is thus an "emblem of closure" indeed. And, like the nautical morality Barthes described, "the possessive nature of the man on a ship," which "makes him at once the god, the master and the owner" (67), maternal affection is not separate from the realm of the proper, from possessiveness. Analogously, both Freud and Lacan wondered whether the preoedipal period is an exclusively dual relation; assuming that the father interferes even before the oedipal conflict, Lacan spoke of a "pre-Oedipal triangle" (qtd. in Laplanche 396). According to Barthes's "mythology of seafaring," the only "means to exorcise" possessiveness on the ship is "to eliminate the man and to leave the ship on its own. The ship then is no longer a box, a habitat, an object that is owned; it becomes a travelling eye, which comes close to the infinite; it constantly begets departures." It "can make man proceed," he concludes, "from a psychoanalysis of the cave to a genuine poetics of exploration" (67). Just as they are part of Moore's "martial arts," curiosity and a sense of adventurousness may have been part of her attraction to the shell. No longer a habitat, it serves to transport new meanings. The "white on white" graft on its surface, the metonymic mark of dyadic relation, traces another economy of meaning. Without the absence of the love object there is no such "poetics of exploration."

When, in May 1940, Crane brought a copy of Moore's poem "A Glass-

Ribbed Nest" to Key West, Bishop expressed a particular favor for its final part: "I admire especially," she wrote, "from 'wasp-nest flaws—of white on white,' to the end. The whole poem is like a rebuke to me, it suggests so many of the plans for the things I want to say about Key West and have scarcely hinted at in 'José's House,' for example."[34] Bishop was well aware how her own work had "nurtured" Moore's. Like Moore's "glass-ribbed nest," Bishop's "house" is a perishable "love nest" made of paper, from writing in fact. Consisting of eight stanzas of detailed observation, placed in sets of two beside each other, "Jerón-imo's House" forms a kind of nest on the page by itself, leaving blank spaces, "flaws of white on white" in its center(s). Moreover, both Bishop's and Moore's poem present the interior space of their house or shell as an image of protection, nurture, and origin of discourse. Bishop's "writing-paper / lines of light" compare to the "flaws of white on white" on the nautilus' "paper." Unlike Moore, however, Bishop does not project writing as mothering and home as wholeness and enclosure, as a place of "integration too tough for infraction" (Moore, *CPMM* 147). Bishop's house is a palace yet no fortress but, instead, a "decentered" dwelling, compartmentalized like a chambered nautilus. Whereas Moore's poem concludes with a close-up of the textures of affiliation and the figure of maternal love, Bishop has public "voices on [the] radio" penetrate the apparent privacy of home. The temper of her poem is temporariness, discontinuity, departure, displacement ("When I move / I take these things"); her speaker is familiar with homelessness and hurricanes rather than fortresses of maternal affection. Bishop escapes domesticity by imagining new and unfamiliar domiciles, whereas for Moore, "fortitude" is, as Kalstone claims, "linked to staying home" (89). And so is her sense of heroism, which only seems to disrupt the gendered binarism of private and public.

## Maternal Heroism

Moore's poem "He 'Digesteth Harde Yron,'" for instance, employs the ostrich to suggest that the provision of nurture, care, and compassion is not a concern reserved exclusively for the biological mother.

> This bird watches his chicks with
> a maternal concentration—and he's
> been mothering the eggs
> at night six weeks—his legs
> their only weapon of defense.
>
> (*CPMM* 99)

This poem reminds us that, among birds, fishes, and mammals, some males do provide maternal care and develop close contact with their offspring. We should not, however, take this as an anticipation of Chodorow's call for shared parenting. Instead, the poem enhances instinctual behavior as a counterbalance to uncivilized excesses of culture, such as the serving of "six-hundred ostrich-brains . . . at one banquet." As the bird displays the human quality of maternal care and the ostrich-eating humans turn into predators, mothering and nature are being realigned.

Similarly, Moore's poem "The Hero" irritates conventional notions of gender by starring a male human who is capable of mothering. At the same time, heroism gets reconceptualized by portraying the hero as

> tired but hopeful-
hope not being hope
until all ground for hope has
vanished; and lenient, looking
upon a fellow creature's error with the
feelings of a mother—a
woman or a cat.

>                                        (*CPMM* 8–9)

Whereas legends distinguish heroes from common mortals by emphasizing their extraordinary strength and courage, this specimen stands out because he abnegates such authority. Identifying heroism as "emotion," as the "feeling of a mother, negligent of power," and as "compassionate unreason,"[35] Moore reinforces traditional notions of femininity in turn.

"Bird-Witted" (1936), by comparison, calls the conventional correlation between maternal nurture and pacifism into question by foregrounding a fundamental difference between human culture and animal kingdom. Throughout mythology and the history of Western civilization, as Nancy Huston points out, war has been a field of activity reserved for males exclusively. Whereas virginity reads as a sign of female power whose loss consequently makes women vulnerable, motherhood supposedly deprives women of their capacity to fight. As a consequence, mothers have been excluded from war and hunting activities not only because giving birth seemed incompatible with taking lives; warring and other forms of violence "have been institutionalized as the *sacred privileges* of the male" (130). In the animal kingdom, by contrast, "there is nothing more ferocious than a mother" (129). Accordingly, in Moore's poem the instinct of the heroic mother bird "wages deadly combat, / and half kills / with bayonet beak and cruel wings." As she wins against cat intellect, the gap between maternal and mental power widens. The use of terms such as *deadly combat, kill, bayonet beak,* and *cruel wings* instead aligns animal morphology with militarism and motherly instincts, thus playing upon the "analogy between war and childbirth" (Huston 131). Maternal fortification turns into heroism at the home front.

"The Paper Nautilus" allies heroism and the maternal and delineates early ontogenesis with reference to common myth.

> as Hercules, bitten
>
> by a crab loyal to the hydra
> was hindered to succeed
> the intensively
> watched eggs coming from
> the shell free it when they are freed,—

Even though the nautilus is the agent ("they [the eggs] *are* freed"), it does not take the hero's part. Like Hercules, who proved his prodigious strength in his infancy, it is the offspring that accomplishes the heroic act: it frees the shell. The nautilus' heroism consequently consists of giving birth to heroes. This is a "heroism of abstinence"[36] and sacrifice, rather than triumph. In addition, the passage holds a subtle contempt for the mother. As Moore compares the postponed liberation of "the intensively watched eggs" to Hercules' delayed success of freeing the region of Argolis from the plague of the Lernean hydra, she parallels mother and hydra. The poem thus presents yet another version of the "Medusa-face of the world" that Jarrell found amiss in Moore's texts (184). Capable of reproducing any of her nine heads yet decapitated by Hercules, the hydra both symbolizes the fear-inflicting part of female reproductive powers and embodies female lack. She gets displaced, however, by the nautilus, whose eight arms "knew love" before loss and lack.

*Breaking the Mirror*

The first poem Moore published after her mother's death was entitled "A Face."

> "I am not treacherous, callous, jealous, superstitious,
> supercilious, venomous, or absolutely hideous":
>> studying and studying its expression,
>> exasperated desperation

>                    though at no real impasse,
>                    would gladly break the mirror;
>
>          when love of order, ardor, uncircuitous simplicity
>          with an expression of inquiry, are all one needs to be!
>                    Certain faces, a few, one or two—or one
>                    face photographed by recollection—
>                         to my mind, to my sight,
>                         must remain a delight.
>
>                                             (*CPMM* 141)

Face-to-faceness suggests unmediated closeness, mirroring, the delights and dangers of identification. Here the speaker's reliance upon the (m)other shows in the double function of the *I* as subject of both the quoted discourse and the lines that follow. In turn, the subsequent deletion of the *I* where one expects its repetition ("though at no real impasse / would gladly break the mirror") indicates that mirroring effects the loss of subjectivity, that only the breaking of the mirror—which is both an image of death and separation—constitutes the subject. The speaker's desire to escape this specularity is outbalanced, however, by her sense of obligation to preserve the (m)other's memory.

Significantly enough, after a troubled period of mourning her mother and fighting health problems, Moore's first larger project, if not her largest project, was to translate La Fontaine's *Fables*. Not only does the quotation from La Fontaine in "Marriage" attest to her early interest in the writer; translation also reconnected Moore with the origins of her own writing and the "revolution in modern poetry," which, as Howard Nemerov noted in his review of the fables, was "accompanied by a special uprising . . . in the translation business" (qtd. in Molesworth 383). It is thus not surprising that Pound, in particular, encouraged Moore's enterprise. Due to their "wonderful detail," however, her translations became, as Bishop claimed, "almost the reverse of Pound's 'translations.'"[37]

More than "ground[ing] her literary efforts in the period of uncertainty after her mother's death" (Molesworth 385), Moore's translation work displaced processes of mirroring onto a different scene of writing. Although translation is a kind of mimicry, her interpretation of La Fontaine's texts proves that translation does not simply transmit language "from one place or state of being to another," without really touching it (Homans, *Bearing* 31). Especially when the translator is an experienced writer, translation also inscribes one voice onto another, leaves a graft on a given ground, comparable to the marks that the nautilus' eggs leave on its protective shell. In the course of Moore's four revisions her own graft more and more covered the foreign ground.

Whereas critics tended to object to the predominance of Moore's own voice in La Fontaine's text, Bishop valued the double-voicedness of her translations. Fascinated "to see [the fables] emerging like a moth from a cocoon," Bishop praised their originality, their particular turns of Moore's phrases—"surprising, amusing, sharp or 'eccentric,'" "always unmistakeably Miss Moore while yet remaining true to La Fontaine's feelings on the subject, too."[38] Moore had similarly cherished Bishop's translation of the Brazilian classic *Minha Vida de Menina* (1942), the diary of a young girl living in the mining town Diamantina in the 1890s. In her review of *The Diary of "Helena Morley"* (1957) she wrote: "That a translator should share the qualities of work translated, Miss Bishop exemplifies in her gift for fantasy, her use of words and hyper-precise eye. The attitude to life revealed by the Diary, Helena's apperceptiveness, and innate accuracy, seem a double portrait" (*Prose* 524). Moore closes her review as follows: "We see furthermore, as Miss Bishop says, 'that happiness does not consist in worldly goods but in a peaceful home, in family affection,—things that fortune cannot bring and often takes away'" (526). It is unlikely that Bishop would have made such a claim. In fact, the quotation Moore ascribes to Bishop is taken from Helena Morley's own introduction to *The Diary*. Putting Morley's words into Bishop's mouth, Moore makes Bishop mimic her own morals about domesticity and the maternal, even echo the distinction "The Paper Nautilus" makes between the realm of the proper and the realm of the gift, and in this way reproduce mimicry.

For Moore the maternal and motherhood belong with the domestic scene. Asked in 1957 whether "the net result of women's 'coming out of the kitchen' [has] been helpful or detrimental to society," Moore considered the "net result" helpful yet objected to what she called "delegated motherhood."

> With regard to careers outside of the home, delegated motherhood can be a threat, for I believe that our integrity as a nation is bound up with the home. Good children are not the product of mothers who prefer money or fame to the well-being of their families. Did not the Apostle Paul, in his ardor to afford Timothy a steadying influence, bid him remember his mother, Eunice, and his grandmother, Lois?

Evidently, the act of remembering foremothers meant something quite different to Moore than to Rich. Advocating the logic of the "feminine mystique," this statement spells out the politics inherent in both Moore's "Paper Nautilus" and "Marriage," a politics that finds "good family relations" being "basic to the well-being of society in general" (*Prose* 678). Moore's aesthetic radicalism thus correlates with a political conservatism and "an old-fashioned domesticity" (Kalstone 8). Bishop's more conventional forms, by contrast, transport a more radical politics.

We are thus not surprised that Rich's recent revision of modernism works through Bishop, not Moore; that the reassessment of the "'Miss Bishop' of Adrienne Rich's youth" (Kalstone, *Becoming* x) foregrounds the very aspects of Bishop's work that Moore subjected to censorship; that Rich's attempt "to suggest new ways of entering [Bishop's] work" (*Blood* 134) also tends to disregard Bishop's close affiliation with Moore. Acknowledging Bishop's parentless upbringing, lesbianism, and political convictions, Rich's essay "The Eye of the Outsider: Elizabeth Bishop's *Complete Poems, 1927–1979*" (1983) discusses her work from the perspective of a shared "outsiderhood" (127). Deploring a lack of personal poems, Rich finds herself rewarded by texts on unequal affiliations, singling out for discussion Bishop's "Songs for a Colored Singer." The perspectives Moore and Rich take upon this poem mark a difference within a shared, "indifferent" interest. While Moore's review of Bishop's collection *North and South* focused on unity, wondering whether "every phase [has] the feel of the rest of the words" (*Prose* 408), Rich concentrates on the author's "respectful" yet "risky undertaking" of speaking with a black women's voice (*Blood* 131). "What I value," Rich writes, "is her attempt to acknowledge other outsiders, lives marginal in ways that hers is not" (131). Preferring Bishop to Moore, Rich repeats the pattern that dominates many of her own explorations of the maternal: she represses the mother and turns toward Bishop the daughter, the other, marginal woman. At first, however, she herself engaged in mimicry.

> Beyond the issues of marriage and divorce, beyond the issue
> of motherhood, lies the implacable political necessity for
> women to gain control of our bodies and our lives.
> —Rich, *On Lies, Secrets, and Silence*

## Reproductions of Mimicry and the Matrix of Female Subjectivity: Rich's Body Poet(h)ics

Comparisons of the use of quotation and allusion in Moore's and Rich's poem show that not only are there diverse forms of mimicry; the ways in which women authors' rehearse other texts themselves have a history. Moore's poem "Marriage" exposes the interdependence of women's silence and her institutionalized subordination. While Dickinson either dismisses marriage as a social constraint or adapts the term as an emblem of female empowerment, Moore identifies marriage with "sexual commerce" and clearly distinguishes between marriage, sexuality, (male) monologue, and female silence, on the one hand, and single(minded)ness, chastity, dialogue, and (female) subjectity, on the other. Written at a time when American women had just achieved the status of political subject, Moore's poem "Marriage" manipulates fragments of discourse without adapting the positions they entail. Composed when the female subject readapted to a "feminine mystique," Rich's poem has its speakers be seduced by the subtleties of sexual bias. Taking various positions yet, in each, repeating the very misconceptions meant to be undone, Rich's poem reproduces the very operation of mimicry. Torn in their loyalties, her speakers themselves transform into daughters-in-law, while the depicted daughter-in-law turns victim and accused at once. The poem thus foregrounds that the "recov[ery of] the place of [woman's] exploitation by discourse" reinforces the very "sameness" to which Irigaray objects: the uniformity and apparent universality of a language that "reproduc[es] the same history," the "same attractions and separations," the "same difficulties, the same impossibility of making connections" (*This Sex* 205). Both Moore and Rich thus put Irigaray's early notion of the subversive potential of mimicry into perspective. Rich, however, makes perfectly explicit what Moore suggests only subtly: mimicry may parody yet also tends to reinforce the postures it intends to undermine. As Rich's text furthermore correlates mimicry with woman's dispossession of her own body and with a dismissal of the mother, she also insinuates how crucial the recovery of the maternal may be for the construction of another sexual economy and discourse.

The Reproduction of Mimicry: Rich's "Snapshots
of a Daughter-in-Law"

"Snapshots of a Daughter-in-Law" is the title poem of a volume written during the years 1954 and 1962, a time when Rich was "reading in fierce snatches, scribbling in notebooks, writing poetry in fragments" (*On Lies* 44). Early readers heavily criticized the poems' "woman-oriented" material, making Rich feel "slapped over the wrists," assured, however, "that these were important themes" (qtd. in Bennett 197). Yet by 1971 she had herself grown uncomfortable with the collection and its protofeminist attitudes and ambiguities. Eventually, the poems themselves were seen as snapshots, as something brief and transitory, less "forceful," as Wendy Martin puts it, than Rich's later work, a "beginning," though, "of a personal and political pilgrimage" (181). Like

Moore's "Marriage," Rich's "Snapshots of a Daughter-in-Law" quotes, repeats, and raises many voices yet comments upon marriage more indirectly than Moore's texts. Focus is not on the institution itself but on women's situation in it and, more generally, in a culture based on paternal law. Unlike Moore's poem, Rich's text searches for solutions, for a way out of marriage as well as for woman's own voice. Portraying matrimony through the depiction of women as daughters-in-law, the poem paints a bleak picture of past and present yet seeks to envision a promising future. Marginal in "Marriage," women-to-women relations are central to Rich's poem. Instead of projecting another economy of desire, however, they keep reproducing what Irigaray calls the "economy of the same."

While feminist variations of the subject of marriage occur throughout Rich's work of the 1970s and early 1980s—in poems such as "A Primary Ground" (1972), "Paula Becker to Clara Westhoff" (1975–76), "For Memory" (1979), and "For Ethel Rosenberg" (1980)—marriage has been an issue in her poetry from the start. Its early treatment resonates with modernist texts in a way that provoked Jarrell to compare the experience of reading Rich's second collection to "getting one of Auden's old carbons for Christmas" ("New Books" 128). Suggestive as it may seem in this context, Jarrell's association of Rich's poems and Auden's carbons nonetheless glosses over the very aspect that distinguishes Moore's and Rich's versions of mimicry. Poems such as "Autumn Equinox" and "The Penennial Answer" do not reproduce fragments from Frost verbatim. They adapt "the voices of the trapped, lonely, desparate wives who inhabit Frost's dramatic monologues" (Kalstone, _Temperaments_ 143). Thus, even if Frost was "'one of the renewers of the speaking voice,'" as Moore quotes in a review (_Prose_ 584), Rich's poems only echo such renewals, allowing their author "to enter the scene guardedly" (Kalstone, _Temperaments_ 145).

"Autumn Equinox" and "The Penennial Answer" differ from "Marriage" _and_ render parallel views. In both poets' texts marriage figures as a contract between men ("Lyman came to ask me of my father" [_Diamond Cutters_ 64]). Like Adam and Eve, who come together to be "alone together," Rich's husbands and wives are strangers to each other and to themselves. "I thought he looked a stranger" (65), one recalls her wedding picture; another feels "a stranger / on [her] own doorstep" (76). For Rich, as for Moore, such estrangement is due to failed dialogue but also to a false trust in the powers of language. In her poem "A Marriage in the Sixties" (1961) "Two strangers [are] thrust for life upon a rock." They "may have at last the perfect hour of talk / that language aches for." And, still," it comes down to "two minds, two messages" (_Snapshots_ 46).

Examining Moore's and Rich's wedding pictures more closely, funda-
mental discrepancies come to the fore. Against "the statesmanship of an archaic
Daniel Webster"—Moore's essence of the matter of marriage—Rich projects

> the semblance of a bride and groom
> Static as the figures on a mantelpiece,
> As if that moment out of time existed
> Then and forever in a dome of glass,
> Where neither dust nor the exploring fly
> Could speck its dry immutability.
>
> *(Diamond Cutters* 65)

Whereas Moore depicts marriage as a public shelter for private feelings, Rich
sees it as a place apart from communal life and politics, a kind of imprisonment,
or exile, a "room so strange and lonely one needs to look outside for warmth"
(75). Like the image of two strangers stranded upon a rock, the wedding picture
preserved under glass like a museum piece suggests isolation. It is a secure space,
lacking exchange and pleasures, a hoard of wholeness that man and woman
alike have outgrown (*Diamond Cutters* 103). "Marriage," Rich has Paula Becker
tell Clara Westhoff in a later text, "is lonelier than solitude" (*Dream* 43).

The distance between Moore's and Rich's views on marriage depend on
biography as well as history. For Moore's generation negotations between a
professional life and the fulfillment of traditional female roles turned out to be
either-or questions, though, of course, Moore's commitment to her mother
meant being female in very conventional ways. Rich, by comparison, had
attempted to fit all under one roof. By the mid-1950s she had had her share of
the feminine mystique, a college education, a book published and praised, and
a family life. Coming out as a lesbian, however, effected the real "change of
world."

In between a conformist apprenticeship and the search for a supposedly
authentic female voice and lesbian identity, Rich's work went through a tran-
sition period, during which the voice of the universal "I" or "we" that domi-
nated her first collections got fragmented. Instead of pictures of couples, the
reader is offered a series of "Snapshots of a Daughter-in-Law," taken from a
double-minded perspective. Having abandoned the dramatic monologue, Rich
wrote "double monologues"—double due to their highly ambivalent voice,
monologous because they reproduce a "language of sameness." Rich's "Double
Monologue" (1960) presents this irresolution as a conflict between mimicry and
identity. Like the speaker of that poem, Rich became increasingly reluctant to

"mime illusions for others" and eventually transformed her poetic and political agenda into this "one thing: to know / simply as I know my name / at any given moment, where I stand" (*Snapshots* 33). The dominant speaking position taken in "Snapshots of a Daughter-in-Law," in contrast, compares to the position "Double Monologue" itself takes within the collection. Placed between "Juvenalia" (1960) and "A Woman Mourned by Daughters" (1960), the poem wavers between two ambivalences: that toward the law of the father ("Juvenalia") and that toward the lack and powerlessness of the mother ("A Woman Mourned"). Situated in this kind of symbolic oedipal triangle, the poem hints that, for a daughter-in-law, knowing one's name, finding one's (speaking) position, is not as simple a matter as "Double Monologue" seems to suggest. As displayed in Rich's "Snapshots," woman's position is torn between loyalties; it oscillates between feelings of attraction and rejection toward both paternal and maternal heritage.

In her essay "When We Dead Awaken: Writing as Re-Vision" (1971) Rich herself described "Snapshots" "as too literary, too dependent on allusion," objecting that, in writing the text, she "hadn't found the courage yet to do without authorities, or even to use the pronoun 'I'—the woman in the poem is always 'she'" (*On Lies* 45). Unlike "Marriage," "Snapshots" indeed quite literally depends on allusion and authorities, rehearses monumental voices of cultural heritage, and reinforces male principles, less in person than in perspective. One finds parody of Horace and paraphrase of Baudelaire, echoes of Yeats and citations from Cortot, Diderot, and Samuel Johnson. The master text of Rich's poem, however, is Eliot's *The Waste Land*.

Restricted to canonical texts, Rich's manner of quoting compares to Eliot's practice more than to Moore's. It does not share Eliot's sense of history, though, which "compels a man," as he claims, "to write not merely with his own generation in his bones, but with a feeling that the whole of literature . . . has a simultaneous existence and composes a simultaneous order" (*Sacred Wood* 49). "Snapshots," by comparison, transports the notion that the whole of literature and culture has excluded or misrepresented women. Quotation and allusion are neither employed fancifully here, nor do they inscribe their author into an established tradition. Instead, as Rich's speakers compete with the adapted voices, "Snapshots" reverts to the device of irony, whose effect is diminished, however, as her speakers' surrender to the adapted discourse. Thus, they enact the very phenomenon that the text's irony denies: the silence of women.

Even though Rich's snapshots distinguish their citations typographically and in this way create a flexible distance between her own speakers and the voices they call upon, the text is neither collage nor dialogue. Orchestrating polyvocal echoes of common misconceptions of femininity, the poem exposes, but also reproduces, the very positions it sets out to undo, thus inscribing the operation of mimicry as woman's very speaking position. Unlike "Marriage," which refrains from commenting upon the attitudes it represents and thus produces a polylogue of equally valid voices, Rich's poem blends its own voices with the tone and temper of the material it borrows. As a consequence, throughout the poem voice is fragmented, dislocated, and transformed from omniscient third person and universal "I" to communal "we." It remains yet another monologue that, disguised as multivoicedness, mimes the very misconceptions and myths it seems to oppose and reproduces the very operation it rejects: mimicry.

From the very beginning Rich's text depicts woman as a performer of pre-fabricated texts, in this way suggesting that *"the feminine occurs only within models and laws devised by male subjects"* (Irigaray, *This Sex* 86), here exemplified by the outmoded ideal of the Southern belle.

> You, once a belle in Shreveport,
> with henna-colored hair, skin like a peachbud,
> still have your dresses copied from that time,
> and play a Chopin prelude
> called by Cortot: *"Delicious recollections*
> *float like perfume through the memory."*
>
> Your mind now, mouldering like wedding-cake,
> heavy with useless experience, rich
> with suspicion, rumor, fantasy,
> crumbling to pieces under the knife-edge
> of mere fact. In the prime of your life.
>
> Nervy, glowering, your daughter
> wipes the teaspoons, grows another way.
>
> (*Snapshots* 21)

Prone to maintain a shaky identity based on the youth of her body, on a beauty figured as nature ("the skin like a peachbud"), the mother copies her old style of dress to make up for the loss of her peachbud skin. Yet even her originally "natural" charm was no more than an imitation of an ideal whose artificiality ("henna-colored hair") resonates with the very text she interprets: "Delicious recollections / float like perfume through the memory." As the poem's fifth snapshot suggests, by juxtaposing Horace's voice and women's practice of leg shaving, mimicry mutilates women both physically and mentally: "*Dulce ridens, dulce loquens,* / she shaves her legs until they gleam / like petrified mammoth-tusk."

Comparing woman's state of mind to a moldering wedding cake, the poem not only echoes and recontextualizes Eliot's preoccupation with cultural decline, sexual sterility, and vegetation rituals. It also recalls Dickinson's sense of marriage as loss of pleasure or even death. Invoking a sense of decay and disintegration ("crumbling to pieces"), the word *mold* suggests that woman, just like nature, grows to bloom and flower. Once deflowered and reproducing, she dwindles without further development. As a superficial growth on damp or decomposing organic matter, mold, like mildew, covers and discolors organisms just as the old dresses cover woman's body. Woolly in appearance, the mold on the wedding cake resembles and replaces the "peachbud skin." At the same time, the term discloses marriage as mold, as a frame in which woman is constructed, as a design that, like the old dress cut, is an inflexible and outmoded pattern. Rooted in the old English word *molde,* meaning soil, the term moreover invokes the circularity of natural processes from fertility to death. Mold denotes a soil particularly suited to plant growth, the surface of the earth, the earth of a burial ground, and in a more archaic meaning, the earth as a substance of the human body. The simile's overall effect is to redefine marriage as mimicry and to deconstruct a self-conception solely built on physical appearances and reproductive functions. Accordingly, the women pictured in "Snapshots" are "battling with [their] years" (*Diamond Cutters* 73); the "drained and flagging bosom of our middle years" signals a losing battle.

At the same time, the poem insists that woman's silence and identifications of femininity with nature are historically grown and culturally reproduced, that they are differences of gender, not biology.

> When to her lute Corinna sings
> neither words nor music are her own;
> only the long hair dipping
> over her cheek, only the song
> of silk against her knees
> and these
> adjusted in reflections of an eye.
>
> Poised, trembling and unsatisfied, before
> an unlocked door, that cage of cages,
> tell us, you bird, you tragical machine—
> is this *fertilisante douleur?* Pinned down
> by love, for you the only natural action,

are you edged more keen
to prise the secrets of the vault? has Nature shown
her household books to you, daughter-in-law,
that her sons never saw?

(Snapshots 22–23)

Just like the mother presented in the first snapshot, Thomas Campion's
Corinna stars as a mimic of male discourse. Even the body she believes to be
her own is but a mirror image of male projections. Reminiscent of the female
figure in Eliot's "The Fire Sermon" who "smoothes her hair with automatic
hand," her posture is imprisoned by the male gaze (*Collected Poems* 62).
Excluded from knowledge and cultural production, her familiarity is with
nature's "household books," with a circular and silent economy of birth and
death ("the secret of the vault").

Echoing Yeats and Eliot, among others, the first part of section 3 further
binds woman to nature.

A thinking woman sleeps with monsters.
The beak that grips her, she becomes. And Nature,
that sprung-lidded, still commodious
steamer-trunk of *tempora* and *mores*
gets stuffed with it all:    the mildewed orange-flowers,
the female pills, the terrible breasts
of Boadicea beneath flat foxes' heads and orchids.

(Snapshots 22)

In the context of Rich's text the allusion to Yeats's "Leda and the Swan,"
which evolves a new cultural order in terms of rape, projects the violence
involved when male molds are imposed on female matter. At the same time,
Rich's paraphrase is self-referential: the speakers indeed become the beak that
grips them. Her critique of mimicry turns out reinforcement. Accordingly, the
following lines align femininity with nature. The "orange-flowers" and
"orchids" recall the sense of lavishness, the "fiddle-head ferns," and "lotus
flowers" Moore associates with the rituals of marriage. Meanwhile, though,
such metaphors are tainted with mold. Fertility and the abortion of woman's
own body have become two sides of the same coin. And both, as Rich's allu-
sion to Eliot's "A Game of Chess" ("female pills") suggests, result in further
physical exhaustion.

If the mother could not shake off the self-destructive mold, the daughter
will. She, the reader is reassured, "grows another way." The organic metaphor,
however, hints that even an "other way" will take her to the same place.

Banging the coffee-pot into the sink
she hears the angels chiding, and looks out
past the raked gardens to the sloppy sky.
Only a week since They said: *Have no patience.*

The next time it was: *Be insatiable.*
Then: *Save yourself; others you cannot save.*
Sometimes she's let the tapstream scald her arm,
a match burn to her thumbnail,

or held her hand above the kettle's snout
right in the woolly steam. They are probably angels,
since nothing hurts her anymore, except
each morning's grit blowing into her eyes.

(*Snapshots* 21)

Whereas the mother is paralyzed by images and ideals from the past, the daughter is lured into a future of self-centered independence. Rejecting her mother as an insufficient role model, she herself, however, gets paralyzed by apathy in the process and seeks self-assurance in self-mutilation. "The rejection of the mother," writes Irigaray, "is accompanied by the rejection of all women, herself included" (*This Sex* 69). Mother and daughter thus "grow" the same way: They listen to others but themselves lack a voice. They are supposed to view the world from the (dis)position of nature, across "raked gardens," yet are dispossessed of their bodies.

The fourth snapshot juxtaposes the self-congratulatory pose of a paternal literary lineage that the poem's third section alludes to (and which I briefly discussed in the introduction) with the isolated and ambivalent position of the female author.

Knowing themselves too well in one another:
their gifts no pure fruition, but a thorn,
the prick filed sharp against a hint of scorn . . .
Reading while waiting
for the iron to heat,
writing, *My Life had stood—a Loaded Gun—*
in that Amherst pantry while the jellies boil and
                                                scum,
or, more often,
iron-eyed and beaked and purposed as a bird,

dusting everything on the whatnot every day of
                                        life.

                                        (*Snapshots* 22)

The proposed familiarity among women ("Knowing themselves . . .") results
not from their intimacy. It stems from their successful internalization of con-
ventional ideas on femininity ("pure fruition"), which conflict with the "phal-
lic" elements of female creativity ("thorn") and self-defensiveness ("prick").

Employing the iron to symbolize the pressures of conformity, the lines
"Reading while waiting / for the iron to heat" make reference to Tillie Olson's
short story "I Stand Here Ironing" (1953–54). Significantly enough, Olson tells
a tale about a female impersonator, a young girl who "out of despair" began to
"imitate happenings or types at school" (18). In this way she authorizes herself
by mimicry and travesty, by a "deadly clowning" that make her "as imprisoned
in her difference as she had been in anonymity" (19). Combining the allusion
to Olson's story with Dickinson's line creates a line of "tradition." Unlike the
intertextual network between Baudelaire, Eliot, Lowell, and C. K. Williams
that connects generations of modern poetry, continents, and cultures, women's
lineage is not based on a continuous discourse. It, rather, bespeaks the silences
of "household books" and the common experiences of obstacles to creative
work. Whereas Eliot's speaker "shored" fragments from the great tradition
"against [his] ruins" to "set [his] lands in order" (*Collected Poems* 69), Rich's
speaker sees women drown in a continuous stream of household chores. This,
however, also disregards the complexity of Dickinson's denials.

Section 7 quotes from and comments upon Wollstonecraft's first book
*Thoughts on the Education of Daughters* (1787).

> *"To have in this uncertain world some stay*
> *which cannot be undermined, is*
> *of the utmost consequence."*
>                           Thus wrote
> a woman, partly brave and partly good,
> who fought what she partly understood.
> Few men about her would or could do more,
> hence she was labelled harpy, shrew and whore.

                                        (*Snapshots* 23)

Partly rendered in iambic pentameter, the passage accuses Wollstonecraft of a
limited understanding and thus takes on the very perspective that the author had

rebelled against. Fighting identification of women, nature, and emotion, Woll-
stonecraft was dedicated to the defense of women's rationality and reason. Her
*Vindication of the Rights of Women* (1792) was the first substantive treatise calling
for women's emancipation through coeducation—a radical claim for its time. In
fact, Wollstonecraft's prose anticipated many of the arguments that feminists
have been rehearsing ever since; Rich's poem itself is indebted to her thought.
At the same time, by addressing women "in a firmer tone" (9) and pleading for
equal rights, Wollstonecraft's text itself inflects with a highly pitched mimic
voice. As Rich's commentator presents herself as a further enlightened subject,
she both rejects the other woman's mimic voice and takes on her position of
mimic, thus reproducing mimicry. Similarly, opening with a fragment from
Samuel Johnson's infamous comparison of a woman preaching and a dog walk-
ing on his hind legs (*"Not that it is done well, but / that it is done at all?"*), section
9 features another speaker who internalized and accepted the prejudices she
rehearses. In this way, the poem insinuates, mimicry turns against women
themselves.

> Bemused by gallantry, we hear
> our mediocrities over-praised,
> indolence read as abnegation,
> slattern thought styled intuition,
> every lapse forgiven, our crime
> only to cast too bold a shadow
> or smash the mold straight off.
>
> (*Snapshots* 24)

Adapting a passage from the conclusion of Simone de Beauvoir's *Le deux-*
*ième sexe* (1949), Rich's final snapshot attempts to "smash the mold straight off"
suddenly yet merely throws a bold shadow, instead. The projected vision of
femininity, freed from cultural constraints, remains consistent with the preced-
ing portraits of the "daughter-in-law." While the speaker shifts position from
first-person plural to first-person singular, future woman remains at a far dis-
tance, represented by the "mute anonymous 'she'" that Rich's poems continu-
ously fall back upon (Lamos 104).

>                      Well,
> she's long about her coming, who must be
> more merciless to herself than history.
> Her mind full to the wind, I see her plunge
> breasted and glancing through the currents,

taking the light upon her
at least as beautiful as any boy
or helicopter,
           poised, still coming
her fine blades making the air wince
but her cargo
no promise then:
delivered
palpable
ours.

(Snapshots 24–25)

Resonating with de Beauvoir's voice, these lines juxtapose the previously rehearsed misconceptions of femininity with a feminist view that partly corresponds to Rich's own perspective, partly explains the cultural dynamic upon which her poem's travesty relies. The central claim of *Le deuxième sexe* is that women are not born but, rather, made women. De Beauvoir not only insisted that throughout history women have been reduced to the position of other, object, and immanence, that notions of women's predetermination by hormones and natural instincts are culturally inscribed and perpetuated. Women themselves, she claimed, have reproduced such views because, confronted with a long history of misrepresentation, they necessarily internalized the discourse of their own suppression. De Beauvoir therefore called for a transcendence of sexual differences, for the equality of the sexes, a "brotherhood" of men and women. Confined to immanence, de Beauvoir claimed, woman has so far attempted to draw man into her own prison. Nowadays, she concludes, women seek "to emerge, herself, in the light of transcendence" (717).[39]

The image of female subjectivity projected by Rich's last snapshot ("taking the light upon her") visualizes this claim. It also refers to the following passage from *La deuxième sexe,* which Rich offers as a source:

elle arrive du fond des ages, de Thèbes, de Minos, de Chichen Itza; et elle est aussi le totem planté au coeur de la brousse africaine; c'est un helicoptère et c'est un oiseau; et voilà la plus grande merveille: sous ses cheveux peints le bruissement des feuillages devient une pensée et des paroles s'échappent de ses seins. (*Snapshots* 64)[40]

These lines derive from a discussion of the resistance against female emancipation. In order to maintain the status quo, de Beauvoir points out, opponents of women's liberation—afraid of having to do without the "feminine charm" and mystery that makes man's life cheerful (729)—frequently emphasize the potential losses it supposedly involves. Ironically projecting woman as totem, bird, and helicopter, de Beauvoir suggests that, as long as woman decorates, disguises, and exhibits herself, she may win men's adoration and awe yet remains fixed in an object position that disguises her subjectivity. "Torn between the past and the future," woman in the middle of the twentieth century "appears," de Beauvoir argues, "most often as a 'true woman' disguised as a man, and she feels herself as ill at ease in her flesh as in her masculine garb. She must shed her old skin and cut her own new clothes" (725). Rich's final vision of woman, by contrast, employs the very dress codes that de Beauvoir had urged women to take off. Shielded and armed with "blades," she resembles Moore's freelancing figures. "Plung[ing] breasted," she compares to the fallen fighter Rich described in "The Knight." "At least as beautiful as any boy," she heralds the troubled androgynous figures of Rich's later poetry. Woman's own "cargo," however, is not yet delivered. As hinted by the pronoun *ours,* language itself, the source of female subjectivity, is still to be repossessed. Rich's final appropriation of de Beauvoir's authority, however, begins to reinscribe, no matter how ambivalently, the female subject as a speaking subject who speaks if not her own language, then at least her own mind.

Rich's claim that woman "must be / more merciless to herself than history" echoes de Beauvoir's view of woman's reemergence from prehistory, a view that not so much mourns lost origins but emphasizes a long tradition of female travesty. Evoking Freud's comparison between "the discovery of the Minoan-Mycenaean civilization behind that of Greece" and psychoanalysis' insight into the importance of the preoedipal phase for female subject formation, de Beauvoir's image, however, connotes what both her own and Rich's projection of female subjectivity omits. Just like de Beauvoir's transcendent sense of sexual equality, Rich's prophetic vision of liberated womanhood denies the maternal as historical and physical origin.

In her own poetic explorations of women's affiliations, Irigaray herself projects mimicry in a shade of difference. Her essays "When Our Lips Speak Together" and "The One Doesn't Stir without the Other" (1979) see mimicry as a self-destructive, rather then a joyfully subversive, force that produces distance between women by reproducing sameness. "Exiled from yourself," the daughter confronts her mother in the first essay,

> you fuse with everything you meet. You imitate whatever comes close. You become whatever touches you. In your eagerness to find yourself again, you move indefinitely far from yourself. From me. Taking one

model after another, passing from master to master, changing face, form, and language with each new power that dominates you. You / we are sundered; as you allow yourself to be abused, you become an impassive travesty. (*This Sex* 210)

What was once perceived as "playful repetition" has turned into "impassive travesty." Deploring "the ebb and flow of our lives spent in the exhausting labor of copying, miming" (207), Irigaray indirectly objects to her own labor, the skillful manipulation and deconstruction of "master discourse" in her earlier work. Curiously enough, the daughter's reproach of the mother ("You become whatever touches you") echoes Rich's lines ("the beak that grips her / she becomes"), which themselves echo Yeats. Irigaray's turn against the mother itself turns out to be an act of mimicry. "Speaking sameness," both Rich and Irigaray impersonate the common notion that subjectity is based on the suppression of maternal origins. Both Rich's poem and Irigaray's essays, however, call upon another type of woman, instead. For both mimicry remains an interim strategy that ultimately fails, however, to construct a "different" voice and "make connections." Accordingly, Rich's essay "Motherhood and Daughterhood" opens as follows: "A folder lies open beside me as I start to write, spilling out references and quotations, all relevant probably, but none of which can help me to begin" (218).

## Claiming the Matrix of Female Subjectivity

Rich's view of motherhood and mother figures has always been highly ambivalent. For the most part she has associated both with a lack or loss of subjectivity. Continuous with "Snapshots of a Daughter-in-Law," whose vision of a new woman depends upon the negation of the mother and her mimic voice, Rich's prose of the 1970s rejects motherhood, like marriage, as an institution detrimental to female self-affirmation. "To be a female human being trying to fulfill traditional female functions in a traditional way," she claimed in her essay "When We Dead Awaken: Writing as Re-Vision" (1971), "*is* in direct conflict with the subversive function of the imagination" (*On Lies* 43). Throughout the 1970s Rich politicized this view and, not wholly incomparable to Moore's position on marriage, argued it serves to institutionalize women's oppression. In 1976 she defined "motherhood as enforced identity and as political institution" (197); in 1978 she paralleled "patriarchal motherhood" with "economic exploitation" and "compulsory heterosexuality" as "institutions by which women have traditionally been controlled" (*Blood* 24). Rich's most comprehensive excursus into motherhood remains her highly controversial book *Of Woman Born: Motherhood as Experience and Institution* (1976).[41] Interestingly enough, its appearance coincided with two other publications, both of which dramatize their own particular "return" to the mother. One is Rich's essay "Vesuvius at Home: The Power of Emily Dickinson" (1976), whose intention was, among other things, to "repossess" Dickinson "as a source and a foremother" (*On Lies* 167) and which will be discussed in detail in chapter 3. The other is the collection *Twenty-One Love Poems* (1976), the first texts in Rich's oeuvre to deal explicitly with lesbian relationships and to attempt to reclaim women's sexuality as a material basis of female subjectivity.[42] This synchronicity of a critique of motherhood, on the one hand, and the symbolic act of repossessing the "nonmother" Dickinson (*On Lies* 196) and the maternal body as matrix of women's existence, on the other, is more than a coincidence. Reimagining maternity and mother figures, Rich tried to recuperate from the realm of mother-daughter and woman-to-woman relations the "stone foundation" (*Dream* 77) of what Rich's essay "Compulsory Heterosexuality and Lesbian Existence" (1978) conceptualizes as a "lesbian continuum," of the "range—through each woman's life and throughout history—of women-identified experience" (*Blood* 51).

I myself begin with a reading of the essay "Motherhood and Daughterhood," which, according to Rich, constitutes the center of her book *Of Woman Born*. I will show that Rich's ambivalence toward motherhood led her to distinguish between mother figures and a realm of the maternal. As a consequence, her writing retained the image of the mother as mimic while at the same time reinventing the maternal as a variable figure of origin and identity. I take this tendency as the main drive of *The Dream of a Common Language* (1978), a collection of poems that problematize motherhood yet redefine the maternal as a "ground-note" of both the "lesbian continuum" and "a whole new poetry." As this matrix of female subjectivity turns out to be a province of silence more than speech, the ultimate importance of Rich's poetic return to the mother is not to reaffirm referentiality but, rather, to accept the necessary losses on which signification and constructions of subjectivity depend.

## Reinventing the Mother

*Of Woman Born* introduces motherhood as a "crucial, still relatively unexplored, area of feminist theory" (15). The "cathexis between mother and daughter," in particular, writes Rich in the chapter "Motherhood and Daughterhood," remains "the great unwritten story" (225). Composed in ten sections—and thus structured like "Snapshots of a Daughter-in-Law" and *Of Woman Born* itself (but unlike any other of the book's chapters)—the essay reassesses her previous views of mother-daughter relations. Oscillating between the projection of a "subliminal, subversive, pre-verbal" knowledge that aligns mother and daughter (220) and the "desire to become purged, once and for all of our mothers' bondage, to become individuated and free" (236), the essay creates a duality that eventually effects the displacement of the (biological) mother by a surrogate mother, another woman, a female lover.

The essay opens with a rhetorical dismissal of mimicry that is presented as the very precondition for a rediscovery of maternal origins.[43]

A folder lies open beside me as I start to write, spilling out references and quotations, all relevant probably, but none of which can help me to begin. This is the core of my book, and I enter it as a woman who, born between her mother's legs, has time after time and in different ways tried to return to her mother, to repossess her and be repossessed by her. (218)

The metaphor "spilling out references" visualizes the ejection of a patriarchal heritage and echoes Rich's poem "A Woman Mourned by Daughters" (1960), whose daughters repudiate a self-sacrificing and suffocating maternal affection geared to reproduce traditional gender roles.

. . . . . . . . . . . . . . . .
What is it, if not you,
that settles on us now
like satin you pulled down
over our bridal heads?
What rises in our throats
like food you prodded in?
Nothing could be enough.
You breathe upon us now
through solid assertions
of yourself: teaspoons, goblets,
seas of carpet, a forest
of old plants to be watered,
an old man in an adjoining
room to be touched and fed.
. . . . . . . . . . . . . . . . . . . . . .

Introjection and incorporation of objects signify processes of identification, their expulsion the rebellion against an internalized identity, here that of the mother as a powerless caretaker. Both poem and prose suggest that their speaker has been nourished on an indigestible food, on traditional roles, on "references and quotations." Still, there is a significant shift of emphasis. Whereas the poem still resonates with the very mimic tone of female self-contempt characteristic of Rich's "Snapshots," the prose takes patriarchy itself as its target. And, whereas the poem imagines the maternal body dead and drained, the prose reshapes that body into the very "nourishment" of female subjectivity. The phrases "What rises in our throats" and "Spilling out references" thus signify two different kinds of separation. The rejection of the mother has turned into the rejection of mimicry upon which the rise of the female subject supposedly depends.

The daughter's refusal of maternal nurture metaphorizes the original separation from the maternal body and thus recalls Irigaray's essay "And the One Doesn't Stir without the Other" (1979). This text revises the earlier "When Our Lips Speak Together" by recreating the process of female subject formation as a development from a close affiliation to a phase of division to a redefined desire for and final reconnection with the mother. The first (preoedipal) stage is reimagined as a timeless, indifferent state of mirroring and melting, located "before there are any images" (63) and characterized by a continuous flow of energy, a reciprocal process of nourishment and endless exchange of substance. Alienation sets in the moment the daughter feels overfed and fears paralysis: "you feed me / yourself too much, as if you wanted to fill me up completely with your offering. You put yourself in my mouth, and I suffocate. . . . I want no more of this stuffed, sealed up, immobilized body" (61, 62). As a consequence of this aversion, the daughter choses another love object and attempts "to walk behind" the father (62). In the second stage of subject formation the daughter mourns the mother's "death" after this separation took place. "Trapped in a single function—mothering," she complains, the mother is left without memory, subject position, and sense of self: "When the one of us comes into the world, the other goes underground. When the one carries life, the other dies." Emphasizing the importance of separation, Irigaray still proposes a third stage of female subjectivity, in which mother and daughter interrelate yet do so as separate subjects: "What I wanted from you, Mother, was this: that in giving me life, you still remain alive" (67).

Rich's poem "A Woman Mourned by Daughters" dramatizes this process of separation, moving from the suffocating nurture entailed in dyadic unity to an ambivalent turn toward the father (the "old man in an adjoining / room"), accompanied by an angry mourning of the mother's death. Like Irigaray's text, it insists that the process of "doubl[ing] up" (Kristeva, "Stabat Mater" 167) traditionally leads to self-denial. "Typically, under patriarchy," Rich explains in *Of Woman Born*, "the mother's life is exchanged for the child; her autonomy as a separate being seems fated to conflict with the infant she will bear" (166). Accordingly, the symbolic return to the mother projected in "Motherhood and Daughterhood" proposes to reconstitute the mother: "This is the core of my book, and I enter it as a woman who, born between her mother's legs, has time after time and in different ways tried to return to her mother, to repossess her and be repossessed by her" (218). Claiming to repossess the first love object and being repossessed by the mother's desire simultaneously, these lines reimagine a preoedipal identity of subject and object. The simile that transforms the first person into a third person ("I enter it as a woman who") testifies that repossessing the mother means reinventing her as well as remaking oneself into an other woman.

In Rich's essay the reinvention of the mother entails a rereading of her own mother's biography, which had served as a subtext for "Snapshots." Focused on her life before marriage now, the prose resuscitates the mother's skills and dedications and presents her as a successful concert pianist and composer, as a talented, determined person, as a scholar and enthusiastic reader. As the depiction merges the image of the unmarried independent woman with that of a female figure starring in the final snapshot, remaking her as "an explorer in new realms" who "lives in the present and future, not the past" (224), we realize that, like Rich's final snapshot, this portrait is a projection. "As daughters we need mothers," Rich explains,

> who want their own freedom and ours. We need not be the vessels of another woman's self-denial and frustration. The quality of the mother's life—however embattled and unprotected—is her primary bequest to her daughter, because a woman who can believe in herself, who is a fighter, and who continues to struggle to create livable space around her, is demonstrating to her daughter that these possibilities exist. (247)

Like Irigaray, Rich demands a different kind of nurture, not "the old, institutionalized, sacrificial, 'mother-love' which men have demanded: we want courageous mothering" (246). In this way Rich recreates Moore's maternal hero as a maternal heroine.

Having shared with the reader memories of her own mother, Rich's essay shifts toward "the gulf between 'mothers' and 'nonmothers'" (249), an issue that foreshadows the turn her interest in motherhood was going to take. Supposedly deviant and resistant to the pressures of patriarchal culture, "to the law of heterosexual pairing and bearing" (*Of Woman Born* 252), the childless woman turns into yet another figure of identification that finally displaces the mother. The silence projected upon the childless woman—"throughout recorded history," Rich writes, "the 'childless' woman has been regarded . . . as a failed woman, unable to speak for the rest of her sex" (251)—allows Rich to project her own voice.

Along with Margaret Fuller, Emily Brontë, Dickinson, Woolf, and de Beauvoir, Rich finally remembers her own childless black nurse as mother. "My Black mother was 'mine' only for four years, during which she fed me, dressed me, played with me, watched over me, sang to me, cared for me tenderly and intimately. 'Childless' herself, she *was* a mother." Exposing this figure of ultimate otherness as both provider of nurture and "nonverbal" communication *and* object of erotic desire, Rich displaces both the freelancing androgynous figure from "Snapshots" and her natural mother by a politically more appealing surrogate mother.[44] In fact, the black female turns out to have been the object of desire all along. "When I began writing this chapter," Rich adds in the next-to-last paragraph, "I began to remember my black mother again: her calm, realistic vision of things, her physical grace and pride, her beautiful soft voice" (254). Retrospectively situated as object of primal desires, this figure also triggers Rich's final revision of the oedipal conflict. "At the edge of adolescence," Rich concludes, "we find ourselves drawing back from our natural mothers . . . toward men. . . . Women are made taboo to women. . . . In breaking this taboo, we are reuniting with our mothers; in reuniting with our mothers, we are breaking this taboo" (255). In the end lesbian sexuality both violates paternal law and enacts a symbolic return to the mother. Representing the supposed parallel between lesbian love and mother-daughter reunion through a chiasmic sentence structure, Rich acknowledges that the desired closure, wholeness, and identity are being achieved rhetorically.[45] Such circularities reappear in *The Dream of a Common Language,* in relation to which "Motherhood and Daughterhood" reads like a preface.

*Silences and "Secret Circles of Fire":*
*The Limits of a Common Language*

Rich's collection *The Dream of a Common Language* reimagines the "reun[ion] with our mothers" as a return to the female body, which prompts visions of a "new language" (75) and a genuinely female voice. Exploring the "lesbian possibility, an engulfed continent which rises fragmentarily into view from time to time only to become submerged again" (*Blood* 50), the poems authorize new frontiers and attempt to map a location not yet marked by language. This attempt in itself is the truly radical aspect of this particular collection. Throughout *The Dream of a Common Language* the projected place of origin figures as a state of preoedipal unity, a preliminary stage on the way to another discourse, not a discourse in itself but a pretext of lesbian sexuality, "the [preverbal] knowledge flowing between two alike bodies" (*Of Woman Born* 220). Exploring the material basis of female subjectivity, Rich comes to acknowledge the body as a realm of suppressed rhythms and sounds, women's sexual encounters as a secret but silent "circle of fire" and specularity, and the retreat into the closed circles of intimate lesbian relations as a form of self-marginalization, a deprivation of power. This process both redefines lesbian sexuality as a counterforce against the "myths of separation" (*Dream* 11) and entails an acceptance of the symbolic order. Restoring its very fundament, Rich's new conception of subjectivity would, however, still not accept language as an "order of sacrifice." Instead, it restores the female body as its fundamental part, resonating within women's multiple voices.

As a consequence, Rich's poems discriminate between different kinds of silence that may be explored by tracing her frequent use of the word *float*. Employed in poems such as "To a Poet" and "Sibling Mysteries," the verb *float* echoes "Snapshots," in which the mother's sense of self is built on "Delicious recollections [that] float like perfume through the memory." In Rich's later poems, however, the word connotes fluidity, boundlessness, and dissemination and, like poststructuralism does, distinguishes femininity from firm, self-centered male subjectivity and symbolic modes.[46] Recurring throughout the collection, the term's meaning itself shifts and floats yet remains associated with muteness as much as mutuality. Whereas in "To a Poet" *float* links mothering activities and its metaphors (*milk, tears*) with a loss of language and the lack of another vocation, in "Sibling Mysteries" it denotes a fulfilled, desireless, though also "languageless" (Moore, *CPMM* 46) state of dyadic unity. The fundamental difference between the silences of motherhood and mother-child symbiosis is that, in the former, loss of language entails finality, the death ("abortion") of a potential female author(ity); in the latter, a liberation from a worn-out discourse, a new beginning as well as a homecoming to the silent origin of a "new language."

We cut the wires,
find ourselves in free-fall, as if
our true home were the undimensional

solitudes, the rift
in the Great Nebula.
No one who survives to speak
new language, has avoided this:
the cutting-away of an old force that held her
rooted to an old ground

(*Dream* 75)

The poem "Origins and History of Consciousness" envisions such "cutting away," the "drive to connect," and redefines "the true nature of poetry" as a cathartic experience in the course of which the speaker "floats" back into presymbolic conditions.

I have dreamed of going to bed
as walking into clear water ringed by a snowy wood
white as cold sheets, thinking, *I'll freeze in there.*
My bare feet are numbed already by the snow
but the water
is mild, I sink and float
like a warm amphibious animal
that has broken the net, has run
through the fields of snow leaving no print;
this water washes off the scent—
*You are clear now*
*of the hunter, the trapper*
*the wardens of the mind—*

yet the warm animal dreams on
of another animal
swimming under the snow-flecked surface of the pool,
and wakes, and sleeps again.

No one sleeps in this room without
the dream of a common language.

(7–8)

The "snowy wood" and whiteness recall the "whiteness of the wall / behind the poems, planks of books / photographs of dead heroines" (7) that, at an earlier point in the poem, insinuated the lack of an adequate discourse and literary tradition—a lack that turns into liberation. The cleansing releases the speaker

from language and conventional meanings ("the scent") as well as from tradi-
tional subject-object relations, from male dominance over female creativity and
nature, figured by the hunter, which invokes poems such as "Orion" and
"Transcendental Etude." The described floating condition dissolves such hier-
archies in an image of wholeness, an identity of "I" and "you," hinted at by a
sudden address of the "I" as "you" and highlighted by the italic print. As the
dreams of catharsis and common language blur, rhetorical figures are being lit-
eralized. Whereas, initially, the animal figures the condition of the speaker ("I
float and sink *like* a warm amphibious animal"), the parallelism of *dream* and *sleep*
finally fuse speaker and figure.

In the poem's second part the dream materializes as the sexual encounter
of two women, which is compared to a "drowning" or, to use Kristeva's words,
"an underwater, trans-verbal communication between bodies" ("Stabat Mater"
182).

It was simple to meet you, simple to take your eyes
into mine, saying: these are eyes I have known
from the first. . . . It was simple to touch you
against the hacked background, the grain of what we
had been, the choices, years. . . . It was even simple
to take each other's lives in our hands, as bodies.

What is not simple: to wake from drowning
from where the ocean beat inside us like an afterbirth
into this common, acute particularity
these two selves who walked half a lifetime untouching—

. . . . . . . . . . . . . . . . . . . . . . . . . . . . . . . . . . . .

It's simple to wake from sleep with a stranger,
dress, go out, drink coffee.
enter a life again. It isn't simple
to wake from sleep into the neighborhood
of one neither strange nor familiar

(*Dream* 8–9)

As in Dickinson's poems about Eden, the look into another's eyes/I's suggests
identity. The alliance of two lovers with "bodies, so alike, . . . yet so different"
(*Dream* 30), "neither strange nor familiar," even recalls Moore's maternal econ-

omy of difference in indifference. Here, however, paradise is the practice of lesbian love, projected as a return to preoedipal reciprocity.

The term *afterbirth,* which pictures the experience of lesbian love as a kind of rebirth, in which both partners play the part of mother and child, subject and object ("Conceived / of each other, conceived each other"), suggests that, as in Dickinson, such extreme proximity is indeed no place to linger. Referring to the placenta and fetal membranes expelled after delivery, *afterbirth* also symbolizes the texture of connection that, unlike Moore's nautilus shell, which survives as a souvenir, is eliminated in order to separate "into this acute particularity / these two selves." Whereas women's sexual relations seem a "simple," because after all "original," affair, the separation into two individuals, or what Lacan calls "the deflection of the specular I into the social I" (*Écrits* 5), marks a moment of crisis. The penetration of "a ring of the telephone, a scream of someone beaten up far down in the street," the sounds of "this city, / this century, this life" forces such separation just as father and phallus intervene in the dyadic union. In contrast to heterosexual relations, which are handicapped by a "natural" distance between the partners, lesbian affiliations are endangered by a surplus of intimacy, a "lure of spacial identification" (Lacan 4), the closure and confinement of a "secret circle of fire."

>                                [. . .] Conceived
> of each other, conceived each other in a darkness
> which I remember as drenched in light.
>                          I want to call this, life.
>
> But I can't call it life until we start to move
> beyond this secret circle of fire
> where our bodies are giant shadows flung on a wall
> where the night becomes our inner darkness, and sleeps
> like a dumb beast, head on her paws, in the corner.
>                                       *(Dream 9)*

After a deictic signal of presence and closure ("I want to call this, life") the poem begins to reconsider ambivalently the speaker's inclination to regress to a safe, preoedipal-like state and an illusion of identity. Delineating intimate lesbian love as an inner darkness, "a dumb beast," the poem's final line reestablishes the figurativeness dissolved at the end of its first part; once again dreams and desires dissociate from "reality" and necessities of life. "To live outside the law! Or, barely within it," indeed becomes, as Rich puts it in "Ghazals," "a twig on boiling waters, enclosed inside a bubble" (*Leaflets* 68). With the final image of the "dumb animal" and the focus on the "beyonds" of this "secret circle of fire," on history rather than ontology, the dream of a common language dissolves. Or, more precisely, it turns out to be not a language at all but a silent and circular rhythm ("where the ocean beat inside us"), a mute echo of "our roughly literal life."

In order to make these echoes signify, to recreate physical intimacy on the textual level, Rich's poem employs a discourse that privileges the literal yet also acknowledges that there is no escaping the fundamental figurativeness of language. In fact, the originality of her "Twenty-One Love Poems" stems from the ways in which "sonnets" such as "(The Floating Poem, Unnumbered)" appropriate traditional forms and images for a radically novel subject matter.

> Whatever happens with us, your body
> will haunt mine—tender, delicate
> your lovemaking, like the half-curled frond
> of the fiddlehead fern in forests
> just washed by sun. Your traveled, generous thighs
> between which my whole face has come and come—
> the innocence and wisdom of the place my tongue has found there—
> the live, insatiate dance of your nipples in my mouth—
> your touch on me, firm, protective, searching
> me out, your strong tongue and slender fingers
> reaching where I had been waiting years for you
> in my rose-wet cave—whatever happens, this is.
>
> (*Dream* 32)

These lines reproduce the cathartic ("washed by sun") and specular moments prevalent in "History and Origin of Consciousness." Images of wholeness and closure ("half-curled frond," "whole face," "rose-wet cave"), repetition and echo ("come and come"), as well as deictic markers rewrite the lesbian sexual encounter in terms of the preoedipal mirror stage of subject formation. The image of the lover's face echoing the orgasm of the beloved literalizes both the body's rhythms and sounds and the echo itself, thus suggesting the identity of lover and loved. As Rich herself explains: "The identification with another woman's orgasm as if it were one's own is one of the most intense interpersonal experiences: nothing is either 'inside' me or 'outside' at such moments" (*Of Woman Born* 63). Moving from "whatever happens with us" to "whatever happens, this is," the poem, however, inscribes the identity of "I" and "you" (*us*) into the utterance ("this is"), thus making it as much an intratextual as an interpersonal experience.

Accordingly, whereas the poem's directness resists metaphorization and literary reference, the poem's figurativeness echoes other texts. Here the speaker is not haunted by her own otherness but, rather, by the likeness of another woman's body and of other women's texts. The "fiddlehead fern" recalls Moore's "Marriage," the "traveled, generous thighs" incorporate a well-traveled American motif, the "dance of [the] nipples" manipulate Yeats's dancer and dance. The "rose-wet cave," appropriates a conventional symbol of love ("rose") while also mapping out a highly clichéd topography of the female body ("cave"), reminiscent of the darkest (Freudian) continents and deepest fears of female sexuality. Women's sexual desire, figured as her "wetness," cannot be visualized apart from these common cultural representations. Yet only by recontextualizing these common images can their meanings be multiplied, if not changed. This also implies that the writer has to accept language as it is, to "choose [words] / or choose / to remain silent" (*Your Native Land* 34), without necessarily accepting the notion of language as an "order of sacrifice" (Kristeva) in which substance turns into absence. Silence, as Rich claims in "Cartographies of Silence" (1975), is not necessarily identical with absence but "can be a plan / rigorously executed / the blueprint of a life." The metaphor of the blueprint interestingly intertwines the revision of silence with that of a practice of mimicry and copying. Whereas "Snapshots of a Daughter-in-Law" condemns mimicry as a rehearsal of paternal law, *The Dream of a Common Language* reclaims the realm of the pre-symbolic, of the body as the mute origin and matrix of a fundament of female subjectivity, which for its very muteness requires a "routine / remembering" (*Wild* 22).

Associating the physical world with an "other" poetics and the maternal with a "different" voice, "Transcendental Etude" (1977) works as a coda to the collection (Altieri, *Self* 171). As a summary of its insights, the poem also builds the fundament for work that follows. Central among these insights is the implicit acceptance that any notion of origins depends upon preexisting fictions of origins. Accordingly, the poem is framed by a scenic passage whose echoes of Hopkins, Yeats, St. Vincent Millay, Whitman, and Ashbery foreground that we are traveling occupied territory. Attempting to "cut . . . away from an old force" (*Dream* 75), the poem reclaims culturally colonized domains for a lesbian politics and poetics.

a green so dense with life
minute, momentary life—slugs, moles, pheasants, gnats,

spiders, moths, hummingbirds, groundhogs, butterflies—
a lifetime is too narrow
to understand it all, beginning with the huge
rockshelves that underlie all that life.

(Dream 73)

Appropriating Whitman's catalogue technique, Rich aligns her own poetic
project with Whitman's vision of identity, relocates her work in a tradition of
homoerotic writing, and, in this way, hints at both the belatedness and the rad-
icalism of her work.

What follows, however, is a feminist critique of conventional subject for-
mation. As a way of counterbalancing the "wrenching apart" from the mater-
nal body, the poem proposes to retrieve the "ground-note" of female subjec-
tivity figured here as the sounds of the mother's heartbeat—a metaphor whose
sentimental overtones underline once again how both inapt and yet unavoid-
able worn images are. Rejecting "performance" principles and "theatricality,"
"competitiveness," and "mastery"—that is, the very principles cherished by the
mother figure in "Snapshots"—the speaker opts for the rehearsal of the body to
recuperate the lost maternal territory, a shared language and birthright.

Homesick for myself, for her—as, after the heatwave
breaks, the clear tones of the world
manifest: cloud, bough, wall, insect, the very soul of light:
homesick as the fluted vault of desire
articulates itself: I am the lover and the loved,
home and wanderer, she who splits
firewood and she who knocks, a stranger
in the storm, two women, eye to eye
measuring each other's spirit, each other's
limitless desire,
a whole new poetry beginning here.

(76)

In one way Rich's "fluted vault of desire / articulates itself" by mimicry. Or, as
Colleen Lamos observes: "This 'new poetry' produces its confident assertion by
virtue of its technical brilliance and literary allusions, echoing an entire tradition
of lyric poems that claim to reconcile 'the slayer and the slain,' 'the dancer and
the dance' into a transcendent symbiosis" (115). At the same time, in the given
context these echoes are being appropriated in a way that affects that entire tra-

dition. In order to put the female matrix on the map of subjectivity, Rich suggests, this matrix has to materialize in symbolic modes of discourse and interact with the very order it means to transform.

Like "Origins and History of Consciousness," "Transcendental Etude" resists its own deictic closure ("a whole new . . .") and reopens for an extended metaphor that, like Rich's final snapshot, projects a silent woman.

> Visions begin to happen in such a life
> as if a woman quietly walked away
> from the argument and jargon in a room
> and sitting down in the kitchen, began turning in her lap
> bits of yarn, calico and velvet scraps,
> laying them out absently on the scrubbed boards
> in the lamplight, with small rainbow-colored shells
> sent in cotton-wool from somewhere far away,
> and skeins of milkweed from the nearest meadow—
> original domestic silk, the finest findings—
> and the darkblue petal of the petunia,
> and the dry darkbrown lace of seaweed;
> not forgotten either, the shed silver
> whisker of the cat,
> the spiral of paper-wasp-nest curling
> beside the finch's yellow feather.
>
> (76)

Woman's return to the kitchen, her "care for the many-lived forms," and her creative use of materials reminiscent of Moore's poems ("rainbow-colored shells," "paper-wasp-nest") may come as a surprise. Yet the kitchen itself has turned into a place of cultural practice. As a figure for women's multiple speaking positions, for the differences within their voices, and for their ability to make do with "scraps," the image of the quilt has displaced that of the collage. Reconstructive, synthetic quilt making has displaced analytical deconstructive collage art.

> Such a composition has nothing to do with eternity
> the striving for greatness, brilliance—
> only with the musing of a mind
> one with her body, experienced fingers quietly pushing
> dark against bright, silk against roughness,

pulling the tenets of a life together
with no mere will to mastery,
only care for the many-lived unending
forms in which she finds herself,
becoming now the sherd of broken glass
slicing light in a corner, dangerous
to flesh, now the plentiful, soft leaf
that wrapped round the throbbing finger, soothes the wound;
and now the stone foundation, rockshelf further
forming underneath everything that grows.

(77)

Juxtaposing performance principles with disinterested care, nurturance, and a silent sense of wholeness, this passage projects the image of a woman in harmony with the world of her objects. Having the female figure transform into the materials of her collage art ("the sherd of broken glass," "the soft leaf"), the poem invokes the identity of subject and object and fuses multiplicity and fragmentation with wholeness. It thus visualizes the matrix of an integrated sense of female subjectivity further explored in Rich's collection *A Wild Patience Has Taken Me This Far* (1981), most particularly in the poem "Integrity." Accordingly, Rich writes near the end of her essay "Motherhood and Daughterhood":

> To accept and integrate and strengthen both the mother and the daughter in ourselves is no easy matter, because patriarchal attitudes have encouraged us to split, to polarize, these images, and to project all unwanted guilt, anger, shame, power, freedom, onto the "other" woman. But any radical vision of sisterhood demands that we reintegrate them. (253)

According to Rich, such reintegration or self-identity is a necessary pretext for any acknowledgment of difference among women—a subject matter that preoccupies Rich in her next collection of poems.

Rewriting female subjectivity in terms of women's particular affiliation with the maternal body and materiality, Rich asserts the primacy of the female subject. Whereas her earlier poems find woman as part of a married couple "stranded upon a rock," she now figures as "the stone foundation, rockshelf further / forming underneath everything that grows." Rereading this image through Rich's poem "Mother-Right" (1977), we may indeed discover a new phase of her poetry dawning.

Woman and child   running
in a field   A man planted
on the horizon

The man is walking boundaries
measuring   He believes in what is his
the grass   the waters underneath   the air

the air   through which child and mother
are running   the boy singing
the woman   eyes sharpened in the light
heart stumbling   making for the open

(*Dream* 59)

In the context of this poem any claim to the "rockshelf foundation" reaches out for the space in between grass and water, cuts the ground from under man's feet, expropriates the father, and lays the foundation for a potentially different symbolic order—a different law, that is, not a lawless state.

Similarly, in Irigaray's more recent work the inevitable "economy of nature" does not refer to female difference in any essentialist sense. Instead, it constitutes the basis for a different kind of legislation. Her essay "On the Necessity of Gender-Differentiated Laws" (1989)[47] argues that the specificity of female subject formation requires not so much the equality of the sexes but a reflection of sexual differences within legislation. Irigaray insists, for instance, on laws against the exchange value of virginity and the exploitation of motherhood, legitimating her claims with reference to women's particular needs and previous matriarchal societies that practiced such gender-specific legislation. While there are obvious parallels to the argument of Rich's book *Of Woman Born,* Irigaray no longer dismisses the law of the father and the economy of lack. Instead, she addresses that lack, the insufficiencies of patriarchal law, themselves.[48] Rather than exploring female lawlessness, she insists on gender-differentiated laws that inscribe female subjectivity into the symbolic order. "Making for the open," Rich's "mother-right," in contrast, still longs to claim a space free from inscription. Reformatting her own final snapshot, whose female figure emerged "as beautiful as any boy" from a rejection of the mother, "Mother-Right" acknowledges, however, that change may happen within established symbolic orders, that it should be based not on a dismissal of mother figures but on a redefined notion of both mother and the maternal.

Accordingly, Rich's poetry has continued to converse with mother figures. At no point, however, does she come to terms with them in the way her collection *Sources* (1983) makes peace with father and husband (while completely erasing the mother as a source of a sense of self). Nor does she ever write a text that speaks from the position of the mother. Instead, the figure of the mother as mimic keeps haunting Rich's poetry and reappears in her poem "Solfeggietto" (1985–88). Portraying the mother as a teacher of *solfège,* the poem revises the early poem "Juvenalia." Whereas the latter reminisces on a daughter's first writing exercises under paternal supervision, "Solfeggietto" presents her as a reluctant student of musical scales, the solfa syllables' prescribed text taught by the mother. Presenting the mother as an instructor of mimicry, the text furthermore rehabilitates the father.

The poem's first section offers a snapshot of the mother's piano, depicted as "a black cave / with teeth of ebony and ivory," symbol of a phallic mother, a mysterious dangerously dark realm of femininity that extends into a world structured by binary oppositions, in which male dominates female as white dominates black. "[S]et on the big book on the chair," the daughter was meant "to face," that is, to identify with "the keyboard world of black of white." In sections 2 and 3 the speaker distances herself from the (mother's) position she is expected to imitate, pointing to the political dangers that mimicry bears. Displacing the mother's "moldering" memories by her own recollection of a trip ("Summers of '36, '37, Europe untuned"), the speaker remembers

How we sang out the chorus   how I loved
*the watchfires of the hundred circling camps*
and *truth is marching on* and *let us die to make men free*

                                                (*Time's Power* 4)

The fourth section refocuses on the piano lessons as they symbolize women's "doomed exhaustion their common mystery."

                            the mother cannot teach
the daughter because this is not the story
of a mother teaching magic to her daughter
Side by side I see us locked
My wrists   your voice   are tightened
Passion lives in old songs   in the kitchen
where another woman cooks   teaches   and sings
*He shall feed his flock like a shepherd*
and in the booklined room

where the Jewish father reads and smokes and teaches
Ecclesiastes, Proverbs, the Song of Songs
The daughter struggles with the strange notations
—dark chart of music's ocean    flowers and flags

(4)

The line "side by side I see us locked" invokes Rich's poem "Snapshots,"
which presents woman as "Poised, trembling, and unsatisfied, before / an
unlocked door, that cage of cages" and underscores that mother and daughter
take the same position ("side by side"). Still, the daughter insists on her differ-
ence. She rejects "the dark" and indistinguished "chart of music's ocean,"
which recalls an image previously aligned with lesbian love ("the drowning
from where the ocean beat inside us"), and privileges other, supposedly more
passionate and knowledgeable tunes: the sound of the black nurse's "old songs"
and the father's words. These words maintain the very ethnic tradition that was
threatened by another kind of mimicry, the mass psychosis stirred by the
national socialist movement referred to earlier in the poem. The comfort and
care provided by the black mother and the Jewish father are complementary.
She offers physical nurture, he intellectual care and a historically grown, reli-
giously anchored identity. Both pass on a special knowledge, a deeper wisdom
and compassion, based on their shared marginal position. The mother's lesson,
by contrast, was mainstream mimicry.

Daughter who fought her mother's lessons—
even today a scrip of music balks me—
I feel illiterate in this
your mother-tongue   Had it been Greek or Slovak
no more could your native alphabet have baffled
your daughter   whom you taught for years
held by a tether   over the ivory
and ebony teeth of the Steinway
                                          It is
the three hundredth anniversary of Johann
Sebastian Bach   My earliest life
woke to English Suites   under your fingers
I understand a language I can't read
Music you played streams on the car radio
in the freeway night
You kept your passions deep   You have them still

I ask you, both of us
—Did you think mine was a virtuoso's hand?
Did I see power in yours?
Was it worth fighting for?    What did you want?
What did I want from you?

(5)

Describing the "mother tongue" as an illegible language, this poem echoes "Transcendental Etude" whose speaker's struggles with patriarchal discourse, attempting "to sightread / what our fingers can't keep up with, learn by heart / what we can't even read." Here, however, the mother tongue spells convention, conformity, and a movement along mainstream lines ("Music you played streams on the car radio"). No surprise that the poem's final lines echo Nietzsche and Freud, thus revitalizing and reproducing the practice of mimicry.

Whereas the daughter's attitude toward the mother continues to be dominated by the same old ambivalences, the acknowledgment of the father as an outsider, as one of the "dispossessed" (*Blood* 176), marks a significant change in Rich's position and reflects the course her poetics and politics have taken in the last decade. Ever since the publication of "Split at the Root: An Essay on Jewish Identity" (1982), Jewishness, along with her lesbian feminist orientation, has been the predominant feature of self-definition for the poet.[49] What is so strange about this dedication to Judaism is that it entails yet another ambivalent revision of her maternal lineage. Identifying herself as a Jew, Rich favors the very religious background of her father that she had criticized throughout her book *Of Woman Born* and adopts a system of beliefs that is traditionally passed on through the mother. "If it is true," writes Rich, "that 'we think back through our mothers if we are women' . . . then even according to lesbian theory, I cannot (or need not?) count myself a Jew" (*Blood* 102). Interestingly enough, however, Rich describes her turn to Judaism by the very terms that served her vision of "homecoming" to the mother. The assessment of an "early, primary, and intense relationship" with the father involves the breaking of a "taboo" (104), the "testing [of] a forbidden current" (108), and the "embrace" of a "new and mysterious Jewish world" (115). In this way Rich reclaims Jewishness as another marginal position that integrates maternal and paternal heritage for her conception of a heterogeneous female subject.

For Rich a new poetry indeed begins, as "Transcendental Etude" implied, with the recognition of women's heterogeneous speaking position. This insight made her resume the very poetic practice she once rejected: the use of quotations. Meanwhile, though, these quotations originate from women's texts and underscore their cultural participation and presence. Rich may still comment upon such citations. No longer, however, are they employed to be opposed or appropriated but, instead, stand on their own. Marked and separated from the text by italicization and indention, they evolve their own resonances.[50] Assembling fragments from the writings of Susan B. Anthony, Jane Addams, Elizabeth Barrett Browning, and Dickinson as well as of anonymous, "common" women, they give her poems a kind of quilt character. Rich's more recent texts thus still depend on allusions and authorities. The criteria for what qualifies as "authority," though, have changed significantly over the years as the conceptions of authority themselves have changed. Rich's poem "The Desert as a Garden of Paradise" (1987–88), for instance, a text made up of eleven, loosely structured sections, is as heavy with connotation and reference as Rich's "Snapshots," yet its frame of reference reflects a new set of concerns. Not differences of gender but, rather, of religion and race, not the oppression of women by male power, but various forms of colonization and proselytization of "the other," now preoccupy the poet.

In all this Rich's poetry has come to echo her own writing, thus reinforcing the authority of her own voice. Reappropriating phrases or images previously employed in poems about married life for the context of woman-to-woman relations, Rich underlines both the change of her speaking position and the limits of the symbolic order she has decided to accept. The metaphor of the woman "raking leaves," repeated throughout Rich's dramatic monologues, for instance, reverberates in the poem "For Memory" (1979).

Old words:    *trust    fidelity*
Nothing new yet to take their place.

I rake the leaves, clear the lawn, October grass
painfully green beneath the gold
and in this silent labor thoughts of you
start up
I hear your voice:    *disloyalty    betrayal*
stinging the wires

I stuff the old leaves into sacks
and still they fall and still
I see my work undone

(*Wild* 21)

Here the image of leave raking no longer insinuates the supposed circularity of a woman's life or the transitoriness of female beauty. Instead, the leaves, both like and unlike Whitman's leaves of grass, represent a multitude of differences among women and the many tensions they cause within woman-to-woman relations. In this context "raking" refers to the never-ending project of remembering other women by calling upon their writing and thus constructing one's own subject position as part of an intertextual cultural network. One of the women Rich repeatedly remembers and tries to repossess as a part of the "rock-shelf foundation" of female subjectivity was Emily Dickinson.

# Adrienne Rich and Emily Dickinson: From Absence to Feminist Transcendence—Female Subjectivity as Process in History

Despite the poets' dissimilar sense of subjectivity and representation, feminist literary criticism has repeatedly placed Dickinson and Rich in a historical continuity based on their supposedly related self-conceptions.[1] In most of these readings the poets have served as cornerstones for the reconstruction of a female tradition of American women's poetry in which Dickinson eventually took the center stage and Rich came to be seen as one of the poets who "reveal the impact Dickinson's work continues to exercise" (Diehl, *Dickinson* 186). This focus on the establishment of a female poetic lineage has been part of a larger project geared to make visible the presence of women in history and to write the female subject back into cultural discourse. The concern with the poets' position in literary history thus directly involves the question of the female subject's position in history—a question that French feminist theory has failed to address.

Unlike the affiliations the first two chapters explored within the framework of Kristeva's and Irigaray's theory, the dialogue between Rich and Dickinson therefore locates a blind spot within feminist theory itself. This conceptual lack becomes evident every time modernist-subversive and postmodernist-feminist poetry are being compared, that is, every time the different notions of politics entailed in such categorizations come to clash. The difference between the two, however, is established by our reading practices rather than by the literary texts themselves, by manipulations that are by no means restricted to feminist critical practices. Lacking a methodological approach that mediates Dickinson's and Rich's distinct poetics and politics, my reading interrelates their texts directly in order to explore their particular notions of subjectivity in history and to evolve the poets' own implicit theoretical positions. This procedure will show that Dickinson and Rich engage in strategic constructions of self and world, in a creative practice of subject constitution that depends upon their culture's rhetoric, knows its own fictional nature and from which emerges a heterogeneous, shifting, and often self-contradictory sense of subjectivity. Both authors thus came to understand subjectivity and history as processes performed in language and calling into question conventional notions of history as a chronological chain of events. Only Rich, however, uses this insight in order strategically to inscribe the female subject into the discourse of her work, prose and poetry alike, to tell a story about and to posit a history for that subject.

To be sure, French feminist theory has by no means ignored the issue of history. In fact, Kristeva's essay "Women's Time," concerned with conceptions of time and femininity as well as with the history of feminism, provides us with a valuable set of terms. She distinguishes three types of temporality, two of which entail notions of repetition and eternity and "are traditionally linked to female subjectivity insofar as the latter is thought of as necessarily maternal" (17). The first, cyclical temporality, refers to the "eternal recurrence of a biological rhythm which conforms to that of nature." The second, monumental temporality, for which, as Kristeva admits, "the very word 'temporality' hardly fits" (16), is "all-encompassing and infinite like imaginary space" and associated with mythology, religious beliefs, and the notion of resurrection. The third category, the time of history, encompasses "time as project, teleology, linear and prospective unfolding; time as departure, progression, and arrival" and is associated with "language considered as the enunciation of sentences (noun + verb; topic-comment, beginning-ending)" and male subjectivity (17).

Kristeva argues that these conceptions of temporality relate to "two [successive] generations" of feminism (18) that have defined their position within the social contract and time in distinct ways. Liberal feminism—that of the suffragettes as well as that of de Beauvoir—has aimed at an equality of the sexes in the system of production that depends upon the insertion of women into historical time and upon enunciation. Subsuming the multiplicity of women's voices "under the label 'Universal Woman,'" this earlier women's movement, Kristeva argues, has subscribed to a "logic of identification" (19) with established power structures to the point of denial of traditional female functions such as wifehood and motherhood. Feminism after 1968, by contrast, developed a strong distrust of the political system. "Demanding recognition of an irreducible identity, without equal in the opposite sex" (19), Kristeva explains, this current of feminist protest has situated itself outside linear time, rejoining, instead, mythical memory and the cyclical temporality of marginal movements.

According to Kristeva, the major dilemma of feminism is that neither the identification with nor the rejection of power is likely to escape the symbolic contract. After all, it is the radical *"separation* from a presumed state of nature" that manifests men and women's "common destiny" (23). As a consequence, she argues:

> the very logic of counterpower and of countersociety necessarily generates, by its very structure, its essence as a simulacrum of the combated society or of power. In this sense and from a viewpoint undoubtedly too Hegelian, modern feminism has only been but a moment in the interminable process of coming to consciousness about the implacable violence (separation, castration, etc.) which constitutes any symbolic contract. (28)

Dickinson and Rich are quite aware that "when evoking the name and destiny of women one thinks more of the *space* generating and forming the human species than of *time,* becoming, or history" (15). "Sigh no more, ladies," we can read in "Snapshots of a Daughter-in-Law," "Time is male / and in his cups drinks to the fair." Likewise, for Dickinson time is a male category. The soul's "favor," she claimed, "is the best Disdain / Toward Artifice of Time—or Men" (J 753).[2] Both poets are also aware that "the patriarchal nature of language and culture," as Janet Todd puts it, "must inform the tellings of history" (95). Due to their distinct historical situatedness, however, this insight leads Dickinson and Rich to rather different consequences.

The fact that Dickinson, in a letter to the Norcross sisters, wonders about "the moon . . . at the end" before she worries about the beginning of the Civil War (L 234) is symptomatic of a worldview that, as I argued in chapter 1, privileges the temporality of writing over linear history. This does not, as has generally been assumed, reflect Dickinson's distance to worldly events and political affairs. Her preference of poetry over the prosy world of her father(s) is in fact triggered by her historical consciousness. "The world is sleeping in ignorance and error," she defends her favor for rhetorical figures, for "what they call a metaphor in our country." Therefore, she insists, "we must be crowing cocks, and singing larks, and a rising sun to awake her; or else we'll pull society up to the roots, and plant it in a different place. We'll build Alms-houses, and transcendental State prisons, and scaffolds—we will blow out the sun and the moon, and encourage invention" (L 34). Overdetermined by irony, this passage still indicates that Dickinson's "escape" from history to poetry is hastened by a critical distance to her own culture's politics, its philosophy ("transcendental") and institutions ("State prisons"), as well as by the awareness that her own concerns were of little avail. Projecting the course of historical time as a "brief masquerade" (J 70), Dickinson anticipates Paul de Man's conception of the textuality of history, his belief "that the basis for historical knowledge are not empirical facts but written texts, even if these texts masquerade in the guise of wars and revolutions" (*Blindness and Insight* 165). Not only did she agree with Emerson's view that history is no more than "a fable agreed upon" (*Collected Works* 2:6)—and a transient fable for that matter. She also realizes that we all take part in that masquerade, performing different dramas for different audiences, on different days, in different poems. As Dickinson's father acts "Chief Marshal of the day" (L 127) and "steps like Cromwell" (L 339), her speakers transform from beggar into queen as we turn a page. This sense of performativity entails an alternative sense of temporality that accommodates what is habitually excluded, including her own unorthodox cultural practice.

Dickinson's sense of female subjectivity in history originated from her early reception of the myth of biblical Eve and Eve's particular position in discourse. As Homans so convincingly argues, Dickinson aligns herself with Eve's disobedience, her doubt toward orthodoxy, and her desire for knowledge and linked the myths of "Original Woman" with her own position within cultural discourse. Such affinity to "the mother of irony" (*Women Writers* 171) is inextricably bound with Dickinson's insight into the fictionality of language (169–71, 173–78) and into what Kristeva calls "the inseparable conjunction between the sexual and the symbolic" ("Women's Time" 21). This conjunction is responsible in part for the lack of evidence on Eve's fate. Not only is Eve a figure of a fairly mysterious, motherless origin; she is also, as Dickinson points out, deprived of death (L 9). Such absences themselves, however, are fundamental to Dickinson's poetic enterprise, since they point toward "something" beyond "literal life":

> Something besides severe colds, and serpents, and we will try to find *that* something. It cant be a garden, can it, or a strawberry bed, which rather belongs to a garden—nor it cant be a school-house, nor an Attorney at Law. O dear I dont know *what* it is! Love for the absent dont *sound* like it, but try it, and see how it goes. (L 31)

This "Love for the absent," postulated against both nature ("garden") and culture ("school-house," "Law"), makes history a minor concern indeed. Recording the evident, traditional history disregards the absent, unknown, and dark, the very phenomena that escaped Emerson's visions but captivated Dickinson's. Though comparable to tragic historical events— "Feet, small as mine—,"

Dickinson wrote, "have marched in Revolution" (J 295)—pain and death are excluded from historical records. Death "Hadn't any playmates," Dickinson wrote, "Or 'Early history'" (J 153). An "unclaimed Hat and Jacket," may "Sum the History" of an anguished drowning (J 923). And

> One Crucifixion is recorded—only—
> How many be
> Is not affirmed of Mathematics—
> Or History—
>
> (J 553)

Women's cultural practice, as conceived by Dickinson, remains similarly absent from history books. Associating women's writing with witchcraft "hung, in History" (J 1593), poems such as "I think I was enchanted" (J 593) relocate female art not within historical temporality but as part of a lineage of conspiratorial cultural practices. Including figures as distinct as Eve, Anne Hutchinson, Barrett Browning, and herself, who decided to "sing . . . because she [could] not pray" (L 278), this lineage frequently involves alternative religious rituals and other challenges to orthodoxy. Browning's writing, so Dickinson's poem suggests, converts the mind to an alternative creed, thus having poetry displace religion. Itself resistant to representation ("I had no power to tell," "I could not have defined the change," "Is witnessed, not explained"), such conversion experience challenges "common sense" and linear thought, transcends time, and brings about a new perception of the world. Unlike Emerson, whose essays evolve a "home-grown" American poetry through acts of forgetting,[3] Dickinson's sense of writing and female subjectivity involves remembering without, however, affecting the (dis)courses of history. After all, "To Tomes of solid Witchcraft - Magicians be asleep." Instead, by transposing witchcraft into poetic present ("History and I / Find all the Witchcraft that we need / Around us, every Day—" [J 1583]) and eternity alike ("Magic—hath an Element / Like Deity—to keep—"), Dickinson's speaker wants both witchcraft and women's poetry out of the spheres of immanence and cyclical rhythms, those "meanest Tunes" of nature. She aligns it with monumental time, with the timeless rhythms of poetic language, instead ("The Days—to Mighty Metres stept—").

This view of the location of women's cultural practices and their impact on dominant culture sides with Cixous rather than with de Beauvoir. According to de Beauvoir, witchcraft is a practice located apart from society, law, and time. It calls upon one of the oldest and widespread myths of femininity as ultimate otherness, as a power that lures men into women's "darkness of immanence" and death (175). Poststructuralist French feminism, by contrast, has celebrated witches as emblems of an uncivilized power, "healers" "in direct contact with nature," specialists of the unconscious, the body, and female desire (Gauthier 201, 200). Cixous and Catherine Clément align the sorceress with the hysteric, thus realigning history and psychoanalysis and rereading history as hysteria; both the sorceress and the hysteric, the authors argue, are part of culture's imaginary zone of exclusions, a zone "we must try to remember *today*."

> It will be a history read differently, at once the same in the Real and an other in the Imaginary. These narratives, these myths, these fantasies, these fragments of evidence, these tail ends of history do not compose a true history. To be that, it would have to pass through all the registers of the social structure, through its economic evolution, through analysis of the contradictions that have made and are making its history. . . . Instead, it is a history, taken from what is lost within us of oral tradition, of legends and myths—a history arranged the way tale-telling women tell it. (6)

Seen from this perspective, Dickinson rewrites conceptions of history themselves. In doing so, however, she was not necessarily beyond her time. Her turn away from history's masquerade is set in a culture that did not yet know a historical female subject. Poststructuralist preferences of female otherness, by contrast, represent a conscious choice directed against the (supposed legal) sameness of all political subjects.

In some sense the conception of femininity and history implicit in Rich's writing can be read as roughly following the development Kristeva delineated in "Women's Time." Eventually, however, it goes beyond these categories. Rich's early poems work according to a "logic of identification" with established powers—if, in fact, the discourse of late modernism can be considered as such—and aspire toward a monumental timelessness. The poetry of the early 1960s transitional phase was followed by collections that repudiate paternal authorities, demand a female power and discourse instead, and first appeal to the cyclical temporality of nature then to a supposedly universal female history. During the late 1960s Rich revalues femininity for its supposed immanence, its very detachment from history and paternal heritage. By the early 1970s, however, she finds the knowledge of women's past fundamental to female subjectivity and begins to practice a rhetoric of revision that is geared toward reconstructing female lineages by remembering women of the past. In this way Rich's texts of the 1970s combine the first two positions Kristeva describes, oscillating between the desire for an "*insertion* into history" and a "radical *refusal* of the subjective limitations imposed by this history's time on an experiment carried out in the name of the irreducible difference" ("Women's Time" 20). Exploring that difference in *Dream of a Common Language,* Rich came to accept the symbolic contract, granted that it be used and appropriated for "feminist measures."[4] Having acknowledged the various differences among women as well as their distinct historical situatedness by the early 1980s, Rich rewrites female subjectivity in history as a process of past memories and present positions. As she drafts that historical female subject, she accepts her as being constructed but also insists on her part as an agency on behalf of that subject.

In this way Rich's feminist poetics surpasses Kristeva's account of the feminine in history, which after all reaffirms the traditional association of women with space and keeps reducing femininity to the maternal. In fact, Rich puts into practice the third generation of feminism envisioned in Kristeva's essay. This third position, which Kristeva "strongly advocate[s]" and "imagine[s]," "implies less a chronology than a *signifying space,* a both corporeal and desiring mental space" in which the "very dichotomy man/woman as an opposition between two rival entities may be understood as belonging to *metaphysics."* It will be accompanied, she claims, by a "demassification of the problematic of *difference . . .* between the sexes," by "a retreat from sexism (male as well as female)" and based upon *"an interiorization of the founding separation of the sociosymbolic contract"* (34). Rich's sense of subjectivity is therefore much closer to poststructuralist positions than feminist criticism has been willing to admit.

Differences, of course, remain. Insisting on agency (as Irigaray does) without developing a concept of history or conceptualizing temporality (as Kristeva does) without allowing for agency, French feminism lacks a sense of the female subject as an agent of her own history. Rich, in contrast, designs a female subject that by continuous displacements of prior, outdated subject positions reconstructs herself as a process of past and present. By following the development of this sense of subjectivity, which is feminist in the sense of its politics and poststructuralist in its notion of discourse as a site of subject constitution, this chapter reassesses Rich's importance as a feminist theorist. For, unlike Dickinson and Moore, she is that. More than that, my argument shows that Rich plays an important and mostly unacknowledged part in the emergence of what came to be known as poststructuralist feminist thought by appropriating its insights for political strategies. More than being a significant mediator between (radical) feminist and poststructuralist positions, Rich's work highlights the fundamental interdependence between these two perspectives. At the same time, Rich's feminist poetics and sense of female subjectivity in history cannot be reduced to a theoretical position or program. Instead, it develops in the interspaces between her poetry and prose, in a "signifying space" that had already served Dickinson well. Unlike Dickinson, Rich makes use of this space for a new conception of "women's time."

Discontent with traditional historiography surfaces in Rich's work long before women's history and female identity became one of her dominant agenda. Rich's earlier texts, though, do not deplore the gaps in history but, rather, its detachment from contemporary consciousness and existence. Incapable of providing the knowledge that the moment demanded, learned books and "memorabilia" had lost their function (*Snapshots* 37). In the early 1960s "to 'know how it was'" seemed to mean "to forget how it is" (39), with history becoming a documentation of useless, distorted facts and "moulding" memories. "Readings of History" (1960), Rich wrote, "show us nothing / but pieces of ourselves, detached, / set to a kind of poetry, / a kind of music" (38). Knowledge no longer needed to derive from the records of past experiences or the timelessness of (modern) literature. It was relocated in subjective experience, in political action, and in the act of writing poetry itself. Poetry, as Altieri pointed out, was preserved "as a unique way of knowing the world and discovering or creating significance within it" ("Symbolism" 606). Accordingly, Rich claimed in 1964, "what I know, I know through making poems" (in Gelpi and Gelpi 89).

In between the timelessness of her early work and the later emphasis on historicity, Rich's poetry features speakers disconnected from time and texts focused on presence and process. The volume *Necessities of Life* (1966), for instance, moves, as Kalstone observed, from presenting an "emerging self" to performing "vanishing acts" (152). *Leaflets* (1969), by comparison, demands to be read as a journal or a series of pamphlets, privileges a Whitmanian "now," and reclaims eternity as a physical experience: "Eternity streams through my body: / touch it with your hand and see" (65). And yet, despite such preference for presence, both *Necessities of Life* and *Leaflets* anticipate future concerns with a female past, in fact are pretexts to her feminist project. In the title poem, "Necessities of Life" (1962), for instance, the subject performs the very transformation hinted at in the final section of "Snapshots"—a move that dismisses the past for a more promising future without, however, pointing the direction.

So much for those days. Soon
practice may make me middling-perfect, I'll

dare inhabit the world
trenchant in motion as an eel, solid

as a cabbage head. I have invitations:
a curl of mist steams upward

from a field, visible as my breath,
houses along a road stand waiting

like old women knitting, breathless
to tell their tales.

(Necessities 10)

This is Rich's version of a subject in in-between position whose options, how-
ever, are quite distinct from Dickinson's subjectivity on edge. Dismissing both
transcendence ("a curl of mist steams upward") and a linear path ("along the
road"), Rich's speaker turns toward a domestic space ("houses"), toward imma-
nence and silence ("breathless")—a silence that longs to release the tales of an
other, an oral history, tales that, like that of witchcraft, are yet to be told.

The poem's process, during which the subject separates from the past to
embrace the future yet pauses in the present to claim another heritage, is a
recurrent pattern in Rich's work. In *Necessities of Life* Dickinson functions as a
representative of such an alternative heritage, as a historical person without his-
tory, as a "breathless" female tale teller well versed in the idiosyncratic art of
silence. Though Rich's poem "I Am in Danger—Sir—" (1964) deplores that
Dickinson is not to be known ("who are you?") and remains "equivocal to the
end," Rich does not attempt to "repossess" Dickinson. Instead, Dickinson's
centrality in *Necessities of Life* is due to parallels of poetics and sense of subjec-
tivity. Imagining speakers whose existence is an "Angled Road" (J 910), Rich's
work of the mid-1960s came closer to Dickinson's than it would ever be again.

Like *Necessities of Life,* Rich's collection *Leaflets* inscribes female figures
into its texts. These inscriptions, however, are not yet geared to reclaim femi-
ninity for history. Quite the opposite: femininity gets privileged in part for its
very absence from history, for its supposed authenticity. The speaker in "Abne-
gation" (1968), for instance, trades her past for the kinship of a wild animal and
an "immaculate present." More than a decade later *Sources* (1982) recalls this
"foxy" figure as "long dead" but once "an omen, surviving" (9).

I go along down the road
to a house nailed together by Scottish
Covenanters, instinct mortified
in a virgin forest,
and she springs toward her den

every hair on her pelt alive
with tidings of the immaculate present.
They left me a westernness,
a birthright, a redstained, ravelled
afghan of sky.
She [the red fox] has no archives,
no heirlooms, no future
except death
and I could be more
her sister than theirs
who chopped their way across these hills
—a chosen people.

*(Leaflets* 38)

This poem seems clearly to juxtapose Western male culture and history, violence against "original existences" (*Sources* 14), and illusions of transcendence with (female) nature, Eastern exoticism, immanence, and death. Accordingly, it contrasts literary connotation ("the apotheosis of Reynard / the literature of fox-hunting") with denotation ("the red fox, the vixen"). Expressing a preference for the secondary and supplementary, the speaker tries to abnegate power and thus declares herself independent. Still, the poem bears two significant ironies. As the speaker repudiates the colonial forebearers for a female "foremother" who is supposedly undetermined by history, she cannot help but reinforce traditional romanticizations of nature, immanence, and the literal. The ambivalence entailed in a such move shows in the condescending attitudes toward women that the poem's "foxy" figure expresses. Moreover, the speaker's desire to renounce her "birthrights," to escape the temporality of history, to dismiss her paternal heritage for the kinship of a figure free from the burdens of time and manifest destiny, and to revert to a *tabula rasa* place, a virginal page upon which to inscribe a new identity—such desire reproduces the very impulse that brought the rejected ancestors to the New World, the supposedly "virginal" promised land. The poem's abjection thus equals the move modernism has always already made: "Modernity," as de Man writes in his essay "Literary History and Literary Modernity," "exists in the form of a desire to wipe out whatever came earlier, in the hope of reaching at last a point that could be called a true present, a point of origin that marks a new departure. This combined interplay of deliberate forgetting with an action that is also a new origin," de Man assumes, creates a "curiously contradictory" relation between modernity and history (*Blindness and Insight* 148, 151). As history depends on modernity for its duration and renewal, he argues, modernity cannot assert itself without being reintegrated into historical processes. Rich's negation is consequently part of an American identity politics and its ongoing modernity. The same holds for Dickinson, yet her claims are different to begin with.

Dickinson's poem "I'm ceded—I've stopped being Their's—" (J 508), for instance, repudiates paternal past, religious background, and inherited birthright yet acknowledges that changes of identity are first of all matters of rhetoric.

I'm ceded—I've stopped being Their's—
The name They dropped upon my face
With water, in the country church
Is finished using, now,
And They can put it with my Dolls,
My childhood, and the string of spools,
I've finished threading—too—

Baptized, before, without the choice,
But this time, consciously, of Grace—
Unto supremest name—
Called to my Full—The Crescent dropped—
Existence's whole Arc, filled up,
With one small Diadem.

My second Rank—too small the first—
Crowned—Crowing—on my Father's breast—
A half unconscious Queen—
But this time—Adequate—Erect,
With Will to choose, or to reject,
And I choose, just a Crown—

Rejecting her given name, the speaker consciously claims her own identity, unapproved by religious rites yet still effecting a fundamental conversion ("the Crescent dropped"). "Called to [her] Full," the speaker cannot, as Rich would have it, "cut . . . away of an old force that held her / rooted to an old ground" (Dream 75). Depicting this ground as her "Father's breast," the speaker insinuates that paternal heritage is taken in with mother's milk.

Accordingly, Dickinson's text may indeed be, as Rich suggests, a poem of self-confirmation yet without, as she claims, "transcending the patriarchal condition of bearing her father's name" (On Lies 172). Instead, Dickinson appropriates the name of the father, establishes speaking positions *on* but not *with* her own terms. In fact, adopting "the accoutrements of royalty," her "second baptism," as Diehl puts it, "is more Catholic than her first" (111). Throughout her work Dickinson exploits religious orthodoxy as well as conventions of womanhood to provide her with "Scaffolds" (J 1142) for her "Columnar" selves (J 789). In this way she shatters the very cultural codes she exploits without, however, dismantling them.

Both Rich's and Dickinson's speakers trade inherited birthrights for kinships of their own choice. Yet the choices they make are ultimately different. Rich dismisses (paternal) culture for (maternal) nature and celebrates the ideal of a "down to earth" sisterhood. In this way she anticipates her later concern with a "common world of women" (*On Lies* 203), with the network of a female counterculture that "abnegat[es] power for love" (*Dream* 11), and is repeatedly figured in terms of natural processes. Dickinson, in contrast, erects authority apart from nature and commonness, common womanhood in particular. Her consciously chosen "Grace" is a wholly different matter than the "grace" that is woman's only possession (J 810), in that it allows access to the heights of a hierarchically structured universe ("supremest name"). Rich admired Dickinson's sense of power, though she developed her own notion of what counts as power and authority. And, while both poets yearn for integrity and wholeness ("Called to my Full—The Crescent dropped— / Existence's whole Arc—filled up"), Dickinson offers only glimpses of identity, scattered throughout the course of her writing—an identity that, as chapter 1 has shown, was not all that desirable after all. Rich, by contrast, transforms such longing into a poetic-political program.

This enterprise entails a reconstruction of Rich's own past that thrives toward comprehensiveness, continuity, and wholeness. Whereas Dickinson transforms Emerson's self-reliant "trust thyself" (*Collected Works* 2:28) into a more tentative "explore thyself," based less on confidence than on negative capability, Rich's imperative became to "find thyself," "to know," as she prophetically formulated in "Double Monologue," "simply as I know my name / at any given moment, where I stand." Born from a modernist sense of impersonality, a "capacity for detachment from the self and its emotions" (Auden, "Foreword" 10), Rich's writing strove "to give birth to" "a recognizable, autonomous, self, a creation in poetry and life" (*Of Woman Born* 28). Whereas Dickinson perceived her speakers as "supposed persons," created anew in the processes of each poem's enunciative situation and "unhinged" from all the contexts that had them emerge (Cameron 24), Rich claimed to collapse biographical and enunciative subject into one speaking position, to make "the woman in the poem and the woman writing the poem become the same person" (*On Lies* 47). Such a project does not necessarily derive from a naive faith in mimesis. It depends upon an awareness of the textuality of subjectivity and history that inspired a desire to inscribe oneself and other female figures into history.

Accordingly, Rich presents her work and life as an ongoing transformation based on a growth of consciousness and knowledge. Such development is not easily discernible in Dickinson, whose poems tend to repeat and reformulate a series of highly complex existential concerns. Dickinson did not record dates of composition nor vary her speakers' gender, and very rarely created nor poems in male and female versions. Revising early texts, Rich, by comparison, displaces male pronouns by female ones and retrospectively interprets her decision to date her poems as "an oblique political statement . . . a declaration that placed poetry in a historical continuity, not above or outside history" (*Blood* 180). For the "lesbian archeologist" the past became a locus of discovery and renewal, for "Sifting her own life out from the shards she's piecing" (*Wild* 53). Dickinson's life, as Cameron observes, is made into a myth, a text that readers turn to whenever her poems resist making sense. Rich's readers, in contrast, turn toward her prose, which interprets Rich's own "revisionary myth-making" (Ostriker) and functions as a kind of "Reader's Guide to Adrienne Rich's Poetry," a manual to her poems' meanings. The relation between prose and poetry, however, is not one of correspondence but, rather, of dialogue and conflict.

While Dickinson displaced history by an unorthodox temporality of poetic presence, Rich has promoted revisionism, "the act of looking back, of seeing with fresh eyes, of entering an old text from a new critical direction" (*On Lies* 35). Significantly enough, her essay "When We Dead Awaken: Writing as Re-Vision" (1971) uses her own biography to illustrate this strategy, thus resonating with Emerson's claim that "civil and natural history, the history of art and literature must be explained from individual history" (*Collected Works* 2:10). Rich thus shares Emerson's view that "all history becomes subjective"—that, "in other words, there is properly no History; only Biography" (*Collected Works* 2:6). Dickinson, by comparison, severely doubted the historicity of biographical writing. "Biography," she claimed, "first convinces us of the fleeing of the Biographied—" (L 972). For her the fictionality of language was the bottom line. If, as a consequence, history equals fiction, a fiction moreover that excludes her own sense of subjectivity, why not project one's own fictions? Write what cannot be lived but make it larger than life! This Dickinson may have had in mind. Rich, in contrast, has put her insights into the limits and potential of language to a different use. Reconsidering "what a poem used to be for me, what it is now" (qtd. in Gelpi and Gelpi 89), selecting only particular early poems for republication, or writing a "last address" to Dickinson (*Wild* 43), she made her personal history a continuous process of self-(re)construction.

Likewise, her poems have employed revision to recreate female subjectivity as an ongoing dynamic. Like Dickinson, Rich thus creates "subjects-in-process." Unlike her, she desires to write these subjects into a "real" of history, which gets inextricably entangled with the history of her own writing.

As Dickinson believes history to be a fiction and Rich insists on poetry's potential to reinvent history, their writings imply distinct theoretical leanings. Dickinson's sense of subjectivity as fictional and ever changing sympathizes with Butler's sense of performativity (which itself relates to an Irigarayan sense of mimicry). In contrast, Rich's sense of subjectivity as continuous revision of preceding subject positions is an identity practice that projects a sense of identity "made up of heterogeneous and heteronomous representations . . . an identity that one decides to reclaim from a history of multiple assimilations, and that one insists upon as a strategy" (de Lauretis's "Feminist Studies" 9). The main difference between Dickinson's and Rich's sense of a subject-in-process is that Rich's notion of process incorporates the subject into a continuous narrative, a history. In this way Rich rewrites history as well. Claiming the female subject from a history that is being invented and written by her very practice of "writing as re-vision," identity practice turns history, and history becomes identity practice. Rich's poetics thus throws light upon and bridges, at least in part, the gap in French feminist theory.

This chapter first explores Rich's construction of female subjectivity as process between past and present by exploring her ongoing dialogue with Dickinson. The "dialogue with brave and imaginative women who came before us" (*On Lies* 205)—first with exceptional women or "heroines" then with women who were heroic in their very ordinariness—has been one of her central strategies in repossessing the past. From the late 1950s to the early 1990s, a period marked by "Snapshots of a Daughter-in-Law," "The Spirit of Place" (1981), and her recent prose piece "Beginners" (1993), Dickinson has been a significant addressee in this dialogue. My reading focuses both on Dickinson's resistances against being "repossessed" and on the workings of Rich's identity practice—that is, on the ways in which, by rereading Dickinson, Rich engages with the history of her own poetics and politics. Taking the reader back to *Diving into the Wreck* (1973) and *Leaflets* (1969), Rich's revision of Dickinson proves that, as Moore once put it, "in connection with personality, it is a curiosity of literature how often what one says of another seems descriptive of one's self" (*Prose* 514).

The analysis of Rich's essay "Vesuvius at Home: The Power of Emily Dickinson" (1976) and of poems that relate to Dickinson allows us to register the changes within Rich's identity practice and her continuous processes of subjectivity. In this way Rich's essay exemplifies how revision works as identity practice, how biography and history correlate, how the attempts "to achieve access to a female past" dialogue past and present. Put in psychoanalytical terms, Rich's perspectives on Dickinson develop from an identification to an ambivalent acknowledgment of difference and a final separation. One can also, however, depict her reading of Dickinson as a movement from a "literalization" of Dickinson's metaphors toward a distrust of such literal readings: while her essay "Vesuvius at Home" re-presents Rich's visit to Dickinson's Amherst room as an entrance into the poet's mind, her volume *A Wild Patience Has Taken Me This Far* (1981) acknowledges that Dickinson is nowhere to be found but in her words and that, after all, the mind is not a room. The development of Rich's dialogue with Dickinson thus follows both the paradigm of mother-daughter relations and the transformations of her own feminist poetics and politics, her changing views of history and subjectivity.

Rich's reading of Dickinson has been part of her efforts to undo "the erasure of women's political and historic past" (*On Lies* 9), "to define a female consciousness" (18), and "to found a culture of our own" by breaking the silence passed over "the entire history of women's struggle for self-determination" (11). These efforts themselves make Rich an agency, a figure of integration, "destined to piece together . . . the history of the dispossessed" (*Blood* 176). The second part of this chapter will therefore show how in the 1980s both her criticism and poetry took new directions, how her interest in women's history as a source of power and identity shifted toward an understanding of the female subject as a process of present and past—both her own and that of others. As my analysis of Rich's poem "The Spirit of Place" (1980) shows, this change of perspective acknowledges the subject's fragmentation in history yet never abandons the desire for wholeness and identity.

"Thank you for remembering me. Remembrance—mighty word."

—Emily Dickinson, L 785

## Reading an Other: Female Subjectivity as Dialogue and Identity Practice

Rich's essay "Vesuvius at Home: The Power of Emily Dickinson" (1976) is a milestone in the reception of Dickinson's work and a paradigmatic example of early feminist literary criticism, geared to empower what had been neglected, belittled, and underestimated for a long time: Dickinson's life and work as well as the weight of the female critic's own voice. Approaching Dickinson in terms of her greatness, Rich presents her in a new attire—in a dress stripped of its laces—yet discloses as much about her own identity practice as about Dickinson's poetics. "As a women poet," Rich writes, "finding my own methods, I have come to understand her necessities, could have been witness in her defense" (*On Lies* 158). Throughout her essay she affirms this claim by aligning Dickinson's poetry with different stages of her own work. The introductory part recalls a visit to the Dickinson Homestead, where, analogous to her poem "Diving into the Wreck" (1972), Rich attempts to find "the [poet] herself and not the myth" (*Diving* 23). The main part presents Dickinson by a selection from her work that takes the reader back to Rich's own collection *Leaflets*. The historical frame of Rich's reading of Dickinson is thus her own writing.

"The Thing Itself and Not the Myth": Repossessing Dickinson

One of Rich's intentions has been to take Dickinson "seriously," which meant literally at times. Dickinson's claim "Home is not where the heart is, but the adjacent buildings," for instance, is translated into "New England realism, a directive to be followed" (*On Lies* 158). Relating her visit to the Dickinson Homestead, Rich literally returns to the poet's scene of writing, joining those who, in the words of Wolff, "regard this House almost as a holy place, making the trek to Western Massachusetts as if to a saint's shrine, seeking some ineffable truth" (3). At the same time, Rich's trip, or better the tale thereof, reconstructs her own past. Remembering her undergraduate weekends in Amherst and the publication of the different Dickinson editions as a subtext to her literary apprenticeship, "Vesuvius at Home" also rewrites her essay "When We Dead Awaken." While the latter identifies the male modernists as *the* crucial impact on her work, its reprinted version is supplemented by the following footnote:

> A. R., 1978: Yet I spent months, at sixteen, memorizing and writing imitations of Millay's sonnets; and in notebooks of that period I find what are obviously attempts to imitate Dickinson's metrics and verbal compression. I knew H.D. only through anthologized lyrics; her epic poetry was not then available to me.

Remembering Dickinson, Rich rescues a female origin from "beneath the conscious craft" of her work (*On Lies* 40).

By presenting her revision of Dickinson as a pilgrimage and expedition, Rich moreover recontextualizes her feminist enterprise and recalls the allegorical movement of her poem "Diving into the Wreck" (1972). The simile Rich employs to describe her previous approach to Dickinson—"for months, for years, for most of my life, I have been hovering like an insect against the screens of her existence" (*On Lies* 158)—aligns her with the masked diver who "crawl[s] like an insect down the ladder" and into the wreck of submerged mysteries. Accordingly, Rich's trip to Amherst and the diver's expedition share common goals:

> I came to explore the wreck.
> The words are purposes.
> The words are maps.
> I came to see the damage that was done
> and the treasures that prevail.
>
> . . . . . . . . . . . . . . . . . . . .
>
> the thing I came for:
> the wreck and not the story of the wreck
> the thing itself and not the myth
>
> (*Diving* 23)

Like the diver who takes words for maps, Rich reads Dickinson's words as "a directive to be followed." The "thing" she meant to recover was not the famous "myth" of Amherst but Dickinson herself, the woman behind the "mask . . . of innocuousness and of containment" (*On Lies* 169).

Like the diver, Rich seeks to lift the veil of legend that "has gotten in the way of her being repossessed" (167), aims to retrieve Dickinson "at her true worth" (164), "in her fullest range" (167), to grasp the poet's "essential," "creative and powerful self" (175), and her work's "complex sense of Truth" (183). Like Karl Keller, who was to take her as a teaser indulging in "show biz" in order to make sure that "no one takes over or dares by presumptuousness [to] lay claim or even enter in" (*Feminist Critics* 75, 72), Rich grants Dickinson a "deliberate strangeness" (*On Lies* 166). Yet, after years of "trying to visit, to enter her mind, through her poems and letters," she attempts to enter Dickinson's mind by penetrating the privacy of her bedroom (159), thus literalizing Dickinson's metaphors of rooms and houses.

Entering the wreck excavated from the subject's prehistory and unconsciousness, Rich's diver discovers the silent origin, the polar yet complementary androgynous nature of the self, and returns to a seemingly secure, circular primal scene of simultaneous division and wholeness apart from history.

> This is the place.
> And I am here, the mermaid whose dark hair
> streams black, the merman in his armored body
> We circle silently
> about the wreck
> we dive into the hold.
> I am she: I am he
>
> . . . . . . . . . . . . . .
> We are, I am, you are
> by cowardice or courage
> the one who find our way
> back to this scene
> carrying a knife, a camera
> a book of myths
> in which
> our names do not appear.

At a comparatively climactic moment in her essay Rich relates how she stepped into Dickinson's room/mind.[5]

> Upstairs at last: I stand in the room which for Emily Dickinson was "freedom." The best bedroom in the house, a corner room, sunny, overlooking the main street of Amherst in front, the way to her brother Austin's house on the side. Here, at a small table with one drawer, she wrote most of her poems. Here she read Elizabeth Barrett's *Aurora Leigh*. . . . Here I become, again, an insect, vibrating at the frames of windows, clinging to panes of glass, trying to connect. The scent here is very powerful. Here in this white-curtained, high-ceilinged room, a red-haired woman with hazel eyes and a contralto voice wrote poems about volcanoes, deserts, eternity, suicide, physical passion, wild beasts, rape, power, madness, separation, the daemon, the grave. Here, with a darning needle, she bound these poems. . . . Here she knew "freedom," listening from above-stairs to a visitor's piano-playing, escaping from the pantry where she was mistress of the household bread and puddings. . . . From this room she glided downstairs.
> (*On Lies* 161)

With its recurrent deictic marker ("here") and its awkward account of sensual impression ("The scent here is powerful"), this passage aims at authenticity and close contact. Like the diver who arrives carrying the same old "book of myths / in which / our names do not appear," however, Rich's essay tends to reproduce the infamous myths. The desired connection does not happen: "Here I become, again, an insect, vibrating at the frames of windows," Rich admits, echoing Dickinson, who found "Hunger"—or desire—"a way / Of Persons outside Windows— / The Entering—takes away—" (J 579). Entering Dickinson's bedroom, this emblem of her exclusion from history, yet remaining locked out of the vastness of her consciousness, Rich insinuates that Dickinson is not to be repossessed by a literal reading.

Remembering Dickinson while driving back to Boston, as "that genius" "in the trail [of which] my mind has been moving," Rich acknowledges that the poet was a "foremother," not in the sense of providing maternal origins but as a muse called upon to displace prior male muses and the many projections of paternal power that predominated Rich's own poetry. Rich's insistence, in both her essay on Dickinson and her poem "Diving into the Wreck," on the primacy of the thing marks both her debt to a Puritan heritage, which survived in Emerson as well as in Imagist poetry, and a fundamental difference from Dickinson, who herself asserted the primacy of the word.[6] This difference is the subtext of Rich's essay on Dickinson, which surfaces in the text's main part.

## "An Ambivalence toward Power, Which Is Extreme"

The main part of Rich's essay presents Dickinson through an unusual selection from her work, concentrating on her "poetry of extreme states" (182) and on poetological poems that reflect gender-related ambivalences by featuring powerful male figures. This focus on the masculine—for Dickinson a figure of multiple indeterminate meanings, for Rich a figure of patriarchy and "the naked and unabashed failure of patriarchal politics and patriarchal civilization" (*Poems* xv)—marks a point of crossover in the poets' work. For a discussion of this matter Rich singles out "My Life had stood—a Loaded Gun—" (J 754), a text that readers have counted among Dickinson's best as well as her most baffling texts.

My Life had stood—a Loaded Gun—
In Corners—till a Day
The Owner passed—identified—
And carried Me away—

And now We roam in Sovreign Woods—
And now We hunt the Doe—
And every time I speak for Him—
The Mountains straight reply—

And do I smile, such cordial light
Upon the Valley glow—
It is as a Vesuvian face
Had let it's pleasure through—

And when at Night—Our good Day done—
I guard My Master's Head—
'Tis better than the Eider-Duck's
Deep Pillow—to have shared—

To foe of His—I'm deadly foe—
None stir the second time—
On whom I lay a Yellow Eye—
Or an emphatic Thumb—

Though I than He—may longer live
He longer must—than I—
For I have but the power to kill,
Without—the power to die—

Rich considers this poem "the real 'onlie begetter' of [her] thoughts here about Dickinson" and "for us, at this time, . . . a central poem in understanding Emily Dickinson, and ourselves" (*On Lies*, 172, 174). In this way she appropriates the text as a missing link between nineteenth- and twentieth-century women, as an expression of collective female awareness. Yet, "if there is a female consciousness in this poem," she qualifies, "it is buried deeper than the images: it exists in the ambivalence toward power, which is extreme" (174). More than anything else, this interpretation acknowledges Rich's own ambivalences toward Dickinson. Since at the time Rich found the "idea of power inextricably linked with maleness, or the use of force" (*Of Woman Born* 70), her emphasis on the "power of Emily Dickinson" both reconceptualizes power and marks a clear distance from the nineteenth-century poet as well as, through the subtle parallels her essay creates, from her own earlier work. Rich had not only "mused over, repeated to myself, taken into myself over many years" the poem "My Life had stood—a Loaded Gun—" (*On Lies* 172). She had also rephrased it into her own text "Orion" (1965). By rereading Dickinson's poem, Rich therefore reassesses the protofeminist poetics and politics that informs her own work of the mid-1960s.

Tending toward narrative, Dickinson's poem "My Life had stood—a Loaded Gun—" seems to present a chronological series of "events," the story of a life, structured by seemingly clear-cut binary oppositions such as Owner/Gun, self/other, night/day, life/death, etc. Due to its multiple resonances (of the myth of the American frontier, e.g.) and its intertextual references (to Dickinson's "Master letters," e.g.), the poem has been read in various ways, all of which revolve around matters of subject-object relations.[7] Yet, though "sense is to be found," as Cameron puts it, "it is not in the telling of the story" (65). The text tempts the reader into reading referentially while ultimately resisting such reading. Paraphrases of the poem, Cameron rightfully observes, face their own inadequacy once they confront the last stanza. Depriving its speaker of "The privilege to die" (J 536), the text is deprived of an ending and makes us realize all the more that what we deal with is not a story but an allegory. As such, it tends "toward narrative, the spreading out along the axis of an imaginary time in order to give duration to what is, in fact, simultaneous within the subject" (de Man, *Blindness and Insight* 225). Nor is it an allegory of someone's life. Speaker and "Owner" are, as Robert Weisbuch perceptively argues, configurations of someone's life, not identifiable persons but, rather, personifications of a life's conditions or, as I want to suggest, of subject formation itself.

Turning metaphor into allegory, the poem in fact delineates two distinct moments in subject constitution. Its comparison of life and a loaded gun substitutes an abstract entity referring to the speaking subject ("My Life") by an object ("Gun") that is passive, immobile, cornered, and closeted ("had stood") yet potentially powerful and, when triggered, destructive, dangerously explosive, and even murderous ("Loaded"). Displacing subject by object, the poem foregrounds the very operation underlying all signification: a "Life," an animate subject, can only be represented in language by turning into an object (language). The "gun" stands for "life," which itself stands for the absent subject, and only through this chain of displacements the speaker ("I") comes into being. "To take the name of Gold— / And Gold to own—in solid Bars," Dickinson wrote in one of her poems, "The Difference—made me bold—" (J 454). The difference between taking the name of gun and owning a gun makes for the semantic loadedness of "My Life had stood—a Loaded Gun—."

After having turned *life* into *gun,* the poem's speaker dismisses her fiction of initiation, takes the metaphor of the "Loaded Gun" literally and, "carried away" by the verbatim meaning, spins out her hunting narrative in the course of which the initial relation between "Owner" and "gun" transforms. The very moment the "We" dissociates into "I" and "He," the original power structure ("The Owner passed—identified—") is reversed ("I speak for Him"). In this way the speaker is empowered to name, thus to structure, her relation to the objective world. As a consequence, the poem shifts its focus to the level of subject-object relations represented as the difference between the Me (or "We") and the Not-Me ("Woods," "Doe," "Mountains").

By use of parataxis, parallelism, and anaphor, the second and third stanza associate roaming, hunting, and smiling with speaking and speaking with killing. Outward bound—in fact, aggressively other directed—these activities are aimed at taking possession of otherness. And yet the figure of the echo ("The mountains straight reply") indicates that the gap between subjectivity and language, on the one hand, and the silence of nature, on the other, is not to be bridged. Instead, looking at the world meant "looking . . . / In an abyss's face" (J 1400) to Dickinson. More than that: figuring speech—the smile that "enlightens" the "Valley glow"—as a volcano's eruption ("as a Vesuvian face / Had let its pleasure through"), she insists on language's destructive powers. In this way, as has been argued most convincingly by Diehl, Hagenbüchle, and Homans, Dickinson recognizes nature as antagonist to the speaking subject. For Dickinson creativity and subjectivity "begin with an acknowledgment that the rest of the world is not to be possessed" (Homans 17). In the few instances in which her speakers take an Adamic position, authority remains a fleeting empowerment, a brief entry into foreign territory, the taste of a forbidden fruit (J 430). Dickinson's "ambivalence toward power" is thus due to more than the sense that "active willing and creation in women are forms of aggression" (Rich, *On Lies* 174). For Dickinson acts of naming and identification are themselves acts of aggression. In this way she calls into question the very functions of language on which Emerson and Whitman as well as Rich rely: its power to confer identity and to refer directly to a "reality" beyond itself.

Rich's reading of "My Life had stood" shows little concern with matters of representation and focuses, instead, on its male figure, for Rich an antecedent to what Keats called the "Genius of Poetry" (174) and a "daemon," an animus figure Dickinson was "possessed" by. Both "genius" and "daemon" express a Romantic sense of creativity and subjectivity and relate to Rich's own projections of the "Genius of Poetry" featured in *Leaflets,* particularly in poems such as "Orion" and "The Demon Lover." Rich's reference to Keats subtly acknowledges that, as Diehl argues, Dickinson's preoccupations with "the self's relation to nature, the power of the imagination as it confronts death, a heroic questing that leads to a trial of the limits of poetic power—are the primary concerns of Romanticism as well" (7). It tends to pass over, however, Dickinson's "distinct version of an American Romanticism" (Diehl 8), which diverged from the Romantic tradition in the very ways that Rich's own poetry related to it. According to Emerson, nature gains significance through the perceiving consciousness, and words are directly fastened to visible things. Language thus becomes "the marriage of thought with nature" (2:335), and the business of the poet or philosopher is "to leap over the chasm of the unknown." In this way the dialectic processes of the imagination "repeat[ ] the traditional paradigm of male mind subduing female matter" (W. Martin 122), exemplifying what de Beauvoir considered man's dream of the penetration of all things by his will. Dickinson, by contrast, recognizes nature's defiance of human understanding, be it scientific or philosophical, and revalues perception itself (J 1071). She grants natural phenomena an independent existence resistant to appropriation and representation. "Nature and God," she claimed, "I neither knew"; both remain strangers (J 835), different worlds whose secrets are not to be revealed. No matter how close the human mind deems itself to nature,

> "nature is a stranger yet;
> The ones that cite her most
> Have never passed her haunted house,
> Nor simplified her ghost"

> (J 1400)

By using the word *cite* here, Dickinson opposes science, philosophy, and Emersonian poetics alike. As a picture language, a heavily symbolic and "sacred text, ready to reveal all if we read it right," for Emerson (Diehl 162), nature for Dickinson remains an alien and unreadable script, "written in a foreign tongue" (Hagenbüchle, "Emerson and Dickinson" 145).

While Emerson proclaims perfect wholes, Dickinson "cut herself off from the comforts of compensatory philosophy" (Diehl 165). Rejecting Emerson's idealism and teleology, she insisted on the separation between self and other as a fundamental condition for subject formation. Though she belongs with the "outcasts and isolates, prophets crying in the wilderness" (Bercovitch, *Jeremiad* 180), Dickinson's wilderness is a particular space. Rereading Emerson's "trust thyself" as "Explore thyself" (J 832), she reverses the direction of the errand and transfigures the struggle between subject and material world into the self's struggle with the other within—at the risk of referentiality. Knowing that nature would not answer the questions that preoccupy her, she turns toward the landscape of her own psyche, where she finds another version of the division between subject and object (see Diehl 183–86). If at all, healing was to be achieved in writing itself.

The distance between Emerson's and Dickinson's sense of subjectivity also determines the authors' conflicting views of history. According to Emerson, "history is to be read and written" in the light of "two facts, namely that the mind is One, and that nature is its correlative" (*Collected Works* 2:21). He assumed that

> along with the civil and metaphysical history of man, another history goes daily forward—that of the external world,—in which he is not less strictly implicated. He is the compend of time: he is also the correlative of nature. His power consists in the multitude of his affinities, in the fact that his life is intertwined with the whole chain of organic and inorganic being. (2:20)

This sense of subjectivity in history is as far from Dickinson as it is close to Rich's occasional utopian views. Amid confusion, destruction, and rage her speakers salvage the vision of "a world / of women and men gaily / in collusion with green leaves" (*Diving* 30) or return to the place where the rift between self and other, male and female, first showed.

> this is the saying of a dream
> on waking
> I wish there were somewhere
> actual we could stand
> handing the power-glasses back and forth
> looking at the earth, the wildwood
> where the split began
>
> > (*Diving* 10)

Whereas Dickinson presented naming as an inadequate means for (female) self-empowerment, Rich's revisionary practice builds upon acts of "renaming." Well aware that one "would simplify / / by naming the complexity" (*Poems* 240), she kept her faith that words may "break through this film of the abstract" (*Dream* 17), that truth may evolve from discourse like a sprout pushes from the earth's darkness into the light of day.

> If from time to time I envy
> the pure annunciation to the eye
>
> the *visio beatifica*
> if from time to time I long to turn

like the Eleusinian hierophant
holding up a simple ear of grain

for return to the concrete and everlasting world
what in fact I keep choosing

are these words, these whispers, conversations
from which time after time the truth breaks moist and green.

(*Dream* 20)

Like Dickinson, Rich knows that language marks our *"separation* from a presumed state of nature, of pleasure fused with nature so that the introduction of an articulated network of differences, which refers to objects henceforth and only in this way separated from a subject, may constitute meaning" (Kristeva, "Women's Time" 23). Where Dickinson pushes the limits of language into a beyond, Rich, not unlike Whitman, tends to deny the distinctions between words and things and appropriates images of nature for her identity politics. This also leads her to misread Dickinson. Granted there was more space, Rich concludes in "Vesuvius at Home," she would have liked to "simply to examine the poems in which [Dickinson] is directly apprehending the natural world" (*On Lies* 183). Undoubtedly, Dickinson's texts would have resisted such a reading—a reading that corresponds to her own integrated, and not Dickinson's "edgy," sense of subjectivity. It is this desire for integrity that gets negotiated in Rich's second interpretation of Dickinson's masculine pronoun, an interpretation that also serves Rich to reassess and distance herself from her own earlier writing.

## "Possession by the Daemon"; or, Historicizing Projections of Patriarchy

According to Rich, Dickinson is possessed by a "daemon—her own active, creative power" (*On Lies* 170), and "My Life had stood—a Loaded Gun—" reads as a poem about such

possession by the daemon, about the dangers and risks of such possession if you are a woman, about the knowledge that power in a woman can seem destructive, and that you cannot live without the daemon once it has possessed you. The archetype of the daemon as masculine is beginning to change, but it has been real for women up until now. (173)

Unlike Rich's alliance of Dickinson's male pronouns and Keats's "Genius of Poetry," which positions Dickinson in literary history, this reading approaches Dickinson through Greek mythology and Jungian psychology, sets her apart from historical contexts, and appeals to fantasies of wholeness, instead.

For the Greeks the *daimon,* or genius, was a guardian spirit, a higher self with positive or negative power over the individual. In the analytical psychology of C. G. Jung it became a primordial image of the collective unconscious, of an "unconscious mythology" that is the "common heritage of mankind" and whose archetypes "constantly recur . . . in the course of history and appears wherever creative fantasy is freely expressed" ("Relation" 817). According to Jung, anima and animus are two major archetypal images, which personify, respectively, the female elements of man's and the male elements of woman's unconscious. Characterized by eros' connecting powers but short on intellect, woman's conscious being has to recover logos' powers of discrimination and knowledge from the archetypal image of her animus (9:2:23). Retrieved into conceptional language, such images, Jung claimed, keep structuring human consciousness, psyche, and self across cultures.

Jungian thought has appealed to feminism because it seemed to reconceptualize and solve central questions of feminist debate. Jung's theory of individuation proposes, for instance, to integrate conscious and unconscious, male and female, elements into a wholeness of being and, by granting woman access to the universal, to transcend the supposed "destiny" of anatomy. This belief finds various repercussions in Rich's work. Her poem "Diving into the Wreck" allegorizes Jung's notion of the psyche's sexual polarity and his belief that the "Urmensch" was androgynous (9:2:218). Her claims that "feminism—woman's consciousness" needs "to break down that fragmentation of inner and outer in every possible realm" (qtd. in Gelpi and Gelpi 114), that a "nonpatriarchal society" would have all binarisms discarded (Gelpi and Gelpi 119), echo his postulate of wholeness.

At the same time, Rich's belief that "the archetype of the daemon as masculine is beginning to change," curiously contradicts Jungian thought. Feminist critics realized that not only was Jung's theory blatantly misogynist; it also rests soundly on a belief that "all that exists is based on opposition" (9:1:41),[8] on a set of binary terms that reinforces what Cixous calls the "universal battlefield" of man's dualistic symbolic systems (*Newly Born Woman* 64). Like Cixous, who discredited androgyny as "merger-type bisexuality" ("Medusa" 288), Rich thus came to reject her "bisexual vision" for its masculine bias (see *Of Woman Born* 76–77). The fact that Rich's Jungian reading of Dickinson coincides with her critique of androgyny suggests that one of its functions is to revise and distance herself from the poetic designs inspired by Jung's psychology. While the first part of Rich's essay reproduces the allegorical movement of "Diving into the Wreck," and in this way foregrounds the limited value of allegory as a method of historical analysis, Rich's reading of Dickinson's poems reaches back to the central theme of her earlier collection *Leaflets:* her own "ambivalence toward power," or what Craig Werner describes as Rich's "tension between her desire to repudiate patriarchy and her desire to assume 'masculine' powers" (171).

The poem "Orion" stages this tension as the conflict between a female speaker and a male animus figure that personifies genial creativity, traditional poetic modes, and patriarchal powers alike. All of these have for too long "possessed" female subjectivity and therefore need to be "exorcised."

> Far back when I went zig-zagging
> through tamarack pastures
> you were my genius, . . .
> . . . . . . . . . . . . . . . . .
> . . . . . . . . . . . . . . . . .
> Years later now you're young
>
> my fierce half-brother, staring
> down from that simplified west
> your breast open, your belt dragged down
> by an oldfashioned thing, a sword
> the last bravado you won't give over
> though it weighs you down as you stride
>
> and the stars in it are dim
> and maybe have stopped burning.
> But you burn, and I know it;
> as I throw back my head to take you in
> an old transfusion happens again:
> divine astronomy is nothing to it.
>
> . . . . . . . . . . . . . . . . . . . . . . . .
> You take it all for granted
> and when I look you back
>
> it's with a starlike eye
> shooting its cold and egotistical spear
> where it can do least damage.
> Breathe deep! No hurt, no pardon

out here in the cold with you
you with your back to the wall.

(*Leaflets* 11–12)

Like Dickinson's "My Life had stood—a Loaded Gun—," this is a poem about power, though itself much less powerful than Dickinson's poem. Like its precursor, it figures creativity as a masterful mythical male hunter, though reference is not to American myths but to Greek mythology, thought to be unconfined by history (cf. Levertov, *The Poet* 68). Like Dickinson, Rich allegorizes the relation between subject and other, whose development, however, runs from a time of vitality, identity, and unbroken faith in poetic conventions ("zig-zagging through tamarack pastures") to moments of confrontation and conflict. Clear-cut stanza breaks divide the poem into frame and center, reflecting its themes: the speaker's internal rift, represented by conflicting loyalties; her division between creativity and kinship, between the roles of poet, lover, mother, and wife, between hunter and husband; between separate lives and mixed emotions. In Dickinson's poem a sense of empowerment prevails; here the ambivalence toward power has taken over.

"Orion" gains its particular significance in Rich's oeuvre through her own retrospective interpretation. According to Rich, the text is "a poem of reconnection with a part of myself I had felt I was losing—the active principle, the energetic imagination, the 'half-brother' whom I projected, as I had for many years, into the constellation Orion" (*On Lies* 45). The poem projects this other by means of apostrophe ("you my cast-iron Viking, my helmed lion-heart king in prison"), which constitutes subjectivity in "a temporality of writing" (Culler, *Pursuit* 149). At the same time, unlike Dickinson's poem, Rich's visualizes creativity and female subjectivity in terms of a heterosexual encounter. As Orion holds onto his phallic power, his "last bravado," the "old story" (*Leaflets* 20) remains a current text. In this way the poem literalizes the erotic trope for creation and the notion of male influence. (To "inflow" means, as Shoshana Felman points out, "to have power over another" [122]). This analogy between creativity, subjectivity, and heterosexuality implies that a displacement of the male other would necessarily transform both woman's imagination and art as well as her sense of self and sexuality.

While the irony entailed in Rich's use of apostrophe and obsolete poetic diction ("pastures," "helmed") challenges generic conventions, the poem's subtle literary allusion specifies such discontent. Indicating in the notes that "one or two" of the poem's phrases were suggested by Gottfried Benn's essay "Artists and Old Age,"[9] Rich hints that what is being resisted here is an ahistoric formalism: the "artistry" of the modern, the word's primacy, the meta-physics of forms, the transcendent autonomy of art, and poetry's monologic character delineated in Benn's essay "Probleme der Lyrik" (1951). "Occidental man," Benn wrote in 1934, "conquers the demonic by form, his own demonic power is form, his magic is that which is technical and constructive" (*Sämtliche Werke* 4:108).[10] By including Benn in its subtext, "Orion" subtly interrogates the grounds against which Rich's early poetry projected its figures. And, as she displaces father figures such as Auden, Frost, and Eliot by the "foremother" Dickinson (who is modernism's foremother as well), Rich was forced to confront this heritage once again. That such interrogation of matters of form only disguises a more fundamental gender conflict is made evident in Rich's poem "The Demon Lover." There the primacy of the word—to Benn the "phallus of the mind" (*Gesammelte Werke* 4:1074)[11]—is reenacted as a scene of rape.

A voice presses at me.
If I give in it won't
be like the girl the bull rode,
all Rubens flesh and happy moans.
But to be wrestled like a boy
with tongue. hips, knees, nerves, brain . . .
with language?
He doesn't know. He's watching
breasts under a striped blouse,
his bull's head down. The old
wine pours again through my veins.

(*Leaflets* 20)

Here Rich's animus figure is finally unmasked as a composite personification of patriarchal power and modern poetics, as male "oppressor" (*Will* 18) and "maniac" rapist alike (*Diving* 44).

Throughout Rich's work Orion returns in various disguises. Yet, unlike Dickinson's masculine pronoun, he has ceased to generate multiple meanings. Instead, he gets stripped of his metaphorical layers and is transformed into historical figures, including Rich's "father's personality [that] haunted [her] life" (*Blood* 116), figures that get displaced by female counterparts eventually. In Rich's "Ghazals: Homage to Ghalib," for instance, "Orion" has turned into an outgrown and obsolete superego.

At the drive-in movie, above the PanaVision
beyond the projector beams, you project yourself, great Star.

The eye that used to watch us is dead, but open.
Sometimes I still have a sense of being followed.

(*Leaflets* 70)

In Rich's poems of the 1970s "Orion" is not the rival of lover or husband but, rather, his accomplice or the husband and lover himself.

Your body is as vivid to me
as it ever was: even more

since my feeling for it is clearer:
I know what it could do and could not do

it is no longer
the body of a god
or anything with power over my life

(*Diving* 50)

This male addressee no longer triggers the woman writer's creativity and voice. Instead, he turns out to be the other that women have, for most of their lives, been trying to communicate with. "Trying to Talk with a Man" (1971), for instance, relocates such vain attempts in a politicized combat zone, reminiscent of the "out here in the cold" we encountered in "Orion":

Out here I feel more helpless
with you than without you
You mention the danger
and list the equipment
we talk of people caring for each other
in emergencies—laceration, thirst—
but you look at me like an emergency

Your dry heat feels like power
your eyes are stars of a different magnitude
they reflect lights that spell out: EXIT
when you get up and pace the floor

talking of the danger

as if it were not ourselves
as if we were testing anything else.

(3–4)

By 1974 the "half-brother" Orion is replaced by a "sister," a figure fore-shadowed for years, even in poems such as "The Demon Lover," and finally reaching center stage in Rich's "White Night."

Dawn after dawn, this neighbor
burns like a candle

. . . . . . . . . . . . .

Somebody tried to put her
to rest under an afghan
knitted with wools the color of grass and blood

but she has risen.

. . . . . . . . . . . .

One crystal second, I flash

an eye across the cold
unwrapping of light between us
into her darkness-lancing eye
—that's all. Dawn is the test, the agony
but we were meant to see it:
After this, we may sleep, my sister,
while the flames rise higher and higher, we can sleep.

(*Poems* 228–29)

Echoing other women's writing from Dickinson to St. Vincent Millay, Plath, and Sexton as well as her own work—including the poems "Living in Sin" (1956), "Snapshots of a Daughter-in-Law," "The Roofwalker" (1961), "Moth Hour" (1965), "Orion," "Abnegation," "Women" (1968), "Trying to Talk with a Man" (1971)—this poem crystalizes (literary) history into one "snail-still hour." The women described write in spite of their particular "birthright," that "redstained, ravelled / afghan of sky" ("Abnegation"), yet still carry its burden. Having turned away from both their own mirror reflection and the "starlike eyes" of paternal powers, they recognize one another in one another's eyes / I's, relate neighborly, nonhierarchically. They "burn," but lance dark-ness instead of light and, like the female figure in "Living in Sin," fear the cold "daylight coming / Like a relentless milkman up the stairs" (*Diamond Cutters* 60). They assert their presence against history ("the sleep of the past") but still lack a history of their own.

Dickinson, by comparison, detected both a beautiful dark and a "Lunacy of Light" in another woman's writing yet only "Wastes," "steady Wilderness," and "Infinites of Nought" in the unmediated, "face to face" reflection of another woman's eyes / I's.

> Like Eyes that Looked on Wastes—
> Incredulous of Ought
> But Blank—and steady Wilderness—
> Diversified by Night—
>
> Just Infinites of Nought—
> As far as it could see—
> So looked the face I looked upon—
> So looked itself—on Me—
>
> I offered it no Help—
> Because the Cause was Mine—
> The Misery a Compact
> As hopeless—as divine—
>
> Neither—would be absolved—
> Neither would be a Queen
> Without the Other—Therefore—
> We perish—tho' We reign—

(J 458)

Like Dickinson's poems on eternity, this poem proclaims the identity between self and other; their identical gender, however, makes all the difference. Whereas Dickinson's "One Year ago—jots what?" (J 296) imagines the eternally prolonged gaze upon a (sexual) other as nurturing, the quoted poem is dominated by sensations of a horrifying absence, of pain, and of death. Presenting the other as female, as the same, the speaker recognizes her own powerlessness in the other and identifies with it. "The Misery" is indeed "a [divine] Compact," because it entails wholeness. It is "hopeless," because this wholeness spells silence and lacks mutual nourishment. What the female misses and the male provides is a history, a subjectivity that entails the "power to die."

Though I than He—may longer live
He longer must—than I—
For I have but the power to kill,
Without—the power to die—

(J 754)

Like Eve, whose life story has, as Dickinson observed in her early letters, a dubious beginning and an unknown end, the speaker of the poem "My Life had stood—a Loaded Gun—" is granted subjectivity and the power to kill/speak by her owner. As an inanimate object, though, she remains incapable of dying.[12] Devoid of the "power" or "art" to die, of a history of their own, women fail to reinforce one another's sense of identity. Looking into one another's eyes/I's, they mirror this lack in an endless gaze at the horrors of death, a gaze that, according to Dickinson, never reaches identity.

Rich's poem "White Night," by contrast, attempts to displace the projections of paternal authority by placing female figures into a mutual position of subject and object. Written between the publication of *Diving into the Wreck* and *The Dream of a Common Language,* the poem thus anticipates the project of the latter volume. In "Sibling Mysteries," for instance, the sisters' eyes are described as "drink[ing] from each other;" "Transcendental Etude" speaks of "two women, eye to eye." The poem "The Lionness" (1975) even literalizes the metaphor "seeing through the eyes of an other."

I come towards her in the starlight.
I look into her eyes
as one who loves can look,
entering the space behind her eyeballs,
leaving myself outside.
So, at last, through my pupils,
I see what she is seeing:

(*Dream* 21–22)

This gaze at an other, who is in some sense the same, also imprisons the subject in a circularity, in a "literal life" apart from the temporality of history. Rich's volume *A Wild Patience Has Taken Me This Far* breaks this specularity by returning to matters of history while at the same time redefining history itself. Significantly enough, in this volume Rich addresses Dickinson once again.

Describing the development of her conception of history, Rich's essay

"Notes toward a Politics of Location" (1984) also delineates the changes her feminist perspective has undergone since the mid-1970s. Whereas "years ago" she "would have spoken of the common oppression of women," of a global women's movement, and a "universal shadow of patriarchy," Rich eventually came to reject the "faceless, raceless, classless category of 'all women'" (*Blood* 211, 219). Accordingly, in an essay written in the year of her "last address" to Dickinson, the author refers to Dickinson not as "woman genius" juxtaposed to that "other genius" Whitman (*On Lies* 159) but as a "white woman genius" contrasted by the "Black woman genius" Zora Neale Hurston (*Blood* 55). In Rich's essay "Blood, Bread, and Poetry: The Location of the Poet" (1984)—a historicized and politicized version of "When We Dead Awaken: Writing as Re-Vision"—the reader searches in vain for references to Dickinson but finds Barrett Browning along with de Beauvoir and James Baldwin. While she once rejected the influences of modern poetry, Rich now retrieves Yeats as a poet who taught her that "poetry can be 'about,' can root itself, in politics" (174).[13] Just like Rich's conversion to Judaism, this attitude reflects a de-emphasis of sexual differences, a "retreat from sexism" (Kristeva, "Women's Time" 34). In this move from a separatist to a more inclusive sense of feminist thought, Rich, along with Audre Lorde, was at the forefront. "I am less quick as I once was," Rich claims, "to search for single 'causes' or origins in dealings among human beings" (*Blood* 217–18). In accord with the general tendencies in feminism during the early 1980s, she acknowledged that subjectivity is, as de Lauretis puts it, built upon "heterogeneous and heteronomous representations of gender, race, and class, and often indeed across language and cultures" ("Feminist Studies" 9).

"The creative energy of patriarchy is fast running out," Rich projects at the end of her essay "Writing as Re-Vision," at a time when her most radically "sexist" poems were yet to be written. While, in the meantime, Rich's poetry has ceased to be possessed by the demon of patriarchy,[14] the demon lives on as a "web" or "tangle of oppressions" (*Blood* 218). In 1984 she described her (speaking) position as that of "an American radical, a lesbian feminist, a citizen who opposes her government's wars against its own people and its intervention in other people's lands" (168). Her feminist project is no longer to "repossess" a woman possessed by the "daemons" of a patriarchal universe but, rather, to reconstruct "the history of the dispossessed."

> As a younger and then an older woman, growing up in the white mainstream American culture, I was destined to piece together, for the rest of my life, laboriously and with much in my training against me, the history that really concerned me, on which I was to rely as a poet, the only history

upon which, both as a woman and a poet, I could find any grounding at all: the history of the dispossessed. (175–76)

While her engagement has shifted to include women as well as African Americans and Indians, Hispanics, the homeless, and other social groups that are discriminated against systematically, Rich still conceives of herself as a figure of integration; her concern with history is intended to ground her own sense of subjectivity. "I write for the still-fragmented parts in me, trying to bring them together," Rich claims in the first published version of her essay on the poet's location. "Whoever can read and use any of this, I write for them as well" (540). Writing has turned identity practice, indeed. (Significantly enough, this last sentence is deleted in the version reprinted in *Blood, Bread, and Poetry*.)

Dickinson was the one among Rich's precursors who most explicitly voiced the sense of self-division expressed in Rich's work of the mid-1960s to mid-1970s. Since Rich's projections of the otherness she desired to reintegrate into her sense of self have kept changing, it has become increasingly difficult for her to relate "directly" to Dickinson's sense of subjectivity, the way she had attempted to in "Vesuvius at Home." Neither Dickinson's methods and exclusions nor her "solutions," her dialectics of a subjectivity on edge, have been her own. Instead, Rich's more recent poems try to integrate the difference within women and her own "still-fragmented" sense of self by reconstructing history itself. Trying to rewrite the female subject as a process of past and present, Rich develops a dialectics of subjectivity that encompasses both her own and Dickinson's past. Such dialectics could not be built on notions of immanence but require a conception of transcendence that remembers Dickinson while acknowledging her difference. Instead of transgressing the edge between this life and that, Rich bridges the distance between past, present, and future. Her sense of a feminist transcendence not only historicizes Dickinson's own notion of transcendence but also reclaims her dialectics as an ethics.

## "Living Memory" and "the Power to Forget"

"This is my third and last address to you," Rich writes, evoking Dickinson in her poem "The Spirit of Place." As part of her collection *A Wild Patience Has Taken Me This Far,* this text shares its sense of female subjectivity and history, which builds upon the insights of *The Dream of a Common Language.* "We came together," reads a line from the poem "For Memory" (1979), "in a common / fury of direction / barely mentioning difference" (21). With a renewed emphasis on the specific historical and geopolitical conditions of different women's lives, the 1981 collection, by contrast, acknowledges the limits of a feminist "drive to connect," accepts the difference within women's positions and modes of expression, and recognizes that their "maps diverge" (18). As a consequence, history ceases to appear as a linear, unbroken narrative. As suggested in "Transcendental Etude," history has turned into a kind of quilt composed and continuously being recomposed from different patches of past and present lives and perspectives. This also makes for a new dialectics of subjectivity, in which the past is both antithesis and affirmation of the present and synthesis becomes a process that envisions a future resonating with both present and past.

Rich's new sense of history still encompasses the past of other female figures. In fact, never before did the poet remember so many women, including Susan B. Anthony, Jane Addams, Harriet Beecher Stowe, the Midwest women described in Willa Cather's work, numerous nameless nineteenth-century "heroines," her own mother-in-law and grandmothers, Simone Weil, as well as Dickinson. And yet the memory of these women no longer functions primarily as a source of power. It also constitutes a matrix of female subjectivity in history that demands that present-day women make use of the past in an ethically responsible manner. At the same time, the poems insist on the importance of one's personal history. As Rich writes in "For Memory":

> And did you ever tell me
> how your mother called you in from play
> and from whom? To what? These atoms filmed by ordinary dust
> that common life we each and all bent out of orbit from
> to which we must return simply to say
> *this is where I came from*
> *this is what I knew*
>
> The past is not a husk   yet change goes on
>
> Freedom. It isn't once, to walk out
> under the Milky Way, feeling the rivers
> of light, the fields of dark—
> freedom is daily, prose-bound, routine
> remembering. Putting together, inch by inch
> the starry worlds. From all the lost collections.
>
> (*Wild* 22)

While Dickinson found the loss of knowledge liberating, this speaker is freed by the knowledge of a past whose force depends, however, on the present, on a responsible "routine remembering," on a "Living Memory" (1988), as Rich entitled a more recent text (*Time's Power* 46–50). Instead of postulating the continuity of women's past and present lives, history has been transformed into a "steadying and corrective lens" (*Wild* 55) for one's present sense of self. Subjectivity has become a perpetual process of past and present.

Aware of such interdependence of past and present, Rich came to acknowledge both the limits and the possibilities of memory. Because "change goes on," changing one's own position within it, we will never achieve more than a partial knowledge of the past, and a fragmented picture of ourselves, overdetermined by present perspectives. At the same time, the final emphasis "For Memory" puts on integration indicates that Rich has not abandoned the notion of wholeness; that the awareness of change and instability also triggers a new desire for a comprehensive vision, which "hold[s] in one steady glance/all the parts of [one's] life" (*Dream* 68). As the poems "Integrity" (1978) and "The Spirit of Place" show—texts I chose because they bear different memories of Dickinson—Rich keeps oscillating between an acceptance of the subject's fragmentation and a continuous faith in her potential wholeness and identity. In this way she retains an ambivalence even toward the power of her dialectic sense of subjectivity. Heavily reliant on intertextual references to her own work, the poem "Integrity" intends to "piece together" its author's self-conception by remembering different moments of her identity practice. Eliding those aspects that resist integration, it culminates in a partial vision that masquerades as completion. Rich's sense of integrity consequently requires acts of forgetting. "The Spirit of Place," by contrast, attempts to capture—as Rich's essay on Dickinson does—the connection between the speaker's personal history and the "spirit" of the particular location that she lives in or visits. Here the speaker recognizes the distance between an official history and her personal memories of New England as well as the conflicting positions she has, throughout her life, taken vis-à-vis Dickinson and thus finally accepts her own fragmentation in history. Redefining the history of others as part of her own sense of self, the speaker aligns with the "spirit of place." Bridging the gap between past and present by claiming her position in a transcendent time-space, she "forgets" her own disclaimers of universalist worldviews, her own vote for "the world as it is." Both "Integrity" and "The Spirit of Place" underline that a "living memory" depends as much on "routine remembering" as on habitual acts of forgetting.

The poem "Integrity" announces its intent with its title, which was added to by a dictionary definition—*"the state of being complete; unbroken condition; entirety"*:

A wild patience has taken me this far

as if I had to bring to shore
a boat with a spasmodic outboard motor

(*Wild* 8)

The extended metaphor that follows rephrases Rich's poem "Diving into the Wreck" from a "post-Dream-of-a-Common-Language-perspective." Identified as the poet herself (not a diver with an "awkward mask"), the speaker undertakes a boat trip (not a diver's expedition), with "nothing but [her]self to go by" (no book of myth, no camera, no weapon), arriving at "the arm of an inland sea"—a place that fuses linearity ("arm") with closure ("inland sea"). This is the new location at which to anchor:

*Nothing but myself?* . . . *My selves.*
After so long, this answer.
As if I had always known
I steer the boat in, simply.
The motor dying on the pebbles
cicadas taking up the hum
dropped in the silence.

Anger and tenderness: my selves.
And now I can believe they breathe in me
as angels, not polarities.
Anger and tenderness: the spider's genius
to spin and weave in the same action
from her own body, anywhere—
even from a broken web.

(*Wild* 8–9)

The poem's metaphor gets interrupted as the speaker begins to meditate on subjectivity and reassembles the threads of her life in a series of images and terms that evoke different stages of Rich's work. As is indicated by the colons, Rich's sense of self as two selves not only appropriates a subject conception predominant in Dickinson's work and her Keatsian metaphor of the spider artist, a Romantic figure for (creative) autonomy and integrity. Rich also rewrites her own design of a polar, androgynous self ("I am he: I am she"). This gets underlined by a somewhat awkward note that traces the introduction of the concept integrity into feminist contexts to an essay on "The Illusion of Androgyny"

(1975)—a text Rich had already quoted in her earlier critique of androgyny (*Of Woman Born* 77).

Needless to say, Rich's "Integrity" is far from poems such as Dickinson's "Me from Myself—to banish—" (J 642). The doubleness of selves Rich depicts does not dialogue the speaking position but fragments a (previously unified male) other. Orion, who "plunges" desolate "like a drunken hunter" (*Wild* 44) through a later part of the volume, is here displaced by two guardian "angels." They "breathe" within but still bear likenesses to male figures as those starring in Rich's poem "Gabriel" 1968. Termed "anger" and "tenderness," these two "selves" evoke the very doubleness that dominates Rich's preceding two volumes: the anger toward patriarchy expressed in *Diving into the Wreck* and the tenderness toward women celebrated in *The Dream of a Common Language*. The phrase "Anger and tenderness," moreover, recontextualizes the title of the first chapter of *Of Woman Born,* in which Rich negotiates the conflicting feelings she experienced as a mother, an issue the overtly sentimental conclusion to "Integrity" evokes. Echoing previous perspectives in her present text, Rich attempts to melt past into present and to construct an unbroken identity.

When the phrase "Anger and tenderness" gets repeated, Rich substitutes its apposition ("the selves") with the image of "the spider's genius." Indebted to Keats and Dickinson, this figure has in other contexts suggested a history in the process of being erased. In Rich's poem "From a House in America" (1974), for instance, the cobweb represents a past being "sucked away" by a vacuum cleaner. Comparable to Dickinson's "spider artist" without audience and a nuisance to "every Broom and Bridget," who maintains the (symbolic) order "Throughout a Christian Land" (J 1275), the image works quite differently in Rich's texts. Dickinson urges her readers to sympathize with the "Neglected Son of Genius," to vote for art and fiction and against traditional female roles and literal life. In Rich's poem, which, as Deborah Pope puts it, fuses "the experience of American women, regardless of century, color, or locale, into a prototype of their tale" (154), the destruction of the cobweb foregrounds the text's own ahistoricity.

Rich's poem "Toward the Solstice" (1977) similarly employs the spider as a figure for history. "If history is a spider-thread / spun over and over though brushed away," its speaker speculates, uneasy with metaphor, one can imagine it leading from the present ("from molding or doorframe") back in time. Time itself is projected as a "path into the pinewoods / tracing from tree to tree" into a past envisioned as the location of a "true" and original language. Once again time is transfigured into space: "whatever cellar hole . . . ," the speaker reflects,

whatever fallen shack
or unremembered clearing
I am meant to have found
and there, under the first or last
star, trusting to instinct
the words would come to mind
I have failed or forgotten to say
year after year, winter
after summer, the right rune
to ease the hold of the past
upon the rest of my life
and ease my hold on the past.

(*Dream* 69–70)

This vision provides not so much a sense of continuity but, rather, serves to liberate the speaker from the limitations of the past. The imagined act is not a remembering but a necessary "unremembering."

Similarly, the image of the "spider's genius," which "spins and weaves in the same action / even from her own body, anywhere— / even from a broken web," fosters forgetting. Comparable to the path taken in "Toward the Solstice," "Integrity" finally envisions integration as a homecoming to a familiar domestic space and to physical existence, both shut off from and protected by the (phallic) paternal powers ("the cabin in the stand of pines"). This double dimension is indicated by a pair of hands, a figure of integration that heals the rift between past and present, a synecdoche, a fragment of the body that entails its wholeness, and an image of writing itself.

The hands that hammered in those nails
emptied that kettle one last time
are these two hands
and they have caught the baby leaping
from between trembling legs
and they have worked the vacuum aspirator
and stroked the sweated temples
and steered this boat here through this hot
misblotted sunlight, critical light
imperceptibly scalding
the skin these hands will also salve.

(*Wild* 9)

These hands want to know neither division nor alienation from labor; they rec-
ollect the parts of one's body, life, and work and proclaim their owner as self-
sufficient as a spider. Yet the very enumerative, paratactical, antihierarchical
structure of these lines signal discontinuity and fragmentation. The poem's final
lines remember, thus "piece . . . together" past and present. They also "ease[ ]
the hold of the past" by erasing the anger, the other self, from memory. For
Dickinson "Time is a Test of Trouble / But not a Remedy" (J 686). Rich, in
contrast, insists on time's power to heal, its "power to forget" (J 1464). Integrity
thus depends on amnesia, at least in part.

At the same time, poems such as "The Spirit of Place" and "Transit"—a
kind of counterpiece to "Integration"—affirm the need for a living memory,
now that anger has been displaced by pain. Partly due to personal experience,
physical impediments, and meditations on death—dominant concerns of Dick-
inson's poetry—have preoccupied Rich during the last decade. In the third part
of her volume *Your Native Land, Your Life* (1985) and in *Time's Power* (1989)
especially, they reflect a growing consciousness that integrity is after all impos-
sible. Accordingly, "Transit" reimagines the female subject as divided into a
healthy, self-confident part ("the skier") and a pain-ridden, reflective person
("the cripple").

> When sisters separate they haunt each other
> as she, who I might once have been, haunts me
> or is it I who do the haunting
> halting and watching on the path
> how she appears again through lightly-blowing
> crystals, how her strong knees carry her,
> how unaware she is, how simple
> this is for her, how without let or hindrance
> she travels in her body
> until the point of passing, where the skier
> and the cripple must decide
> to recognize each other?
>
> (*Wild* 19–20)

It is the awareness of the difference within, the very skepsis toward integrity,
that creates the need for recognition, for remembrance, the desire for wholeness
and identity. Unlike Dickinson's "haunted house"–sense of self and her para-
doxical projections of wholeness, Rich's sense of doubleness and identity is
being translated from writing into experience.

Meditating on her biography as well as on her relation to a historical past, Rich's poem "The Spirit of Place" acknowledges that it is impossible to reassemble the past "as it was" into one's present sense of self. At the same time, the poem holds that history resonates with the "spirit" of a place and proposes a historical sense based on an interdependence of time and place. "[A] place on the map," Rich writes in 1984, "is also a place in history" (*Blood* 212), a location that keeps memory alive by involving its visitors with this history. Whereas Rich's account of her visit to the Dickinson homestead was driven by a desire to step into the past directly, "The Spirit of Place" no longer proposes to enter history through the "confined space" of someone else's mind/room. Here the New England landscape resonates a history that both poets share, even though it has held different memories and experiences for each of them. The text proposes neither a common women's history nor a realm of female consciousness nor a collective unconscious. Instead, it projects a subliminal "time-space" that transcends historical linearity without dismissing history.

Composed in five parts, "The Spirit of Place" opens with yet another drive across New England backroads:

Over the hills in Shutesbury, Leverett
driving with you in spring road
like a streambed unwinding downhill
fiddlehead ferns uncurling
spring peepers ringing sweet and cold
. . . . . . . . . . . . . . . . . . . . . . . . . . . .
trying to sense the conscience of these hills

(*Wild* 40)

New England as presented here is "a shadowy country," a location heavy with a dual history of abolitionist movements and master minds, a place that is both steeped in history and a state of mind in and of itself. Associating, in a poem of 1970, a landscape with a particular time, Rich "could say: those mountains have a meaning / but further than that [she] could not say" (*Will* 50). Ten years later she reconsiders this notion of place and time, suggesting that a landscape preserves history as a kind of "conscience"—not "a spiritual life . . . imparted to nature" (Emerson, *Collected Works* 1:34), not man's projection of his own otherness, but women's consciousness of a lived history that, "wild and witchlike," haunts "every swamp."

At the same time, Rich's New England has preserved its wilderness ("The mountain laurel in bloom . . . here in these woods it grows wild"). Such a "dream of innocence" (*Your Native Land* 41) repeatedly pops up in Rich's poetry and prose to counterbalance historical change and civilization. Against all ecological evidence Rich's essay "Notes toward a Politics of Location," for instance, romanticizes nature as a "beauty that won't travel, that can't be stolen away" (*Blood* 223). It is this apparent power of nature, not its historicity, that triggers the speaker's personal memories. Accordingly, Rich's poem remembers the New England landscape as a retreat from cultural constraints, a site that is disconnected and yet able to reassociate "past and present near and far."

> Here in these hills
> this valley   we have felt
> a kind of freedom
>
> planting the soil   have known
> hours of calm, intense and mutual solitude
> reading and writing
> trying to clarify   connect
>
> past and present   near and far
> the Alabama quilt
> the Botswana basket
> history   the dark crumble
>
> of last year's compost
>
> (*Wild* 41)

Not this private "female experience" but, rather, a transcendent sense of history allows the speaker to reaffiliate with Dickinson and still preserve difference and distance between the poets, as the poem's third and central section does. Interestingly enough, this section entails another return to Amherst, a re-revision of her revision, so to speak.

> Strangers are an endangered species
>
> In Emily Dickinson's house in Amherst
> cocktails are served   the scholars
> gather in celebration
> their pious or clinical legends
> festoon the walls like imitations
> of period patterns
>
> (. . . and, as I feared, my "life" was made a "victim")

The remnants pawed   the relics
the cult assembled in the bedroom

and you   whose teeth were set on edge by churches
resist your shrine
    escape
      are found
nowhere
    unless in words   (your own)

              (42)


Envisioning the gathering of scholars, Rich sees predators on a foreign territory, who take over another's habitat, threaten an exceptionally strange "species" with extinction, and bury the poet under legends that reduce her to either saint or clinical case. Rejecting the myths around Dickinson, Rich repeats her critique of 1976. Criticizing the methods of excavation, the "pawing" of "the cult assembled in the bedroom," she renounces her own prior approach to Dickinson by projecting it on others. Accusing the scholars ("them") of victimization, Rich takes the very perspective she once projected on male political poets who, as she claimed, place "The enemy . . . always outside of the self" (*On Lies* 49).

As Rich renders Dickinson's own words in parenthesis and italics instead of quotation marks, she underlines her distance to Dickinson. Still, she is trying to meet her on equal terms. The questions posed by her earlier poems, the "who are you" of "I Am in Danger—Sir—," she implies, are no more than echoes of Dickinson's own texts ("I'm Nobody! Who are you?" [J 288]) never meant to be answered. The poet herself is "found / nowhere / unless in words ([her] own)"—"one woman's meanings," as Rich writes in a later poem, "to another woman / / long after death / in a different world" (*Your Native Land* 55). Having established an authority in its own right, Dickinson "escapes," remains a stranger yet. The poem accentuates this with a citation from one of Dickinson's letters, addressed to Catherine Scott Turner in 1859:

*All we are strangers—dear—The world is not*
*acquainted with us, because we are not acquainted*
*with her. And Pilgrims!—Do you hesitate? and*
*Soldiers oft—some of us victors, but those I do*
*not see tonight owing to the smoke.—We are hungry,*
*and thirsty, sometimes—We are barefoot—and cold—*

              (43)

Underscoring Dickinson's sense that, even though "We introduce ourselves /
To Planets and to Flowers" (J 1214), "nature is a stranger yet" (J 1400), this
passage anticipates her numerous poems on the void between subject and mate-
rial world and the constant desire it causes ("We are hungry . . ."). Leaving
Dickinson's words uncommented, Rich acknowledges that these words neces-
sarily take on a different meaning, "in a different world."

In spite of her objection to scholarly sanctification, Rich builds her own
shrine for Dickinson in the final lines of this section. With a series of ritualistic
images her speaker performs an imaginary "death ceremony" (Erkkila, "Dick-
inson and Rich" 558) and parts with the older poet's "ghost." In a three-liner
that displaces the previously applied broken pattern, the speaker offers three sets
of healing hands, thus calls upon the image of unity applied in "Integrity," in
order to sort out and put to rest a troubled relationship.

> This place is large enough for both of us
> the river-fog will do for privacy
> this is my third and last address to you
>
> with the hands of a daughter I would cover you
> from all intrusion    even my own
> saying   rest to your ghost
>
> with the hands of a sister I would leave your hands
> open or closed as they prefer to lie
> and ask no more of who or why or wherefore
>
> with the hands of a mother I would close the door
> on the rooms you've left behind
> and silently pick up my fallen work

                                                                          (43)

As the speaker transforms from daughter (as figure of protection) and sister (as
figure of tolerance) to mother (as figure of separation), the poem insinuates that
Dickinson has functioned variously in Rich's work, though meanwhile has
ceased to be a figure of origin and identity. "I've been thinking a lot about the
obsession with origins," Rich reminisces in 1984. "It seems a way of stopping
time in its tracks" (*Blood* 227). Presenting herself as the poet's mother, she
acknowledges that her rereading of Dickinson has recaptured as much as it pro-
duced the poet and thus has served her own identity practice.

Rich's "death ceremony," however, may also have taken its clue from

Dickinson herself, who wrote an obituary to Barrett Browning. The speaker of
"Her—'last Poems'—" (J 312) imagines participating in the burial of the
deceased.

> Late—the Praise—
> 'Tis dull—conferring
> On the Head too High to Crown—
> Diadem—or Ducal Showing—
> Be it's Grave—sufficient sign—
> Nought—that We—No Poet's Kinsman—
> Suffocate—with easy wo—
> What, and if, Ourself a Bridegroom—
> Put Her down—in Italy?

Like Rich's speaker, Dickinson projects herself into multiple (though male)
roles ("No Poet's Kinsman," "Ourself," "Bridegroom") to confront another
woman's death, the ultimate darkness of femininity, a particularly destabilizing,
endangering enterprise, as suggested in another poem on the same matter.

> I went to thank Her—
> But She Slept—
> Her Bed—a funneled Stone—
> With Nosegays at the Head and Foot—
> That Travellers—had thrown—
>
> Who went to thank Her—
> But She Slept—
> 'Twas Short—to cross the Sea—
> To look upon Her like—alive—
> But turning back—'twas slow—

(J 363)

Playing upon the ambivalences of literal and metaphorical meanings, this poem
envisions both the speaker's journey and her close encounter with death ("to
cross the sea") as a temptation to "part" from life herself. Whereas Rich's
speaker parts with Dickinson to take up her own business, Dickinson's is
inclined to identify with, rather than separate from, the other woman.

Redefining her earlier reading of Dickinson as an "intrusion," as an act of
wrongly entering upon, seizing or taking possession of the property of another,
Rich keeps her revisions in process. Her death ceremony dismisses the notion

of history as a possession, a "power stolen . . . from the mass of women, over centuries by men" (*On Lies* 210). In fact, the term *repossession,* which reappears throughout "Vesuvius at Home" to outbalance Dickinson's "possession by the daemon," gets recontextualized in another poem of the same year and projected upon a male figure: "your husband," Rich writes in "Heroines,"

> that your husband
> > has the right
> of the slaveholder
> > to hunt down and re-possess you
> > > should you escape
> > > > (*Wild* 34)

Accordingly, the poem "What Is Possible" (1980) repudiates the image of the mind as a room along with strategies of literalization. Once again, Rich revises her own rhetoric, though, once again, without acknowledging it as her own.

> If the mind were simple   if the mind were bare
> it might resemble a room   a swept interior
> but how could this now be possible
> > > > (24)

Closing the door to Dickinson's room, Rich postulates yet another new beginning, "stop[s] time in its tracks." Like "Transcendental Etude," which proposes "a whole new poetry," or "North American Time," whose speaker "start[s] to speak again," the speaker in "The Spirit of Place" "pick[s] up her fallen work." As the New England landscape turns into a common cultural her- itage, Rich projects her reconnection with Dickinson into a transcendent "spirit of place." Claiming "the river-fog . . . for privacy," she acknowledges that her vision of Dickinson necessarily had to be obscured, veiled, could never be the kind of unobstructed "flash / / of an eye across the cold / unwrapping of light between us" imagined in "White Night." And yet her farewell to Dickinson remains undecided. After having accepted historical distance, she expands her vision once again. "Rich is never content with limits," observes Altieri, "unless she can make consciousness of them a bridge to some larger sense of connec- tions and possible actions" (*Self* 188). This is the bridge she projects in the poem's final section:

> Orion plunges like a drunken hunter
> over the Mohawk Trail   a parallelogram
> slashed with two cuts of steel

A night so clear that every constellation
stands out from an undifferentiated cloud
of stars, a kind of aura

All the figures up there look violent to me
as a pogrom on Christmas Eve in some old country
I want our own earth    not the satellites, our

world as it is   if not as it might be
then as it is:    male dominion, gangrape, lynching, pogrom
the Mohawk wraiths in their tracts of leafless birch

watching:    will we do better?
The tests I need to pass are prescribed by the spirits
of place   who understand travel but not amnesia

The world as it is:    not as her users boast
damaged beyond reclamation by their using
Ourselves as we are   in these painful motions

of staying cognizant:    some part of us always
out beyond ourselves
knowing   knowing   knowing

Are we all in training for something we don't name?
to exact reparations for things
done long ago to us and those who did not

survive what was done to them   whom we ought to honor
with grief   with fury   with action
On a pure night   on a night when pollution

seems absurdity when the undamaged planet seems to turn
like a bowl of crystal in black ether
they are the piece of us that lies out there
knowing   knowing   knowing

(Wild 44–45)

The "cold and egotistical spear" ("Orion") has hit hard; "the constellations" have "melted" (*Your Native Land* 10). Exchanging Orion's "simplified west" and the "trail of that genius" Dickinson for the Mohawk Trail, Rich relocates subjectivity in North American time and Native American history. Dismissing symbols and phantoms, she disclaims prior beliefs in a collective unconscious and a universal female consciousness. Reclaiming the "world as it is," "ourselves as we are," she accepts time's "Test of Trouble" and embraces the present and "real." At the same time, she acknowledges that our actions are "prescribed by the spirits / of place who understand travel but not amnesia," that "ourselves as we are" are still determined by some transcendent power. Projecting "some part of us" exceeding the self "that lies out there / knowing knowing knowing," Rich accepts the fragmentation of the subject, reimagines history and its figures as the missing pieces of one's own self, as one's own otherness. Simultaneously, she reunites subjectivity and history under one global vision. This final emphasis on transcendence opposes Dickinson's sense of estrangement while once again foregrounding Rich's ambivalent relation to Emerson. Unlike Emerson, who saw in nature the alienated consciousness of man, Rich reclaims the spirit of place as a history in constant danger of being forgotten. Her revision of subjectivity expresses an Emersonian faith in "energies which are immortal" (*Collected Works* 2:175), energies that are not projected onto a universal mind, however, but onto history.

In this way Rich's "Spirit of Place" comes out a kind of companion poem to "Phantasia for Elvira Shatajev" (1974) and its sense of a feminist transcendence. In the latter text Shatajev, "leader of a women's climbing team, all of whom died in a storm on Lenin Peak, August 1974," addresses her husband from beyond death—from Dickinson's frequent "vantage point" (Hughes 148)—intonating with a "no longer personal," but multiple and communal, voice. The climbers' experience and mutual commitment is reasserted as a heritage for other women. It becomes the model of a female community, a project meant to live on beyond the memory that survives in the tale told by the man who found and buried the bodies.

> When you have buried us   told your story
> ours does not end   we stream
> into the unfinished   the unbegun
> the possible
> Every cell's core of heat   pulsed out of us
> into the thin air   of the universe
> the armature of rock beneath these snows
> this mountain which has taken   the imprint of our minds
> through changes elemental and minute
> as those we underwent
> to bring each other here
> choosing ourselves   each other   and this life

whose every breath   and grasp   and further foothold
is somewhere   still enacted and   continuing

(*Dream* 5)

Projecting the female community as a stream of energy that disperses into the universe, the poem reverses the flow of power described in the poem "Planetarium" (1968), "a companion poem to 'Orion'" in Rich's eyes (*On Lies* 47). Like "Orion," "Planetarium" depicts the subject as the target and interpreter of pulsations and signals she receives. "Phantasia for Elvira Shatajev," by contrast, rewrites the apocalyptic final chapter of Emerson's *Nature*. Whereas for Emerson the "influx of the spirit" of man establishes the "kingdom of man over nature" (1:45), the women imprint their mind and body heat upon the world. This world in turn emits a lasting inspiration, a "spirit of place" resonant with the memory of their experience. The speaker of "The Spirit of Place" is susceptible to these and other, less comforting imprints, produced, as we are told, by history, not fantasy.

Thus, Rich's poem instructs our engagement and defines the task—"prescribed by the spirits / of place who understand travel but not amnesia"—as both a resistance toward forgetting and an acknowledgment of constant change. Shifting her perspectives, Rich has not abandoned the missionary aspects of her feminist errand. She embarks on "another mission," as she puts it in "What Is Possible," on "a different mission / in the universe" (*Wild* 24). While expressing compassion, Rich's portrait of nineteenth-century heroines, for instance, insists that it simply does not suffice, to be "an outlaw," "deviant," "exceptional / in personal circumstances," and to "speak / in the shattered language / of a partial vision" (35, 36). Power is no longer merely a source to be repossessed but an energy to be recycled in an ethically responsible manner and with an awareness of the task's immensity and of one's own shortcomings. "Will we do better?" the speaker asks in "The Spirit of Place." And in the poem "For Julia in Nebraska" she inquires:

How are we going to do better?
for that's the question that lies
beyond our excavations,
the question I ask of you
and myself, when our maps diverge,
when we miss signals, fail—

(18)

Because "there is no finite knowing, no such rest" (*Your Native Land* 27), Rich's own identity practice remains a "map of constant travel" (54). Despite her awareness of one's own self-division, Rich keeps her poems striving for a center, a sense of wholeness, even essence, as her poem "Delta" (1987) does.

Leading from one source into various directions, the delta, with its "five fingers spread," symbolizes the multidimensionality of the (female) subject, her sexuality, and her history. In this way it recalls the final lines of Dickinson's the poem "I dwell in Possibility—" (J 657), whose speaker claims "For Occupation —This— / The spreading wide my narrow Hands / To gather Paradise—." Dickinson explores the possibilities of discourse to undo her historical disposition and expand her sense of subjectivity in her poetry. Rich, by contrast, has all of her stories recenter around some ethically essential truth ("the heart of the matter") and dive "deeper" into the wreck.

If you think you can grasp me, think again:
my story flows in more than one direction
a delta springing from the riverbed
with its five fingers spread

(*Time's Power* 32)

While Dickinson dismissed history and transcendence for the temporality of writing, Rich's sense of subjectivity keeps oscillating between an awareness of one's multiplicity and fragmentation in history, and a desire for a centered integrated identity, unhinged from time's power. This is the edge that Rich's female subjects ponder.

# Self-Fashioning or Subjected in Style? The Intertextual Networking of Female Subjectivity

Just as the understanding of subjectivity as a position in discourse is a fairly recent theoretical concept, so is the notion of female subjectivity. It has challenged the predominant construction of woman as an object and, more precisely, an "object of vision" (cf. de Lauretis, "Eccentric Subjects" 119)—a construction Moore's "poetics of deflection" makes particularly evident (Diehl, *Sublime* 44). Dickinson, Moore, and Rich alike have foregrounded that subject positions are culturally assigned, fashioned according to historically grown conventions, "costumes," and discursive codes. Yet only Rich has been a major participant, in fact an instigator, in conceptualizing the female self or subject and thereby has also insisted on autobiography as self-assertion, not "self-effacement" (De Man). In prose as in poetry she has shown that female subjectivity develops as a negotiation among various discourses, including other women's as well as her own texts, and that, consequently, female subjectivity may also be transformed discursively. In this way Rich's work shows that, as Linda Hutcheon puts it, "to reinsert the subject . . . into the context of its *parole,* its signifying activities (both conscious and unconscious) within a historical and social context, is to begin to force a redefinition not only of the subject but of history" (79). As we acknowledge subjectivity as a partly predetermined, partly self-determined interrogation of discourses, history turns out a dialogue and process mediating between past and present (texts).

In this way, and somewhat surprisingly, Rich emerges as a proponent of what Nancy Fraser calls the "structuralist model" of subjectivity, a model "derived from Saussure, presupposed in Lacan, and abstractly negated but not entirely superseded in deconstruction and in related forms of French women's writing" (86). According to Fraser's critique of "The Uses and Abuses of French

Discourse Theories for Feminist Politics" (1990), this model "brackets questions of practice, agency, and the speaking subject," just as it precludes the "diachronic"; "it will not," the author insists, "tell us anything about shifts in identities and affiliations over time" (87). By recontextualizing Kristeva's and Irigaray's subject theories in this study, I have shown in contrast, that the notion of the female subject as a position in discourse, as located in "authorship," fore-closes neither history nor agency, "the capacity for movement or self-deter-mined (dis)location, and hence social accountability" (de Lauretis, "Eccentric Subjects" 137). On the one hand, Dickinson's threshold glances, Moore's mim-icry, and Rich's feminist rhetoric display that, if subjectivity is discursive, one can indeed not, as Linda Hutcheon rightly points out, be wholly in control of it (85); that to a certain degree all discourse is citation, and we are indeed all spo-ken subjects. On the other hand, the unorthodoxy of their texts underlines that subject and subjectivity are never completely modeled according to prearranged fashions either. Subjectivity—be it historical or fictional—involves selecting from a wide range of institutional frames, discourses, grammars, tones of voice, and imagery that allow for locally transgressive moves and may envision alter-native positions, or "third event[s]." While the symbolic order may not grant the (speaking) subject autonomy, the poetic texts imply that neither is it a straightjacket of norms and conventions but, rather, a flexible structure that allows for agency.

The poets' texts, moreover, foreground that, due to significant transfor-mations of the symbolic order, the radius of agency has been extended in some ways, limited in others, since the days of Emily Dickinson; that female subjec-tivity has covered different ground at different times. Dickinson still had to speculate whether "she who experiences Eternity in Time, may receive Time's omitted Gift as part of the Bounty of Eternity" (L 688). The diminished impact of church and religion on people's lives, women's political enfranchisement, limited as it may have been in political practice, as well as ever-changing family values and lifestyles are only a few phenomena that have altered the institutional and discursive frame of reference for (female) subjectivity in the meantime and, along with it, women's lives. These developments have also transformed the complex relationship between women as historical subjects and fictions of fem-ininity resistant to change. While such transformations, according to Foucault, do not necessarily reduce control and pressures to conform, there is no denying that gendered subjects are posited quite differently in late-capitalist, postmodern symbolic systems than they are in a Victorian universe. This entails that their capacity to act is channeled into other paths and possibilities, that it conforms to, yet also challenges, new fashions.

It is Rich, once again, who has explicitly insisted that subjectivity entails "recognizing our location, having to name the ground we're coming from" (*Blood* 219). Her poetry at the same time, though, demonstrates that naming is in fact a rather limited device, that our location may be grounded in matters that—for better or worse—have not been assigned a name and thus require to be imagined or *re*-presented. This supposedly other kind of representation, this discourse capable of capturing the "unknown" or unnameable—whose content itself has changed over time—has frequently been aligned with the unconscious and celebrated as an element of resistance by authors as distinct as Kristeva, Rich, and de Lauretis. Unlike Kristeva and Rich, however, de Lauretis suggests that "the notion of the unconscious as excess(ive) may be most productive" if one thinks of "excess as *resistance to* identification rather than unachieved identification," or as "a *dis-identification* with femininity that does not necessarily revert or result in an identification with masculinity but, say, transfers to a form of female subjectivity that exceeds the phallic definition," a definition that goes "beyond the conceptual constraint imposed by the term 'femininity' and its binary opposite—its significant other—'masculinity'" ("Eccentric Subjects" 126).

De Lauretis's claim that there are two kinds of processes at work in subject constitution—that of agency geared toward identification and that of resistance striving toward dis-identification—not only rephrases Kristeva's sense of subjectivity as a process of the semiotic and the symbolic. It also reconceptualizes the semiotic in a way that fits the poetic practice explored in this book. While attesting to the usefulness of Kristeva's sense of subjectivity as a process of semiotic and symbolic, the poets' texts also imply a substantial shift of emphasis toward the dialogical and dialectic nature of the processes of subject constitution. In discursive practice we cannot, as Fraser insinuates, distinguish two subjects, one of the semiotic and one of the symbolic (98). In fact, only for analytical reasons can we disengage the semiotic from the symbolic and vice versa: in (poetic) discourse neither exists without the other; neither is in its effects wholly deconstructive or, respectively, reconstructive. Therefore, we do find strategies of dis-identification, such as Rich's late "retreat from sexism," that are quite consciously applied. Likewise, identity practices such as the revision of Rich's own texts implied in her reading of Dickinson may, to a substantial degree, be guided by unconscious processes.

In this context it is crucial to note in Dickinson's, Moore's, and Rich's writing alike a resistance against subjection by the male gaze, a dis-identification from the sense of femininity as "object of vision." In all three poets' texts this is achieved by a refiguration of the subject's own gaze as a metaphor of self-identity. Accordingly, the historical unfolding of female subjectivity in Dickinson's,

Moore's, and Rich's poetry shows not only in a gradual and increasingly self-conscious inscription of female agency into language, moving from strategies of mimicry toward revisionary writing practices. It can also be approached through the fictions of (self-) identity and moments of near silence, figured by images of specularity and mirroring, of "face-to-face" (and "eye-to-eye") encounters that recur in each of the poets' work. The ways in which these figures shift their location and semantic contexts as we move from Dickinson to Rich, likewise corresponds to a historical development of female subjectivity into history.[1]

Finding only "Wastes" and "Wilderness" in another woman's eye / I, Dickinson projected her visions of self-identity into an unknown "beyond." Exploring a "Bodiless," referenceless state beyond the constraints of gender and history, she reimagines the realm conventionally called "heaven" or "Eden" as a space in which sexual differences and social hierarchies have dissolved. Somewhat paradoxically, Dickinson's broken discourse serves to project an imaginary space in which the split that creates the subject is healed; in which self and other reintegrate in the endless embrace of an unmediated gaze of identity. Claiming this gaze in writing, Dickinson trades literal life for a living language in order to "gather Paradise" (J 657) in poetic presence. She strives for an identity that is unattainable on this side of subjectivity yet comes within reach in the fleeting presence of the act of writing itself. Moore, by comparison, explores self-identity in a poetics that allies creativity and maternal nurture, in a discourse that dissolves subject and object boundaries. Having evolved in the context of close relations to other (creative) women, it nonetheless displays significant bias concerning femininity. In Rich's poetry, finally, images of identity are being realigned with an intimacy of another woman's body, with the "secret circle of fire" that makes up the matrix of female subjectivity. Reimagining lesbian sexuality in terms of the preoedipal economy of mirroring, indifference, and identity, Rich also has to acknowledge, though, that the body is a place of silence, rather than discourse. Or, to put it another way, that it is the discourse *about*, not *of*, the body that is being reinvented.

So if, in view of these glimpses of fulfillment, we return once again to Shakespeare's sisters' dinner party, we may realize that it has by no means been a beggars' banquet. Dickinson, Moore, and Rich know how to feast as well as to fast. "Deprived of other Banquet," Dickinson first "entertained [her]self" (J 773), finding that kind of entertainment "a scant nutrition," "an insufficient Loaf," indeed. "[G]rown by slender addings / To so esteemed a size," she could not only "Reserve ["A Berry"]—for charity" but reach for higher goals, "Till for a further food / [she] scarcely recollect[s] to starve": "The Luxury it was / To

Banquet on [another's] Countenance" (J 815). "I tasted—careless—then—,"
she reports, "I did not know the Wine / Came once a World—Did You? / Oh,
had you told me so—," she complained, "This Thirst would blister—easier—
now—." And still, she admits, the "true" "Banquet" (J 296) of "Fleshless
Lovers" (J 625) remains a "doubtful meal" (J 296) making desire and self-dimin-
ishing crash diets, with the prospect of further feasting, a more desirable state
than "the Actual":

> Who never wanted—maddest Joy
> Remains to him unknown—
> The Banquet of Abstemiousness
> Defaces that of Wine—
>
> Within its reach, though yet ungrasped
> Desire's perfect Goal—
> No nearer—lest the Actual—
> Should disenthrall thy soul—

(J 1430)

As for banquets, Moore cherishes abundance yet detests waste. Like Dick-
inson, she would rather let go of a "perishable souvenir of hope" and hold on
to the "imperishable wish" (*CPMM* 151). Similarly, Rich eventually opts for
the "desire to desire," realizing that feeding upon another will leave you hun-
gry, after all. Yet, while Dickinson's "Banquet" takes place in the "beyond,"
Rich reminds us that, as pop star Madonna puts it, "dining out can happen
down below" ("Where Life Begins"). Appropriating, in her "Twenty-One
Love Poems," the metaphor of eating for oral sex and recontextualizing the
lovers' face-to-faceness, their "Heaven of Heavens" (J 625) as the echo of their
mutual orgasms, for Rich as for Dickinson, the mirror image signifies, phrased
in Lacan's words, "the threshold" of another "visible world" (*Écrits* 3).

Still, their worlds remain distinct. In some ways Rich was once close to
Judy Chicago, putting into poetic practice her visual poetics, her "reinterpreta-
tion of the Last Supper from the point of view of women," the re-metaphoriza-
tion of women's history, subjectivity, and sexuality as a luxurious banquet, a
feast whose "honored guests" are represented by individually crafted tablecloths
and vulvomorphic plates (Chicago 11). In some way she was, as Betty Chmaj
claims, to American literature what Chicago is to American art (253). Reading
Rich's most recent prose, however, we are being reminded that, as a writer,
Rich need not put it all on display, up for grabs. Just as she once again rehearses

the myths around Dickinson, recalling her "white dress and neck ribbon," her "gingerbread-baking self-effacement" (*Found There* 92, 94), she celebrates in Minnie Bruce Pratt the "transgressor mother," in her erotic poetry an "undomesticated passsion" (153). "Forgetting" her own beginnings in the domain of lesbian poetry, Rich keeps up the desire that makes writing itself a passion, "an activity of keenest joy" (215). Yet, if it is poetry, as she claims, that "lifts its head and looks you in the eye," "across enormous social, national, geographic tracts," would she look back at Moore and recognize likeness among all the difference? Could she gaze into Moore's eyes/I's and accept that part of "what is found there," of what has for so long seemed to be an "impersonal look," belongs to her just as well? Could she acknowledge that the "enclave of self-protection" she projected in early poems such as "Storm Warnings" has been more than an attempt to "dissociate[ ] poetry from politics" (foreword, *Collected Early Poems* xix, xx)? That Moore's poetry tries to achieve an equilibrium between "excess / and armor's undermining modesty," between self-regard and solitude (*CPMM* 151), a balance that she herself is now searching for?

What Dickinson's, Moore's, and Rich's images of self-identity all have in common, though, is that they project positions at the margins, or in a beyond, of dominant symbolic systems: Dickinson's poems speak from a location termed "eternity"; Moore imagines an economy of discourse—and thus also desire—dissociated from traditional (commercial) exchanges; and Rich situates her lesbian lovers in a countercultural space. De Lauretis sees a singular potential in such self-marginalizations, or, as she puts it, in the position of an "eccentric subject," located not outside power structures but, rather, in a particular textual practice beyond their dichotomies and heterosexual economy. She finds such subjectivity exemplified in Monique Wittig's notion of the "lesbian" who, due to her dislocation from heterosexuality, supposedly resists the category of woman. The poets' projections of such "eccentric subjects," by comparison, make evident that, constructed in discourse, such marginality can only at rare moments "transgress" cultural categorizations and binarisms. In this way they express a desire that informs feminist theory and women's poetry alike. Both Juhasz's sense that "someday there may be no difference" of gender (3) and Kristeva's conception of a "signifying space" in which the dichotomy of man and woman belongs to metaphysics cherish the utopian vision of a nondualistic, thus supposedly better, world. At the same time, however, the poets' sense of eccentric subjectivity insinuates that even the fictions of subversive marginality situated "outside" historical temporality have their own history. They are historically distinctive in that they are increasingly related to women's lives. More precisely, from Dickinson to Rich the (biblical) image of face-to-faceness gets both secularized and sexualized.

In fact, the poets' figures of self-identity can be distinguished by the way they interrogate representations of the (female) body, moving from poetic equivocations that signify the inadequacy of the body as a basis of female subjectivity to a feminist rhetoric that reclaims the female body as the "groundnote" of women's existence. Unlike Kristeva, Rich revalues the preoedipal bond and female body not as a subversive force but as a "rockshelf," or "stone foundation," of female subjectivity, culture, and history. And, while Dickinson's poetry faces the challenge to render bodiless identities in a medium that works by *différance*, Rich declares the female body an identity and presence that cannot be rendered, therefore needs to be remembered in language. This more recent preoccupation of women's literature and feminist theory with the female body itself correlates with a growing awareness of women's objectification of women and the strategies of its cultural legitimization. Since women specify as social beings by way of reproductive labor (see de Lauretis, "Eccentric," 121), it is no coincidence that, at a time when women's historical position is changing, this specificity is being interrogated for both its potential and its limits. Interestingly enough, Dickinson, Moore, and Rich alike tend to dismiss motherhood as a destructive and suffocating female function yet recreate (the maternal as) a realm of intimacy, re-presented by historically specific images of mutual nurturance projected *beyond* the margins of the heterosexual economy.

At the same time, Rich's poems finally acknowledge that the feminist project of reclaiming the female body and dislodging it from heterosexual culture and reproduction can be envisioned, but never enacted, as a return to an authentic female body. Due to our culturally overdetermined sense of the "natural" body, as Judith Butler and Thomas Laqueur, among many others, have shown, this authentic body simply does not exist. Redefining the silences of the female body as a matrix of female subjectivity, as part of "the ground we're coming from," thus accepting the female body as a rhetorical figure, Rich furthers the gradual disappearance of the body, the processes that, since Dickinson's days, have put the sexual body into discourse—a tendency anticipated by Moore's foregrounding of textual surfaces and mimic postures. This may be why Rich's texts turn out the most "chaste" (Gilmore 100), Dickinson's the most sexy, and Moore's not necessarily characterized by an "overt absence of eros" (Diehl, *Sublime* 47) but suspecting that the disappearance of the female body could, in some way, advance the female subject. While Moore's poetry therefore presents us with parodies of traditional representations of femininity, such as Renaissance images of female chastity, Rich's supposedly "radically" new representations of female sexuality reproduce romantic fictions of femininity without necessarily foregrounding their fictionality. In some way this signifies what Jameson depicts as the difference between modernism and postmodernism: the difference between parody and pastiche. While, like parody, pastiche is the imitation of a peculiar or unique style, the wearing of a stylistic mask, only parody refers to a supposed original with which it sympathizes. This original has been lost to postmodernism, which makes pastiche "a neutral practice of . . . mimicry, without parody's ulterior motive, without the satirical impulse, without laughter, without that still latent feeling that there exists something *normal* compared to which what is being imitated is rather comic" (114).

This may be one reason why Cixous's "laugh of the Medusa" or Dickinson's and Moore's "comic power," to use the phrase of Juhasz, Cristanne Miller, and Nell Smith, is lost on Rich. At the same time, however, the awareness of this pastiche character of postmodern discourse, gained in the process of writing *The Dream of a Common Language,* may have affected Rich's return to citation in her volume *A Wild Patience Has Taken Me This Far* (1981). Here citation becomes a feminist strategy to inscribe women into history and to reimagine the female subject as a process of past and present texts. With this strategic use of intertextual reference, Rich may even have had an impact on Susan Howe's handling of quotation—on a poet, that is, whose textual practice seems in so in many ways incomparable to that of Rich's. Through a postmodernist collage technique based on the author's own (literary) associations, Howe authorizes a (female) subject as an intertextual affiliation between historically distinct, frequently marginalized, speaking positions. Just as Rich's more recent theoretical perspective, this poetic practice re-members forgotten male authors/texts just as it recontextualizes fictions of femininity, thereby underscoring that any otherness, marginality, and female subjectivity being reinscribed into (literary) history is not characterized by gender alone. It is "made up of," as de Lauretis put it, "heteronomous representations of gender, race, and class, and often indeed across languages and cultures" (*"Feminist Studies"* 9). Accordingly, when Rich talks about Dickinson in her recent *Notebooks on Poetry and Politics,* she places her alongside Whitman, making her part of "a strange uncoupled couple, moving together in a dialectic that the twentieth century has only begun to decipher," "shar[ing the] problematic status as white poets in a century of slavery, wars against the Indians, westward expansion, the Civil War, and the creation of the United States as an imperial power" (90, 91). Acknowledging both her devotion to and distance from Whitman and Dickinson, Rich also suggests that at this point in (literary) history any notion of woman-authored writing as a "counter" or "alternative tradition" (Diehl, *Sublime* xi) has become somewhat anachronistic.

The fact that marks of gender difference have been my focus throughout this study was therefore not meant to suggest that traces of class, race, ethnicity, and nationality are of no avail in Dickinson's, Moore's, and Rich's constructions of (female) subjectivity. After all, as Cristanne Miller has reminded us, Moore's most famous maternal hero was black;[2] Dickinson's favor for "drop[s] of India" (J 430) and darkness have significant ethnic overtones, not to mention her highly developed sense of class hierarchies;[3] and Rich's more recent identity practice positions her in multiple locations, including that of a lesbian, white, North American, Jewish feminist as well as an aging person whose body may no longer be the most reliable fundament of being. (This heterogeneous self-conception may partly explain why Rich has recently republished her early poems—a step that Moore, unfortunately, never took. It makes poems readily available that, despite the discontinuation of their publication, have always been present, in part due to Rich's vehement dismissal of them.) And, finally, I should recall that the term that has dominated my own discussion of Rich—that of identity practice or identity politics—has itself been derived from the contexts of African-American feminism.

Taking all these parameters of subject constitution into account, displacing Rich by Howe or Lorde or adding Rita Dove as a partner in the poetic dialogues presented here, the intertextual network of female subjectivity would undoubtedly have taken a significantly different shape.[4] Interestingly enough, though, even if we extended the frame of this dialogic analysis, Kristeva's, Irigaray's, and Cixous's theoretical concepts would have remained highly suggestive. For one thing the crisis of the male philosophical subject interrelates not only with the emergence of the female historical subject but with claims for authority and subjectivity made by other previously marginalized or suppressed groups, in the American context first and foremost by African Americans. Likewise, Irigaray's understanding of mimicry as an interim strategy of female subject constitution is a valid historical category that serves not only to conceptualize strategies of an emerging female subjectivity such as sexual/textual cross-dressing, camouflage, and aspirations to transgress gender. As texts from the so-called Harlem Renaissance show, such sense of performativity is likewise functional for an understanding of African-American cultural production.

Finally, we should not forget that it is readers like us, in our particular cultural and theoretical (dis)positions, that construct and reinsert the subject in(to) texts that, at least as far as the work of Dickinson and Moore are concerned, have not been written with the project of writing the female subject back into discourse in mind. We not only are "armed with" but also restricted by a "semiotic history (personal and social), a series of previous identification by which we have been en-gendered" (Hutcheon 80). We are also armed as well as restricted by our political consciousness and theoretical conceptualization of women's objectification. Moreover, our preference for a "subject-in-process," for multiplicity and plurality of identity, cannot be dislodged from the post-modernist/ late-capitalist context in which such concepts themselves emerged. The instability and performativity of the postmodernist subject after all perpetuates, as Linda Singer so persuasively argued, the economic need for a constant transformation of the subject by means of a continuous remodeling of its surface designs and fashions (78). It is with these qualifications in mind that I want to conclude by redefining (female) subjectivity with Dickinson, Moore, Rich, Kristeva, Irigaray, and Cixous as a process that is never coherent and historically continuous but, rather, negotiates between deconstructive and (re)constructive modes as well as between past and present discourses. It entails Rich's knowledge of constructedness that allows for a more direct use of a Dickinson kind of performativity. It requires armor that, to use Moore's words, unlike Mars's, is not "excessive / in being preventive." Unlike Dickinson, who chose one dress for life while constantly changing costumes in her writing, Moore prefers a kind of battle dress that both protects and signifies and thus does "not let self bar / [one's] usefulness to others who were different" (*CPMM* 152). Female subjectivity thus is a matter of intertextual networking, in and across time, performed not by language itself but by those who—both consciously and unconsciously—act in language and keep doing so in the future. So, Shakespeare's sisters' dinner party is indeed no Last Supper. Just imagine, for a moment, it has only just begun and that many "Far fashions—Fair—" (J 473) are still ahead.

# Notes

## Introduction

1. The dinner party motif is derived from Judy Chicago's collaborative art project "The Dinner Party." See Chicago, *The Dinner Party: A Symbol of Our Heritage* (1978).

2. I am referring here to Miller's illuminating and original study *Marianne Moore: Questions of Authority* (1995), which, by exploring Moore's particular "alternative sense of authority" (5) and the ways in which it questions authority, takes on an issue that has been just as discomforting as it has been central to both feminist criticism and Moore scholarship.

3. Whereas French feminist theory was discussed widely and polemically and mostly dismissed by Anglo-American feminist critics in the early 1980s, revisions of French feminism tend to read more closely and to recontextualize the work of Kristeva, Irigaray, and Cixous as well as of Monique Wittig and other French feminists such as Christine Delphy and Colette Guillaumin. See, for instance, *Revaluing French Feminism,* ed. Sandra Lee Bartky (Bloomington: Indiana University Press, 1990); Shari Benstock, *Textualizing the Feminine: On the Limits of Genre* (Norman: University of Oklahoma Press, 1991); Rita Felski, *Beyond Feminist Aesthetics: Feminist Literature and Social Change* (Cambridge: Harvard University Press, 1989); Diana Fuss, *Essentially Speaking: Feminism, Nature and Difference* (New York: Routledge, 1989); and *The Thinking Muse: Feminism and Modern French Philosophy,* ed. Marion Young (Bloomington: Indiana University Press, 1989). Accordingly, essays that engage French feminist theory for poetic analyses appeared with a considerable time lag. They include: Calvin Bedient, "Kristeva and Poetry as Shattered Signification," *Critical Inquiry* 16.4 (1990): 807–29; Marilyn L. Brownstein, "The Archaic Mother and Mother and Mother: The Postmodern Poetry of Marianne Moore," *Contemporary Literature* 30.1 (1989): 13–32; Claire Buck, "'O Careless, Unspeakable Mother': Irigaray, H.D. and Maternal Origin," *Feminist Criticism: Theory and Practice* (Toronto: University of Toronto Press, 1991): 129–42; Lee Upton, "Coming to God: Dickinson, Bogan, Cixous," *Denver Quarterly* 27.4 (1993): 83–94; Jan Montefiori, *Feminism and Poetry* (1987); and, most recently, *Feminist Measures. Soundings in Poetry and Theory* (1995), ed. Cristanne Miller and Lynn Keller. This collection of essays is of particular interest in this context as it approaches both established and less canonized poets by way of (French) feminist theory and challenges that

theory in the process. See also Mary Loeffelholz, *Dickinson and the Boundaries of Feminist Theory* (1991).

4. See Martha Nell Smith, *Rowing in Eden: Rereading Emily Dickinson* (1992).

5. In her essay "Getting Spliced: Modernism and Sexual Difference" (1987) Carolyn Burke retraces central concepts of an American literary modernism, such as the collage and Pound's sense of "logopoiea," to the writings of Gertrude Stein, Mina Loy, and Moore, to make a case for the originality, radicality, centrality, and gender difference of women's modernist texts.

6. Feminist rereadings of American women's poetry appeared from the late 1960s on. Among the central texts are: Rosemary Sprague, *Imaginary Gardens: A Study of Five American Poets* (Philadelphia: Chilton, 1969); Suzanne Juhasz, *Naked and Fiery Forms: Modern American Poetry by Women: A New Tradition* (1976); *Shakespeare's Sisters: Feminist Essays on Women Poets* (1979), ed. Sandra M. Gilbert and Susan Gubar; Margaret Homans, *Women Writers and Poetic Identity: Dorothy Wordsworth, Emily Brontë, Emily Dickinson* (1980); Cheryl Walker, *The Nightingale's Burden: Women Poets and American Culture before 1900* (Bloomington: Indiana University Press, 1982); Wendy Martin, *An American Tryptich: Anne Bradstreet, Emily Dickinson, Adrienne Rich* (1984); Laura Bennett, *My Life a Loaded Gun: Female Creativity and Feminist Poetics* (1986); Alicia Ostriker, *Stealing the Language: The Emergence of Women's Poetry in America* (1986); and Joanne Feit Diehl, *Women Poets and the American Sublime* (1990).

7. For a revision of this conception of a female tradition see, for instance, Betsy Erkkila, *The Wicked Sisters: Women Poets, Literary History and Discord* (1992).

8. My conception of postmodernism goes back to the work of Andreas Huyssen and is not restricted to a specific (postmodernist) aesthetics. I understand postmodernism as the cultural condition after modernism, in relation to which different cultural groups have reacted with rather distinct cultural practices, dependent on their specific history and their particular sense of identity that developed from that history. See Huyssen, *After the Great Divide: Modernism, Mass Culture, Postmodernism* (Bloomington: Indiana University Press, 1986). Ulfried Reichardt's study *Innenansichten der Postmoderne: zur Dichtung John Ashberys, A. R. Ammons', Denise Levertovs und Adrienne Richs* (1991) uses such notion of postmodernism to conceptualize contemporary American poetry.

9. Wendy Martin and Bennett, for instance, defend their exclusion of modernist writers from their "triptychs" with reasons of continuity. Diehl's book *Women Poets and the American Sublime* as well as Leigh Gilmore's essay "The Gaze of the Other Woman: Beholding and Begetting in Dickinson, Moore, and Rich," by contrast, argue the continuity between nineteenth-century, modernist, and postmodernist women's poetry.

10. For a discussion of this phenomenon, termed with reference to de Man's essay "The Resistance to Theory," see Showalter, "Feminist Criticism in the Wilderness," *Critical Inquiry* 8 (Winter 1981); reprinted in Showalter, *New Feminist Criticism;* and Evelyne Keitel, "Frauen, Texte, Theorie" (1983).

11. Translation mine. The German reads: "Er [der Autor] lädt zum Festmahl nicht die Literaturwissenschaftler an seinen Tisch."

12. This conception of subjectivity is partly indebted to Anne Herrmann's study *The Dialogic and Difference: "An/Other Woman" in Virginia Woolf and Christa Wolf* (1989).

13. Translation mine. The original reads: "Literarische Texte eröffnen Möglichkeiten, die die theoretischer Texte überschreiten."

14. *Double-voicedness* is, of course, by no means a new term in this context. In her essay "Feminist Criticism in the Wilderness" Showalter, for instance, claimed that "women's writing is a 'double-voiced discourse' that always embodies the social, literary, and cultural heritage of both the muted and the dominant" (263).

15. I take the term *identity politics* from de Lauretis's introduction to *Feminist Studies/Critical Studies* (1986). The concept originates from the Combahee River Collective's "A Black Feminist Statement" and is discussed by Elly Bulkin, Minnie Bruce Pratt, and Barbara Smith in *Yours in Struggle: Three Feminist Perspectives on Antisemitism and Racism* (Brooklyn: Long Haul, 1984).

16. As Moore informs her reader in the notes, the poem's source is a remark from a conversation with a certain Miss A. M. Homans, professor emeritus of hygiene, Wellesley College. Moore's note in *Observations* (1924) reads: "'My father used to say, 'superior people never make long visits; then people are not so glad when you've gone.' When I am visiting, I like to go about by myself. I never had to be shown Longfellow's grave nor the glass flowers at Harvard" (105).

17. For a more detailed discussion of the relation between Baudelaire, Eliot, and Rich, see Patrick Deane, "A Line of Complicity: Baudelaire—T. S. Eliot—Adrienne Rich," *Canadian Review of American Studies* 18.4 (1987): 463–82.

18. The function of Dickinson's writing can thus be aptly described by Winfried Fluck's conception of "literature as symbolic act" as developed in his essay of that same title (1983).

## Chapter 1

1. My understanding of Dickinson's work is highly indebted to the work of Roland Hagenbüchle. His essays "Precision and Indeterminacy in the Poetry of Emily Dickinson" (1974) and "Sign and Process: The Concept of Language in Emerson and Dickinson" (1979) as well as his study *Emily Dickinson: Wagnis der Selbstbegegnung* (1988) belong with the most insightful readings of the poet.

2. For an analysis of the early reception of Emily Dickinson, see Willis J. Buckingham, *Emily Dickinson's Reception in the 1890s: A Documentary History* (Pittsburgh: University of Pittsburgh Press, 1989); for reprints of early criticism, see Caesar R. Blake and Carlton F. Wells, *The Recognition of Emily Dickinson: Selected Criticism since 1890* (1965); as well as Paul J. Ferlazzo, ed., *Critical Essays on Emily Dickinson* (1984).

3. See, for instance, John Cody, *After Great Pain: The Inner Life of Emily Dickinson* (Cambridge: Harvard University Press, 1971), 11.

4. Brita Lindberg-Seyersted's study *The Voice of the Poet: Aspects of Style in the Poetry of Emily Dickinson* (1968) is quite informative with regard to the gender of Dickinson's art, though the author herself does not make such interrelations explicit. David Porter's study *Dickinson: The Modern Idiom* (1981) acknowledges the poet's "radically feminist intelligence" (280) but dismisses her poetry as a "unique bodiless body of work" (296). (Gary Lee Stonum's *The Dickinson Sublime* [1990] explicitly counters this position by arguing that Dickinson's literary enterprise "is a coherent body of work" [ix]). Feminist literary criticism, in contrast, has interpreted ruptures in Dickinson's writing in the light of their particular position within culture and within the debates around a particular female aesthetics, rather than female subjectivity. See, for instance, Cristanne Miller, "How 'Low Feet' Stagger: Disruptions of Language in Dickinson's Poetry," in *Feminist*

*Critics Read Emily Dickinson,* ed. Suzanne Juhasz (1983), 184; and *Emily Dickinson: A Poet's Grammar* (1987), 160–86.

5. Neither Kristeva's textual analysis, the part "Le dispositif sémiotique du texte," nor her discussion of the political context ("L'état et le mystère") have been translated (the first simply being untranslatable) and thus frequently go unnoticed. Lewis provides a translation of the chapter "Phonétique, phonologie, et bases pulsionelles," along with his informative review of *La révolution du langage poétique.*

6. About 80 percent of Moore's early poems, so Holley calculated, are directed toward, and oftentimes apostrophize, a "you," an anonymous or identified other. Among the seven poems published in *The Egoist* in 1915 all but one—"Diligence Is to Magic as Progress Is to Flight"—contain apostrophes.

7. In her study of "verbal artistry" in Robert Frost, Wallace Stevens, and Moore, Marie Borroff compares the frequency of finite verbs in Moore's poetry (8.1 percent) to the average frequency of conjugated verbs in natural conversation (16.4 percent), newspaper articles (8.7 percent), contemporary scientific essays (7 percent), and Wallace Stevens's poetry (11.4 percent). In Moore's poem "Virginia Britannia," for instance, Borroff counts only fifty finite verbs among nine hundred words.

8. For further analysis of Dickinson's use of the subjunctive, see Lindberg-Seyerstedt, *Voice of the Poet,* 243–52; and C. Miller *Emily Dickinson,* 65–69.

9. Moore marked her handwritten copy of Dickinson's poem "The Soul selects her own Society—" (J 303) with "cf. Mallarmé." Likewise her reawakened interest in Dickinson coincided with her reading of Mallarmé. In her reading diary, detailed notes on Charles Manson's introduction to Roger Fry's translation of Mallarmé (1937) follow upon her notes on the *Unpublished Poems of Emily Dickinson,* ed. Bianchi and Leete, whose second edition appeared in 1936 (Boston: Little, Brown). See Rosenbach, VII.02.03, 1938–42.

10. For a critique of Kristeva's sense of femininity, see, for instance, Jardine, *Gynesis;* as well as Felski, *Beyond Feminist Aesthetics;* Nancy Fraser, "The Uses and Abuses of French Discourse Theories for Feminist Politics" (1990); Ann Rosalind Jones; and Rose, "Julia Kristeva—Take Two" in *Sexuality in the Field of Vision* (1986), 141–64.

11. Reading notebook 1921–22, Rosenbach VII.01.03. On behalf of Marianne Craig Moore, Literary Executor for the Estate of Marianne Moore, I include the following statement: "The quotations which appear in Marianne Moore's notebooks are not evidence of Moore's agreement or disagreement with the ideas expressed in these quotations, which might have been entered in the notebooks for a variety of reasons."

12. The index of her reading notebook of 1921–22 lists four entries under the topic "psychology"; only "life" has more. Among the citations one finds lenghty passages from André Tridon's study *Psychoanalysis and Nietzsche* as well as from Maxwell Bodenheim's study *Psychoanalysis and American Fiction.* Bodenheim, she noted down, takes psychology as a "diagrammed excuse" for writers' indulgence in sensuality, as a "scientific halo for the monotone of flesh." He attacks the "contention that sex forms the whole of man's physical and intangible content" and expresses his dislike of "sensual melodrama," of novels in which "sensuality adopts a heavy, clumsy, naivety" and the stories of Sherwood Anderson "in which young men lie on their backs in cornfields and feel oppressed by their bodies." According to Bodenheim, the mental and emotional confusion of present-day America as well as the lack of "intellectual curiosity, emotional whimsicality, the

decorative touch, . . . strength, and even plausible creation" in contemporary American literature could not spring from sexual longing solely. "Man contains a far more plaintive interior than a sexologist dares to admit" (Rosenbach VII.01.03).

13. This line is quoted from the notes Moore took on reading Dickinson, Rosenbach II.02.05.

14. For a close analysis of Moore's sense of authority, see Cristanne Miller's highly perceptive study *Marianne Moore: Questions of Authority* (1995). As Miller summarizes her argument, she sees "Moore as determined to establish in her writing a communally focused authority that avoided egocentric and essentialist assertions of a subjective self while also avoiding the self-erasure which is their opposite and double" (vii).

15. All translations from Kristeva are my own. The original reads: "Le fonctionnement mixte de ces deux mécanismes ouvre l'usage normatif du langage d'une part vers le corps et la *chora* sémiotique sous-jacents et refoulés, d'autre part vers de multiples déplacements et condensations qui produisent une *sémantique fortement ambivalente* sinon *polymorphe*" (*La révolution* 222).

16. The original reads: "ils reprennent la topographie du corps qui s'y reproduit" (*La révolution* 222).

17. See Moore's notes on Emily Dickinson, Rosenbach II.02.05.

18. Reading notebook, Rosenbach VII.02.03.

19. Translation mine. The original reads: "Leid und Vision bilden das Janusgesicht der dichterischen Erfahrung" (Heinz Ickstadt, *Dichterische Erfahrung und Metaphernstruktur: Eine Untersuchung der Bildersprache Hart Cranes* [1970]).

20. I thank Gary Lee Stonum for calling my attention to the problems entailed in putting Dickinson's dialectics in temporal terms.

21. Rosenbach V.23.32.

22. Albert Gelpi and Barbara Charles Worth Gelpi, for instance, placed Moore into the "category" of women poets who "suspiciously deflect. . . and repress . . . their emotional and sexual nature in the name of intellectual clarity and discursive crispness" (*Rich's Poetry* xi). See introduction, chap. 2 n. 1.

23. The common view has been that Moore's images of armor represent reticence and restraint, suggest an ego in need of protection or self-defense, or function as devices for an exploration of the world. See, for instance, Randall Jarrell, "Her Shield," *Poetry and the Age* 167–187; Donald Hall, *The Cage and the Animal* (New York: Pegasus, 1970); Suzanne Juhasz, "'Felicitous Phenomenon:' The Poetry of Marianne Moore," *Naked and Fiery Forms* 33–56; Bernhard F. Engel, *Marianne Moore* (Boston: Twayne, 1989).

24. All translations from Kittler are my own. The original reads: "eine ganz neue Ordnung der Dinge."

25. The original reads: "Der kontinuierlich-kohärente Tintenfluß, dieses materielle Substrat aller bürgerlichen In-dividuen oder Unteilbarkeiten."

26. The original reads: "ein Kernstück abendländischer Symbolsysteme."

27. "At any rate," Pound claimed, "it is (yr. metric) a progress on something I (more or less, so far as English goes) began" (*Letters* 205).

28. I myself find her poem "To a Chameleon," originally entitled "You Are like the Realistic Product of an Idealistic Search for Gold at the Foot of the Rainbow" (1916), with its allusion to Shakespeare's "Dark King," a more likely source.

29. Asking Higginson, in a letter of July 1862, to point out her "fault," the poet

adds: "Men do not call the surgeon, to commend—the Bone, but to set it, Sir, and fracture within, is more critical" (L 268).

30. See Robert Innes-Smith, *An Outline of Heraldry in England and Scotland* (Cerby: Pilgrim, 1986).

31. Translation mine. The German version reads: "als bloß sinnlicher Gegenstand kann [der Körper] nicht bedeuten; die Kleidung gewährleistet den Übergang vom Sinnlichen zum Sinn" (*Sprache der Mode* 264).

32. Reading notebook, Rosenbach, VII.03.07.

33. Reading notebook, Rosenbach VII.01.03.

34. See my essay *"Engendering the Body:* Kostümierung, Camouflage, und *Cross-Dressing* als feministische Praxis?" in *Gender Matters. Amerikastudien und Geschlechterforschung,* ed. Sielke (forthcoming 1997).

35. Letter to Bryher, 7 July 1921, Rosenbach V.08.06.

36. Kaja Silverman observes a similar phenomenon with regard to the focus of recent film theory. In her introduction to *The Acoustic Mirror* (1988) she proposes that "film theory's preoccupation with lack is really a preoccupation with male subjectivity, and with that in cinema which threatens to constantly undermine its stability" (2). The conceptualization of the gaze itself has been central to film theory and its concern with male and female spectatorship.

37. Poetry notebook, Rosenbach V.04.04. These phrases find themselves among notes taken for the poem "Marriage."

38. New Historicist readings connect the story of the lady with an actual rape case and thus politicize Renaissance views of female chastity. See, for instance, Leah Marcus, "The Milieu of Milton's Comus: Judicial Reform at Ludlow and the Problem of Sexual Assault," *Criticism* 25 (1983): 293–327.

39. Rosenbach V.23.32.

40. Letter to Moore, 9 July 1921. Rosenbach V.23.32.

## Chapter 2

An early version of this chapter appeared as "Snapshots of Marriage, Snares of Mimicry, Snarls of Motherhood: Marianne Moore and Adrienne Rich." *Sagetrieb* 6.3 (Winter 1987): 79–97.

1. See chapter 1, "Moore's Martial Art," note 3, for the position of Gelpi and Gelpi on Moore. In another place Barbara Charlesworth Gelpi interprets Moore's attention "to the world of living forms and shapes and the formal shaping of her verse" as a sign of unacknowledged victimization and dismisses the complexity of Moore's texts as a curiosity (*Shakespeare's Sisters* 272). Albert Gelpi's *A Coherent Splendor: The American Poetic Renaissance, 1910–1950* (1987) still presents Moore as "an oddity among the Modernists," though "a much admired oddity" (257).

2. Ashbery to Moore, 20 November 1960, and to Warner Moore, 14 February 1967, Rosenbach V.02.39.

3. In her essay "Pater-Daughter: Male Modernists and Female Readers" Rachel Blau Du Plessis elaborates this point (*The Pink Guitar* 41–67).

4. This theoretical excursus is indebted to Evelyne Keitel's essay "Weiblichkeit und Poststrukturalismus—Perspektiven einer feministischen Literaturwissenschaft"

(1988) and Nelly Furman's "The Politics of Language: Beyond the Gender Principle?" (1985).

5. Marianne Hirsch's review article "Mothers and Daughters" (1981) (repr. in Jean F. O'Barr, Deborah Pope, and Mary Wyer, *Ties That Bind: Essays on Mothering and Patriarchy* [Chicago: University of Chicago Press, 1990]) renders a sense of how widespread the discussion of the issue was during the 1970s. On the subject, see also *The (M)other Tongue: Essays in Feminist Psychoanalytic Interpretation,* ed. Shirley Nelson Garner, Claire Kahane, and Madelon Sprengnether (Ithaca: Cornell University Press, 1985).

6. We have, however, only relatively recently begun to think of Moore with regard to the maternal; on the subject, see Marilyn L. Brownstein, "The Archaic Mother and Mother and Mother: The Postmodern Poetry of Marianne Moore" (1989); Cristanne Miller, "Marianne Moore's Black Maternal Hero: A Study in Categorization" (1990); Alicia Ostriker, "Marianne Moore, the Maternal Hero, and American Women's Poetry" (1990); and my own essay "Snapshots of Marriage, Snares of Mimicry, Snarls of Motherhood" (1987).

7. This passage is indebted to the first chapter of Homans's *Bearing the Word,* entitled "Representation, Reproduction, and Women's Place in Language" (1–39).

8. For a critique of Irigaray's supposed essentialism, see Jones, "Writing the Body" (1985); for a defense, see Gallop, "Quand nos lèvres s'écrivent"; for an excellent discussion of the concept of essentialism, see Fuss.

9. Public lecture, given at Columbia University 1937, Rosenbach II.09.04.

10. Reading notes, Rosenbach II.02.05. This does not mean Dickinson did not quote, yet she used quotation to a much smaller extent and for different purposes—for example, to make reference to a particular term taken from another author's work, sometimes acknowledged in the text (J 131, J 148), or to mark irony and render emphasis (J 101, J 168).

11. Letter of 1 August 1925, Rosenbach V.23.32.

12. For a discussion of "the dynamics of influence and intertextuality as they affect the woman poet," see also Lynn Keller's essay "'For Inferior Who Is Free?' Liberating the Woman Writer in Marianne Moore's 'Marriage'" (1991).

13. The first version of "Marriage," for instance, did not have notes attached—possibly to avoid associations with Eliot's *The Waste Land.* The notation offered in *Observations* differs from that of her later publications. Moreover, Moore's notes are not necessarily faithful to the original. Often her citations are not annotated at all, at other times documented meticulously. In her essay "Feeling and Precision" (1944), for instance, she marked a quotation from one of her own earlier essays, making note of it with a footnote (*Prose* 402).

14. See Moore's essay "M. Carey Thomas of Bryn Mawr" (*Prose* 416–19).

15. Moore's term *experiment* may be an allusion to Mark Twain's *The Diary of Adam and Eve.* Twain's Eve herself feels like an experiment, and in "Eve's Diary" (1905) the word *experiment* in fact becomes a kind of key term. See *The Unabridged Mark Twain,* ed. Laurence Teacher (Philadelphia: Rung Press, 1979), 2:522–48.

16. Cristanne Miller's essay "Marianne Moore's Black Maternal Hero: A Study in Categorization" (1989) is the first substantial analysis of race issues and their representation in Moore's work. Miller extends this analysis in "'The Labors of Hercules': Cele-

brating and Overcoming Race," chap. 5 of her study *Marianne Moore: Questions of Authority* (1995).

17. Reading notebook, Rosenbach VII.01.02, 1916–21. The following comments on matters of marriage are, if not otherwise indicated, taken from this notebook and from her poetry notebook, Rosenbach VII.04.04, 1923–30.

18. Poetry notebook, Rosenbach VII.04.04.

19. Reading notebook, Rosenbach VII.01.02.

20. Rosenbach VII.04.04.

21. Rosenbach V.08.06.

22. Rosenbach II.01.02.

23. Rosenbach V.08.06.

24. Rosenbach VII.04.04.

25. Rosenbach VII.04.04.

26. I base my observations with regard to the relation between Bishop, Moore, and Crane on my own reading of the correspondence at the Rosenbach Museum and Archives as well as on Costello, "Moore and Bishop;" Keller, "Words Worth a Thousand Postcards"; Kalstone; and Molesworth.

27. Diehl's study *Elizabeth Bishop and Marianne Moore: The Psychodynamics of Creation* (1993) clearly departs from this tendency.

28. See Freud, "Lectures," 156, 162.

29. Poetry notebook, Rosenbach VII.04.04.

30. Letter of 20 February 1937, Rosenbach V.12.27.

31. Letter of 21 February 1937, Rosenbach V.12.27.

32. Carbon, January 1940, Rosenbach I.03.23.

33. Poetry notebook, Rosenbach VII.04.04. (These phrases are themselves among notes taken from the poem "Marriage.")

34. Letter of 21 May 1940; quoted in part by Kalstone (*Becoming* 69) and Keller ("Words Worth a Thousand Postcards" 422).

35. Poetry notebook, Rosenbach VII.04.04.

36. Poetry notebook, Rosenbach VII.04.04.

37. Letter of 19 July 1954, Rosenbach V.05.06.

38. Letter of 19 July 1954, Rosenbach V.05.06.

39. Translation mine. The original reads: "à émerger dans la lumière de la transcendence."

40. Rich quotes the original text. The English translation reads: "she comes from the remoteness of the ages, from Thebes, from Crete, from Chichén-Itzá; and she is also the totem set up deep in the jungle; she is a helicopter and she is a bird; and there is this, the greatest wonder of all: under her tinted hair the forest murmur becomes a thought, and words issue from her breasts" (de Beauvoir, *The Second Sex* 729).

41. The book provoked more reviews than any of Rich's collections of poetry. Helen Vendler's review "Myths for Mothers," *New York Review of Books,* 30 September 1976, 16–18 (repr. in *Part of Nature, Part of Us* 263–270), was particularly hostile; Alexander Theroux's "Reading the Poverty of Rich," *Boston Magazine,* November 1976, 46–47 (repr. in Cooper 304–8), particularly hysterical.

42. The love poems were published as a separate volume by Effie's Press, Emeryville, California, in 1976.

43. In practice, though, Rich's book did not abandon citation but makes constant use of quotation whose "selectivity" Vendler criticized as a "fault common to all ideologically motivated writing" (269–70).

44. Similarly, in "Disloyal to Civilization: Feminism, Racism, Gynophobia" (1978) Rich confirms this position by claiming that "the most unconditional, tender, and, I now believe, intelligent love I received was given to me by a black woman" (*On Lies* 280). In the 1986 edition of *Of Mother Born,* however, she adds a footnote to the passage on her "Black mother," in which she distances herself from the portrayal of the black woman, interpreting it as an "overpersonaliz[ation]" that does not "give enough concrete sense of the actual position of the Black domestic worker caring for white children" (255).

45. In genetics *chiasma* is a term that relates to processes of reproduction. More specifically, it refers to the crossing over of chromatides during the development of germ cells, which effects an exchange of genetic material and thus safeguards variation in reproduction.

46. Cixous and Irigary identify water as a female element; see Cixous, "Medusa" 260; Irigaray, "The 'Mechanics of Fluids,'" *This Sex* 106–18.

47. Translation mine. The German title is "Über die Notwendigkeit geschlechtsdifferenzierter Rechte."

48. Aware that her interest in law may seem to contradict her earlier work, Irigaray is quite eager to explain the continuity between her former and present position (see "Über die Notwendigkeit geschlechtsdifferenzierter Rechte" 346–48).

49. This reorientation was also manifested by Rich's engagement as a cofounder and editor of the journal *Bridges: A Journal of Jewish Feminists and Our Friends,* whose commitment was announced as "combin[ing] the traditional Jewish values of justice and repair of the world with insights honed by the feminist, lesbian and gay movements" (advertisement).

50. In some sense, this effect compares to that of Moore's early use of quotation. In Moore's own late work, by contrast, as Cristanne Miller argues, citations are increasingly used for a "more personal, popular, occasional, and openly appreciative" poetics, a poetics inspired by a "desire to represent the individual as functioning within a community" ("Quotation, Community, and Correspondances," *Marianne Moore* 167–203; 168).

## Chapter 3

1. See, for example, Juhasz, *Naked and Fiery Forms;* Martin, *An American Triptych;* and Bennett, *My Life a Loaded Gun: Female Creativity and Feminist Poetics.*

2. In a letter of September 1859 to the Hollands, Dickinson similarly assigns time the male gender: "When [Vinnie] is well, time leaps. When she is ill, he lags, or stops entirely" (L 207).

3. See, for instance, the tale of an emergent native "genius" related in "The Poet" (Emerson, *Collected Works* 3:7) and the following claim made in "History": Man "must transfer the point of view from which history is commonly read, from Rome and Athens and London to himself, and not deny his conviction that he is the Court, and if England or Egypt have any thing to say to him, he will try the case; if not, let them forever be silent. He must attain and maintain that lofty sight where facts yield their secret sense, and poetry and annals are alike" (2:6).

4. I am echoing the title of the recent collection *Feminist Measures,* edited by Lynn Keller and Cristanne Miller. The essays on "soundings in poetry and theory" collected by Keller and Miller resonate with a range of feminist measures, though, that seems to surpass that of Rich.

5. The essay's first version features a photograph, taken from the top of the staircase in the Dickinson homestead, suggesting Dickinson's own view down into the hall, which compares to the diver's perspective when "crawl[ing] like an insect down the ladder." See *Parnassus* 15 (1976): 49–64.

6. I take this point from Hagenbüchle, "Emerson and Dickinson" 141–42.

7. The poem has been read, for instance, as a frontier romance, "a domestication on American soil of the tradition of courtly love" (C. A. Anderson 174), as a "a poem of aesthetic initiation" (Gilbert 149), as a "dialectic of rage" (Cameron 56), as "an allegory, almost pure in its self-regard, of language speaking itself" (Porter 216), as a "pioneer's terse epic" related to Mary Rowlandson's captivity reports as well as to matters of slavery and the Civil War (S. Howe, *My Emily Dickinson* 35).

8. Translation mine. The original reads: "alles Wirkende beruht auf dem Gegensatz."

9. The phrases inspired by Benn's essay constitute the image of the mirror reflection (stanza 4), the depiction of the speaker's phallic weapon ("cold and egotistical spear"), and Orion's final position ("against the wall"). The first refers to a passage in which Benn pictures the elder Flaubert, having grown distant to his care for form, style, and objectivity and unable to face himself in the mirror without laughing out loud. (The original reads: "er konnte sich beim Rasieren nicht im Spiegel sehen, ohne aufzulachen" [*Gesammelte Werke* 4:1132]). Rich's lines "a woman's head turns away / from my head in the mirror" adapt this image of self-distance, with a gender difference, yet without reproducing its laughs.

The second phrase Rich adapts originates from Benn's final advice to his successors "to keep an eye on the cold and egoistical aspect which belongs to your task. . . . With your back against the wall, in the grief of fatigues and the greys of emptiness, read Job and Jeremiah and hold out." (Translation mine. The original reads: "Behalten Sie das Kalte und Egoistische im Auge, das zu ihrer Aufgabe gehört. . . . Mit dem Rücken an der Wand, im Gram der Müdigkeiten, im Grau der Leere lesen Sie Hiob und Jeremias und halten aus" [4:1144]). In Rich's poem this passage is reformulated into the lines "it is with a starlike eye / shooting its cold and egotistical spear / where it can do least damage" and "with your back to the wall." Her speaker turns against her master by using his very tools, unmasking her muse as a projection, a mirror image of herself. The eyes/I's of both speaker and other are a "pair of eyes imprisoned" (*Leaflets* 71) by the specularity of their own reflection, of self-reflexivity. In addition, Rich's poem echoes the final passages of Benn's "Probleme der Lyrik," which itself adapts a figure from Flaubert to invite young writers to "take up the spear, where we left it behind" ("Nehmen Sie den Speer dort auf, wo wir ihn liegenließen" [4:1096]). Likewise, the title of the poem that follows up on "Orion," entitled "Holding Out" (1965), alludes to Benn.

10. Translation mine. The original reads: "Der abendländische Mensch . . . besiegt das Dämonische durch die Form, seine Dämonie ist die Form, seine Magie ist das Technisch-Konstruktive" ("Rede auf Stefan George" [1934]).

11. Translation mine. The original reads: "Phallus des Geistes."

12. I thank Heinz Ickstadt for drawing my attention to the interrelation between the early letter and the last stanza of "My Life had stood—a Loaded Gun—."

13. In the foreword to her recent *Collected Early Poems,* by contrast, Rich once again claims that she had "had no political ideas of [her] own at the time," that "at twenty," she "implicitly dissociated poetry from politics" (xx).

14. This shows, particularly, in sections 5 and 6 of her poem "Natural Resources," which clearly distinguish among men and masculinities and project "the phantom of the man-who-would-understand" as a "fellow creature."

the lost brother, the twin—

. . . . . . . . . . . . . . . . . . . .

It was never the rapist:
it was the brother, lost,

the comrade/twin whose palm
would bear a lifeline like our own:

decisive, arrowy,
forked-lightning of insatiate desire

It was never the crude pestle, the blind
ramrod we were after:

merely a fellow-creature
with natural resources equal to our own.

(*Dream* 62)

## Chapter 4

1. In this way my findings contradict Gilmore's argument. Gilmore claims that Dickinson, Moore, and Rich are to be paralleled in their strategies of displacing the male gaze by "the gaze of the other woman." The author can only make this claim, however, by projecting the "gaze of the other woman" where in fact there is no such thing. In the poems that are supposed to substantiate his argument about Dickinson and Moore—"I think I was enchanted" and "Marriage"—the speakers do relate to a female other, though not by way of mutual looks and acts of recognition.

2. See Cristanne Miller's essay "Marianne Moore's Black Maternal Hero: A Study in Categorization" (1989).

3. On the subject, see, for instance, Erkkila, "Emily Dickinson and Class" (1992).

4. In "Questioning Authority in the Late Twentieth Century," the final chapter of *Marianne Moore: Questions of Authority* (204–231), Cristanne Miller explores some such other lines of affiliation by comparing Moore's aesthetics and politics to that of Lorine Niedecker, Gwendolyn Brooks, Heather McHugh, Cynthia Macdonald, Susan Howe, M. Nourbese Philip, and Alice Fulton.

# Works Consulted

Abel, Elizabeth, ed. *Writing and Sexual Difference.* Chicago: University of Chicago Press, 1982.

Adams, Hazard, ed. *Critical Theory since Plato.* New York: Harcourt, 1971.

Alcoff, Linda. "Cultural Feminism versus Poststructuralism: The Identity Crisis in Feminist Theory." *Signs* 13.3 (1988): 405–36.

Altieri, Charles. "From Symbolist Thought and Immanence: The Ground of Postmodern American Poetics." *Boundary* 2.1 (1973): 605–41.

———. *Painterly Abstraction in Modernist American Poetry: The Contemporaneity of Modernity.* Cambridge: Cambridge University Press, 1989.

———. *Self and Sensibility in Contemporary American Poetry.* Cambridge: Cambridge University Press, 1984.

Anderson, Charles A. *Emily Dickinson's Poetry: A Stairway of Surprise.* New York: Holt, 1960.

Anderson, Margaret. *Little Review Anthology.* New York: Hermitage House, 1953.

Ashbery, John. "Jerboas, Pelicans, and Peewee Reese." Rev. of *Tell Me, Tell Me: Granite Steel, and Other Topics,* by Marianne Moore. *Book Week,* 30 Oct. 1966, 18.

Auden, W. H. Foreword. *A Change of World.* By Adrienne Rich. New Haven: Yale University Press, 1951.

Bakhtin, Mikhail. *The Dialogic Imagination: Four Essays by M. M. Bakhtin.* Ed. Michael Holquist. Austin: University of Texas Press, 1981.

———. *Die Ästhetik des Wortes.* Ed. Rainer Grübel. Frankfurt a.m.: Suhrkamp, 1979.

———. *Rabelais and His World.* Bloomington: Indiana University Press, 1984.

Barthes, Roland. *Die Sprache der Mode.* Frankfurt: Suhrkamp, 1985.

———. *Mythologies.* New York: Farrar, 1987.

Baruch, Elaine Hoffman. "Two Interviews with Julia Kristeva." *Partisan Review* 51.1 (1984): 120–32.

Bates, Arlo. "Miss Dickinson's Poems." In *The Recognition of Emily Dickinson: Selected Criticism since 1890.* Ed. Caesar R. Blake and Carlton F. Wells. Ann Arbor: University of Michigan Press, 1965. 12–18.

Beauvoir, Simone de. *The Second Sex.* Ed. and trans. H. M. Parsley. New York: Knopf, 1976.

Benjamin, Walter. *Illuminations.* Ed. Hannah Ahrendt. New York: Schocken, 1969.

Benn, Gottfried. *Gesammelte Werke*. Ed. Dieter Wellershof. Munich: DTV, 1975.

Benn, Gottfried. *Sämtliche Werke*. Ed. Gerhard Schuster. Stuttgart: Klett-Cotta Verlag, 1989.

Benet, Laura. "'She Wandereth after Strange Gods . . .'" *Chimaera* 1.2 (1916): 56–57.

Bennett, Paula. *My Life a Loaded Gun: Female Creativity and Feminist Poetics*. Boston: Beacon, 1986.

Benveniste, Émile. *Problems in General Linguistics*. Coral Gables: University of Florida Press, 1971.

Benvenuto, Bice, and Roger Kennedy. *The Works of Jacques Lacan: An Introduction*. London: Free Association, 1986.

Bercovitch, Sacvan. *The American Jeremiad*. Madison: University of Wisconsin Press, 1978.

———. "Fusion and Fragmentation: The American Identity." In *The American Identity: Fusion and Fragmentation*. Ed. Rob Kroes. Amsterdam: University of Amsterdam, 1980.

———. *The Puritan Origin of the American Self*. New Haven: Yale University Press, 1975.

———, ed. *Reconstructing American Literary History*. Cambridge: Cambridge University Press, 1986.

Bishop, Elizabeth. "As We Like It." *Quarterly Review* 4.2 (1948): 129–42.

———. *The Collected Prose*. Ed. Robert Giroux. London: Hogarth, 1984.

———. *The Complete Poems: 1927–1979*. New York: Farrar, 1980.

Blackmur, R. P. "The Method of Marianne Moore." In *Marianne Moore: A Collection of Critical Essays*. Ed. Charles Tomlinson. Englewood Cliffs: Prentice-Hall, 1969. 66–86.

Blake, Caesar R., and Carlton F. Wells, eds. *The Recognition of Emily Dickinson: Selected Criticism since 1890*. Ann Arbor: University of Michigan Press, 1965.

Borroff, Marie. *Language and the Poet: Verbal Artistry in Frost, Stevens, and Moore*. Chicago: University of Chicago Press, 1979.

Browning, Elizabeth Barrett. *The Poetical Works of Elizabeth Barrett Browning*. Boston: Houghton, 1974.

Burbick, Joan. "Emily Dickinson and the Economics of Desire." *American Literature* 58 (1986): 361–78.

Burke, Carolyn. "Getting Spliced: Modernism and Sexual Difference." *American Quarterly* 39.1 (1987): 98–121.

———. "Supposed Persons: Modernist Poetry and the Female Subject." *Feminist Studies* 2.1 (1985): 131–48.

Burnett, Gary. *H.D. Between Image and Epic: The Mysteries of Her Poetry*. Ann Arbor: UMI Research Press, 1990.

Butler, Judith. *Gender Trouble: Feminism and the Subversion of Identity*. New York: Routledge, 1990.

Cady, Edwin H., and Louis J. Budd, eds. *On Dickinson: The Best from American Literature*. Durham: Duke University Press, 1990.

Cameron, Deborah. *Lyric Time: Dickinson and the Limits of Genre*. London: Johns Hopkins University Press, 1979.

Carruthers, Mary. "Imagining Women: Notes toward a Feminist Poetic." *Massachusetts Review* 20 (1979): 281–307.

Chase, Cynthia. Rev. of *Powers of Horror: An Essay on Abjection* and *Desire in Language: A Semiotic Approach to Literature and Art*, by Julia Kristeva. *Criticism* 26 (1984): 193–201.

"Cherchez la Femme." *Diacritics* 12.2 (1982): 1–77.

Chicago, Judy. *The Dinner Party: A Symbol of Our Heritage*. New York: Anchor Press, 1979.

Chmaj, Betty. "'Away with Your Man-Visions!' How Women's Studies Is Challenging American Studies." *Amerikastudien/American Studies* 31 (1985): 241–59.

Cixous, Hélène. "Castration and Decapitation." *Signs* 7.1 (1981): 41–55.

———. "The Laugh of the Medusa." *Signs* 1 (1976): 875–93.

———. *Weiblichkeit in der Schrift*. Berlin: Merve, 1980.

Cixous, Hélène, and Catherine Clément. *The Newly Born Woman*. Minneapolis: University of Minnesota Press, 1986.

Cooper, Jane Roberta, ed. *Reading Adrienne Rich: Revisions and Reviews, 1951–1981*. Ann Arbor: University of Michigan Press, 1984.

Costello, Bonnie. "The 'Feminine' Language of Marianne Moore." In *Women and Language in Literature and Society*. Ed. Sally McConnell-Ginet, Ruth Barker, and Nelly Furman. New York: Praeger, 1980. 222–38.

———. "Marianne Moore and Elizabeth Bishop: Friendship and Influence." *Twentieth Century Literature* 30 (1984): 130–49.

———. *Marianne Moore: Imaginary Possessions*. Cambridge: Harvard University Press, 1981.

———. "Marianne Moore's Wild Designs." *American Poetry Review* 16.1 (1987): 43–54.

Coward, Rosalind, and John Ellis. *Language and Materialism: Developments in Semiology and the Theory of the Subject*. Ithaca: Cornell University Press, 1982.

Crane, Hart. *The Complete Poems and Selected Letters and Prose of Hart Crane*. Ed. Brom Weber. New York: Liveright, 1966.

Culler, Jonathan. *On Deconstruction: Theory and Criticism after Structuralism*. Ithaca: Cornell University Press, 1982.

———. *The Pursuit of Signs: Semiotics, Literature, Deconstruction*. Ithaca: Cornell University Press, 1981.

———. *Structuralist Poetics: Structuralism. Linguistics, and the Study of Literature*. London: Routledge, 1975.

Dahlen, Beverly. "A Reading: Emily Dickinson: Powers of Horror." *Ironwood* 14.2 (1986): 9–27.

De Lauretis, Teresa, ed. "Eccentric Subjects: Feminist Theory and Historical Consciousness." *Feminist Studies* 16.1 (1990): 115–50.

———, ed. "Feminist Studies/Critical Studies: Issues, Terms, and Contexts." In *Feminist Studies/Critical Studies*. Bloomington: Indiana University Press, 1986. 1–19.

De Man, Paul. *Allegories of Reading: Figural Language in Rousseau, Nietzsche, Rilke, and Proust*. New Haven: Yale University Press, 1979.

———. "Autobiography as Defacement." *Modern Language Notes* 94 (1979): 919–30.

———. *Blindness and Insight*. Minneapolis: University of Minnesota Press, 1983.

Derrida, Jacques. *Die Differenz und die Schrift*. Frankfurt a.M.: Suhrkamp, 1972.

Diaz-Diocaretz, Myriam. *Translating Poetic Discourse: Questions on Feminist Strategies in Adrienne Rich*. Amsterdam: John Benjamins, 1985.

Dickinson, Emily. *The Letters of Emily Dickinson.* Ed. Thomas H. Johnson and Theodora Ward. 3 vols. Cambridge: Harvard University Press, 1986.

————. *The Master Letters of Emily Dickinson.* Ed. R. W. Franklin. Amherst: Amherst College Press, 1986.

————. *The Poems of Emily Dickinson.* Ed. Thomas H. Johnson. 3 vols. Cambridge: Harvard University Press, 1979.

Diehl, Joanne Feit. "Dickinson and Bloom: An Antithetical Reading of Romanticism." *Texas Studies on Literature and Language* 23 (1981): 418–41.

————. *Dickinson and the Romantic Imagination.* Princeton: Princeton University Press, 1981.

————. *Elizabeth Bishop and Marianne Moore: The Psychodynamics of Creativity.* Princeton: Princeton University Press, 1993.

————. *Women Poets and the American Sublime.* Bloomington: Indiana University Press, 1990.

Doolittle, Hilda. *Collected Poems.* New York: New Directions, 1983.

————. "Marianne Moore." *Poetry* 3.8 (1916): 118–19.

Du Plessis, Rachel Blau. *The Pink Guitar: Writing as Feminist Practice.* New York: Routledge, 1990.

Eagleton, Terry. *Literary Theory: An Introduction.* Minneapolis: University of Minnesota Press, 1983.

Easthope, Antony. *Poetry as Discourse.* London: Methuen, 1983.

Ecker, Gisela. "Poststrukturalismus und feministische Wissenschaft." *Frauen, Weiblichkeit, Schrift: Literatur im historischen Prozeß. Argument* 14 (1985): 8–20.

*The Future of Difference.* Ed. Hester Eisenstein and Alice Jardine. Boston: G. K. Hall, 1980.

Eliot, T. S. *Collected Poems, 1909–1962.* New York: Harcourt, 1963.

————. Introduction. *Selected Poems.* By Marianne Moore. *Marianne Moore: A Collection of Critical Essays.* Ed. Charles Tomlinson. Englewood Cliffs: Prentice-Hall, 1969. 60–65.

————. "Marianne Moore." In *Marianne Moore: A Collection of Critical Essays.* Ed. Charles Tomlinson. Englewood Cliffs: Prentice Hall, 1969. 48–51.

————. *The Sacred Wood: Essays on Poetry and Criticism.* London: Methuen, 1953.

————. *On Poetry and Poets.* New York: Farrar, 1957.

————. *Selected Essays.* London: Faber, 1951.

————. *Selected Prose.* Ed. and intro. Frank Kermode. New York: Harcourt, 1975.

Emerson, Ralph Waldo. *The Collected Works of Ralph Waldo Emerson.* Ed. Joseph Slater. 5 vols. Cambridge: Harvard University Press, 1971–94.

————. *Emerson's Complete Works.* Riverside Edition. 11 vols. Cambridge: Riverside Press, 1883.

Engel, Bernhard. *Marianne Moore.* Boston: Twayne, 1989.

Erkkila, Betsy. "Dickinson and Rich: Toward a Theory of Female Poetic Influence." *American Literature* 56 (1984): 541–59.

————. "Emily Dickinson and Class." *American Literary History* 4.1 (1992): 1–27.

————. *The Wicked Sisters: Women Poets, Literary History, and Discord.* New York: Oxford University Press, 1993.

Fauré, Christine. "Absent from History." Intro. and trans. Lillian S. Robinson. *Signs* 7 (1981): 71–80.

Felman, Shoshana. "On Reading Poetry: Reflections on the Limits and Possibilities of Psychoanalytical Approaches." In *The Literary Freud: Mechanisms of Defense and the Poetic Will*. Ed. Joseph H. Smith. New Haven: Yale University Press, 1980. 119–48.

Felski, Rita. *Beyond Feminist Aesthetics: Feminist Literature and Social Change*. Cambridge: Harvard University Press, 1989.

"Feminist Readings: French Texts/American Contexts." *Yale French Studies* 62 (1981): 1–240.

Féral, Josette. "Antigone or the Irony of the Tribe." *Diacritics* 8 (1978): 2–14.

Ferlazzo, Paul J., ed. *Critical Essays on Emily Dickinson*. Boston: G. K. Hall, 1984.

Finch, A. R. C. "Dickinson and Patriarchal Meter: A Theory of Metrical Codes." *PMLA* 102.2 (1987): 166–76.

Fitz, Linda T. " 'What Says the Married Woman?' Marriage Theory and Feminism in the English Renaissance." *Mosaic* 13 (1980): 1–22.

Flowers, Betty S. "The 'I' in Adrienne Rich: Individuation and the Androgyne Archetype." In *Theory and Practice of Feminist Literary Criticism*. Ed. Gabriela Mora and Karen S. Van Hooft. Ypsilanti: Bilingual, 1982: 14–35.

Fluck, Winfried. "Literature as Symbolic Action." *Amerikastudien/American Studies* 28.3 (1983): 361–71.

Foucault, Michel. *The History of Sexuality*. New York: Vintage, 1980.

———. *The Use of Pleasure*. New York: Vintage, 1985.

Frankenberg, Lloyd. "The Imaginary Garden." *Quarterly Review* 4.2 (1948): 192–223.

Franklin, R. W. *The Editing of Emily Dickinson: A Reconsideration*. Madison: University of Wisconsin Press, 1967.

Fraser, Nancy. "The Uses and Abuses of French Discourse Theories for Feminist Politics." *Boundary 2* 17.2 (1990): 82–101.

Freud, Sigmund. *Introductory Lectures on Psychoanalysis*. Ed. James Strachey. New York: Norton, 1966.

———. *Sexuality and the Psychology of Love*. Ed. Phillip Reiff. New York: Macmillan, 1963.

Friedan, Betty. *The Feminine Mystique*. New York: Dell, 1963.

Froula, Christine. "When Eve Reads Milton: Undoing the Canonical Economy." *Critical Inquiry* 10 (1983): 321–47.

Furman, Nelly. "The Politics of Gender: Beyond the Gender Principle?" In *Making a Difference: Feminist Literary Criticism*. Ed. Gayle Greene and Coppélia Kahn. London: Methuen 1985. 59–79.

Fuss, Diana. *Essentially Speaking: Feminism, Nature and Difference*. New York: Routledge, 1989.

Gaines, Judith. " 'Beefcake' Advertising Offers New Sex Objects." *Boston Sunday Globe* 5, September 1993.

Gallop, Jane. *The Daughter's Seduction: Feminism and Psychoanalysis*. London: Macmillan, 1982.

———. "*Quand nos lèvres s'écrivent*: Irigaray's Body Politic." *Romanic Review* 74.1 (January 1983): 77–83.

Gallop, Jane, and Carolyn Burke. "Psychoanalysis and Feminism in France." In *The*

*Future of Difference.* Ed. Hester Eisenstein and Alice Jardine. Boston: G. K. Hall, 1980. 106–21.

Garrigue, Jean. *Marianne Moore.* Minneapolis: University of Minnesota Press, 1965.

———. "Notes toward a Resemblance: Emily Dickinson, Marianne Moore." In *Festschrift for Marianne Moore's Seventy-Seventh Birthday.* Ed. Thurairajah Tambimuttu. London: Frank Cass, 1966. 52–57.

Gauthier, Xavière. "Why Witches?" In *New French Feminisms.* Ed. Elaine Marks and Isabelle Courtivron. Brighton: Harvester, 1981. 199–203.

Gelpi, Albert. *A Coherent Splendor: The American Poetic Renaissance, 1910–1950.* Cambridge: Cambridge University Press, 1987.

———. *Emily Dickinson: The Mind of the Poet.* Cambridge: Harvard University Press, 1966.

———. *The Tenth Muse: The Psyche of the American Poet.* Cambridge: Harvard University Press, 1975.

Gelpi, Albert, and Barbara Charlesworth Gelpi, eds. *Adrienne Rich's Poetry.* New York: Norton, 1975.

Gifford, Henry. "Two Philologists." In *Marianne Moore: A Collection of Critical Essays.* Ed. Charles Tomlinson. Englewood Cliffs: Prentice-Hall, 1969. 172–78.

Gilbert, Sandra M. "The American Sexual Poetics of Walt Whitman and Emily Dickinson." In *Reconstructing American Literary History.* Ed. Sacvan Bercovitch. Cambridge: Cambridge University Press, 1986. 123–54.

Gilbert, Sandra M., and Susan Gubar. *The Madwoman in the Attic: The Woman Writer and the Nineteenth-Century Literary Imagination.* Bloomington: Indiana University Press, 1979.

———. *Shakespeare's Sisters: Feminist Essays on Women Poets.* Bloomington: Indiana University Press, 1979.

Gilmore, Leigh. "The Gaze of the Other Woman: Beholding and Begetting in Dickinson, Moore, and Rich." In *Engendering the Word. Feminist Essays in Psychosexual Poetics.* Ed. Temma F. Berg, Anna Shannon Elfenbein, Jeanne Larsen, and Elisa Kay Sparks. Urbana: University of Illinois Press, 1989. 81–102.

Godwin, William. *Enquiry Concerning Political Justice.* Ed. Codell K. Carter. Oxford: Clarendon, 1971.

Goldman, Emma. *Red Emma Speaking.* Ed. Alix Kates Shulman. New York: Vintage, 1961.

Gölter, Waltraud. "Zukunftssüchtige Erinnerungen: Aspekte weiblichen Schreibens." *Psyche* 7 (1983): 642–68.

Goodridge, Celeste. *Hints and Disguises: Marianne Moore and Her Contemporaries.* Iowa City: University of Iowa Press, 1989.

Greene, Gayle, and Cora Kaplan, eds. *Making a Difference: Feminist Literary Theory.* London: Methuen, 1985.

Gregor, Arthur. "'Omissions Are Not Accidents': Reminiscences." *Twentieth Century Literature* 30 (1984): 150–56.

Hagenbüchle, Roland. *Emily Dickinson: Wagnis der Selbstbegegnung.* Tübingen: Stauffenburg, 1988.

———. "Precision and Indeterminacy in the Poetry of Emily Dickinson." *Emerson Society Quarterly* 20 (1974): 33–56.

———. "Sign and Process: The Concept of Language in Emerson and Dickinson."
   *Emerson Society Quarterly* 25 (1979): 137–55.
Halkett, John. *Milton and the Idea of Matrimony: A Study of Divorce*. New Haven: Yale
   University Press, 1970.
Hall, Donald. *The Cage and the Animal*. New York: Pegasus, 1970.
Haller, Malleville, and William Haller. "Hail Wedded Love." *Journal of English Literary
   History* 13 (1946): 79–97.
———. "The Puritan Art of Love." *Huntington Library Review* 5 (1942): 253–72.
Halliday, Mark, ed. *Against Our Vanishing: Winter Conversations with Allen Grossman on the
   Theory and Practice of Poetry*. Boston: Rowan Tree, 1981.
Harari, Josue V., ed. *Textual Strategies: Perspectives in Poststructuralist Criticism*. New York:
   Cornell University Press, 1979.
Hartman, Geoffrey. *Easy Pieces*. New York: Columbia University Press, 1985.
Herrmann, Anne. *The Dialogic and Difference: "An/Other Woman" in Virginia Woolf and
   Christa Wolf*. New York: Columbia University Press, 1989.
Heuving, Jeanne. "Gender in Marianne Moore's Art: Can'ts and Refusals." *Sagetrieb* 6.3
   (1987): 117–26.
———. *Omissions Are Not Accidents: Gender in the Art of Marianne Moore*. Detroit: Wayne
   State University Press, 1992.
Higginson, Thomas Wentworth. *Atlantic Essays*. Boston: James R. Osgood, 1871.
———. "An Open Portfolio." In *Critical Essays on Emily Dickinson*. Ed. Paul J. Ferlazzo.
   Boston: G. K. Hall, 1984. 20–26.
Hirsch, Marianne. "Mothers and Daughters." *Signs* 7 (1981): 200–222.
Hof, Renate. "Feministische Wissenschaft—A New Feminine Mystique?" *Amerikastu-
   dien/American Studies* 33 (Fall 1988): 135–48.
Holley, Margaret. *Marianne Moore: A Study in Voice and Value*. Cambridge: Cambridge
   University Press. 1987.
———. "The Model Stanza: The Organic Origin of Moore's Syllabic Verse." *Twentieth
   Century Literature* 30 (1984): 181–91.
Homans, Margaret. *Bearing the Word: Experience in Nineteenth-Century Women's Writing*.
   Chicago: University of Chicago Press, 1986.
———. "'Syllables of Velvet': Dickinson, Rossetti, and the Rhetorics of Sexuality."
   *Feminist Studies* 11 (1985): 564–93.
———. *Women Writers and Poetic Identity: Dorothy Wordsworth, Emily Brontë, and Emily
   Dickinson*. Princeton: Princeton University Press, 1981.
Howard, Richard. *Alone with America: Essays on the Art of Poetry in the United States since
   1950*. New York: Atheneum, 1980.
Howe, Daniel Walker. "American Victorianism as a Culture." *American Quarterly* 27
   (1975): 507–32.
Howe, Susan. *My Emily Dickinson*. Berkeley: North Atlantic, 1985.
———. *The Nonconformist's Memorial*. New York: New Directions, 1993.
Hoyt, Helen. "Remonstrance with Sleep." *Chimaera* 1.2 (1916): 57.
Hughes, Gertrude Reif. "'Imagining the Existence of Something Uncreated': Elements
   of Emerson in Adrienne Rich's *Dream of a Common Language*." In *Reading Adrienne
   Rich: Reviews and Re-Visions, 1951–81*. Ed. Jane Roberta Cooper. Ann Arbor: Uni-
   versity of Michigan Press, 1984. 140–62.

Huston, Nancy. "The Matrix of War: Mothers and Heroes." In *The Female Body in Western Culture*. Ed. Susan Rubin Suleiman. Cambridge: Harvard University Press, 1985: 119–36.

Hutcheon, Linda. "Subject in/of/to History and His Story." Rev. of *Alice Doesn't: Feminism, Semiotics, Cinema*, by Teresa de Lauretis; and *The Subject of Semiotics*, by Kaja Silverman. *Diacritics* 16.1 (1986): 78–81.

Huyssen, Andreas. *After the Great Divide: Modernism, Mass Culture, Postmodernism*. Bloomington: Indiana University Press, 1986.

Hymowitz, Carol, and Michele Weisman. *A History of Women in America*. New York: Bantam, 1978.

Ickstadt, Heinz. *Dichterische Erfahrung und Metaphernstruktur: Eine Untersuchung der Bildersprache Hart Cranes*. Heidelberg: Carl Winter, 1970.

Innes-Smith, Robert. An Outline of Heraldry in England and Scotland Cerby: Pilgrim, 1986.

Irigaray, Luce. *Speculum of the Other Woman*. Trans. Gillian C. Gill. Ithaca: Cornell University Press, 1985.

———. *This Sex Which Is Not One*. Trans. Catherine Porter. Ithaca: Cornell University Press, 1985.

———. "Über die Notwendigkeit geschlechtsdifferenzierter Rechte." In *Differenz und Gleichheit*. Ed. Ute Gerhard and Mechthild Gansen. Frankfurt a.M.: Helmer, 1990. 338–50.

———. "When Our Lips Speak Together." *Signs* 6.1 (1980): 69–79.

———. "Women's Exile." Interview. *Ideology and Consciousness* 1 (1977): 62–76.

Jakobson, Roman. *Language in Literature*. Ed. Krystyna Pomorska and Stephen Rudy. Cambridge: Harvard University Press, 1987.

Jameson, Frederic. "Postmodern and Consumer Society." In *The Anti-Aesthetic: Essays on Postmodern Culture*. Ed. Hal Foster. Port Townsend: Bay Press, 1983.

Jardine, Alice. *Gynesis: Configurations of Woman and Modernity*. Ithaca: Cornell University Press, 1985.

———. "Pretexts for the Trans-Atlantic Feminist." *Yale French Studies* 62 (1981): 220–36.

Jarrell, Randall. "New Books in Review." In *Adrienne Rich's Poetry*. Ed. Barbara Charlesworth Gelpi and Albert Gelpi. New York: Norton, 1975. 127–29.

———. *Poetry and the Age*. New York: Knopf, 1953.

Johnson, Barbara. *The Critical Difference: Essays in the Contemporary Rhetoric of Reading*. Baltimore: Johns Hopkins University Press, 1980.

———. Translator's Introduction to *Dissemination* by Jacques Derrida. Chicago: University of Chicago Press, 1981. vii–xxxiii.

———. *A World of Difference*. Baltimore: Johns Hopkins University Press, 1987.

Jones, Ann Rosalind. "Julia Kristeva on Femininity: The Limits of a Semiotic Politics." *Feminist Review* 18.4 (1984): 56–73.

———. "Writing the Body: Toward an Understanding of l'Écriture féminine." *The New Feminist Criticism: Essays on Women, Literature and Theory*. New York: Pantheon, 1985. 361–77.

Jones, Richard, ed. *Poetry and Politics*. New York: Morrow, 1985.

Juhasz, Suzanne, ed. *Feminist Critics Read Emily Dickinson*. Bloomington: Indiana University Press, 1983.

———. *Naked and Fiery Forms: Modern American Poetry by Women: A New Tradition*. New York: Harper, 1976.

Juhasz, Suzanne, Cristanne Miller, and Martha Nell Smith. *Comic Power in Emily Dickinson*. Austin: University of Texas Press, 1993.

Jung, Carl Gustav. *Gesammelte Werke*. Ed. Marianne Niehus. Olten: Walter, 1958.

———. "On the Relation of Analytical Psychology to Poetry." In *Critical Theory since Plato*. Ed. Hazard Adams. New York: Harcourt, 1971. 810–18.

———, ed. *Man and His Symbols*. London: Picador, 1964.

Kalstone, David. *Becoming a Poet: Elizabeth Bishop with Marianne Moore and Robert Lowell*. New York: Farrar, 1989.

———. *Five Temperaments*. New York: Oxford University Press, 1977.

Keitel, Evelyne. "Weiblichkeit und Poststrukturalismus - Perspektiven einer feministischen Literaturwissenschaft." *Amerikastudien/American Studies* 33 (1988): 149–66.

———. "Frauen, Texte, Theorie: Aspekte eines problematischen Verhältnis." *Das Argument* 142 (1983): 830–41.

Keller, Karl. "Notes on Sleeping with Emily Dickinson." In *Feminist Critics Read Emily Dickinson*. Ed. Suzanne Juhasz. Bloomington: Indiana University Press, 1983. 67–79.

———. *The Only Kangaroo among the Beauty: Emily Dickinson and America*. Baltimore: Johns Hopkins University Press, 1979.

Keller, Lynn. "'For Inferior Who Is Free?' Liberating the Woman Writer in Marianne Moore's 'Marriage.'" In *Influence and Intertextuality in Literary History*. Ed. Jay Clayton and Eric Rothstein. Madison: University of Wisconsin Press, 1991.

Keller, Lynn, and Cristanne Miller, eds. *Feminist Measures: Soundings in Poetry and Theory*. Ann Arbor: University of Michigan Press, 1995.

———. "Words Worth a Thousand Postcards: The Bishop/Moore Correspondence." *American Literature* 55 (1983): 405–29.

Kendrick, Christopher. "Milton and Sexuality: A Symptomatic Reading of *Comus*." In *Remembering Milton: Essays on the Texts and Traditions*. Ed. Mary Nyquist and Margaret Ferguson. London: Methuen, 1988. 43–73.

Kenner, Hugh. *A Homemade World*. New York: Knopf, 1975.

Kher, Inder Nath. *The Landscape of Absence: Emily Dickinson's Poetry*. New Haven: Yale University Press, 1974.

Kittler, Friedrich. *Grammophon, Film, Typewriter*. Berlin: Brinkmann und Bose, 1985.

Kloepfer, Deborah Kelly. *The Unspeakable Mother: Forbidden Discourse in Jean Rhys and H.D.* Ithaca: Cornell University Press, 1989.

Koch, Vivienne. "The Peaceable Kingdom: Miss Moore's Poems." *Quarterly Review* 4.2 (1948): 153–69.

Kramer, Hilton. "Freezing the Blood and Making One Laugh." Rev. of *The Complete Poems of Marianne Moore*. *New York Times Book Review*, 15 March 1981, 722–23.

Kristeva, Julia. *Desire in Language: A Semiotic Approach to Literature and Art*. New York: Columbia University Press, 1980.

———. *Die Chinesin: Die Rolle der Frau in China*. Munich: Ullstein, 1976.

———. *The Kristeva Reader*. Ed. Toril Moi. Oxford: Blackwell, 1986.

———. "Oscillation between Power and Denial." Interview with Xavière Gauthier. In *New French Feminisms*. Ed. Elaine Marks and Isabelle Courtivron. Brighton: Harvester, 1981. 165–67.

———. "The Pain of Sorrow in the Modern World: The Works of Marguerite Duras." *PMLA* 102.2 (1987): 138–52.

———. *Powers of Horror: An Essay on Abjection*. Trans. Leon S. Roudiez. New York: Columbia University Press, 1982.

———. "Produktivität der Frau." *Alternative* 19 (1976): 166–72.

———. *La révolution du poétique. L'avant-garde à la fin du XIXe siècle: Lautréamont et Mallarmé*. Paris: Édition du Seuil, 1974.

———. "Stabat Mater." In *The Kristeva Reader*. Ed. Toril Moi. Oxford: Blackwell, 1986. 160–85.

———. "Woman Can Never Be Defined." In *New French Feminisms*. Ed. Elaine Marks and Isabelle de Courtivron. Brighton: Harvester, 1981. 137–41.

———. "Women's Time." *Signs* 7.1 (1981): 13–35.

———. "Word, Dialogue and Novel." In *The Kristeva Reader*. Ed. Toril Moi. Oxford: Blackwell, 1986. 34–61.

Lacan, Jacques. *Écrits: A Selection*. New York: Norton, 1977.

———. *Feminine Sexuality: Jacques Lacan and the École Freudienne*. Ed. Juliet Mitchell and Jacqueline Rose. New York: Norton, 1982.

Lamos, Colleen. *Going Astray*. Ph.D. diss., Philadelphia University of Pennsylvania, Dept. of English, 1989.

Laplanche, J., and J. B. Pontalis. *Das Vokabular der Psychoanalyse*. Frankfurt a.M.: Suhrkamp, 1986.

Laqueur, Thomas. *Making Sex: Body and Gender from the Greeks to Freud*. Cambridge: Harvard University Press, 1990.

Leder, Sharon, and Andrea Abbott. *The Language of Exclusion: The Poetry of Emily Dickinson and Christina Rossetti*. New York: Greenwood, 1987.

Lentricchia, Frank, and Thomas McLaughlin. eds. *Critical Terms for Literary Studies*. Chicago: University of Chicago Press, 1990.

Levertov, Denise. "On the Edge of Darkness: What Is Political Poetry?" In *Poetry and Politics*. Ed. Richard Jones. New York: Morrow, 1985. 162–74.

———. *The Poet in the World*. New York: New Directions, 1960.

Levin, Samuel R. "The Analysis of Compression in Poetry." *Foundations of Language* 7 (1971): 38–55.

Lévi-Strauss, Claude. *The Elementary Structures of Kinship*. London: Eyre and Spottiswode, 1969.

Lewis, Philip E. "Revolutionary Semiotics." Rev. of *La révolution du langage poétique,* by Julia Kristeva, *Diacritics* 4.3 (1974): 28–32.

Lindberg-Seyerstedt, Brita. *The Voice of the Poet: Aspects of Style in the Poetry of Emily Dickinson*. Cambridge: Harvard University Press, 1968.

Loeffelholz, Mary. *Dickinson and the Boundaries of Feminist Theory*. Urbana: University of Illinois Press, 1991.

Lowell, Amy. *The Complete Poetical Works*. Intro. Louis Untermeyer. Boston: Houghton, 1955.

———. *Tendencies in Modern American Poetry*. Oxford: Blackwell, 1917.

Lowell, Robert. *Imitations*. New York: Farrar, 1966.

———. "Modesty without Mumbling." Rev. of *Necessities of Life*, by Adrienne Rich. *New York Times Book Review*, 17 July 1966, 5, 30.

Madonna. "Where Life Begins." *Erotica*. Compact disc. Maverick, 1992.

Mallarmé, Stéphane. *Ouevres complètes*. Ed. Henri Mandor and Georges Jean-Aubry. Paris: Gallimard, 1956.

"Marianne Moore." *Sagetrieb* 6.3 (1987): 1–202.

"Marianne Moore Issue." *Twentieth Century Literature* 30.2–3 (1984): i–xxx, 123–371.

Marks, Elaine, and Isabelle de Courtivron, ed. *New French Feminisms*. Brighton: Harvester, 1981.

Martin, Taffy. *Marianne Moore, Subversive Modernist*. Austin: University of Texas Press, 1986.

Martin, Wendy. *An American Triptych: Anne Bradstreet, Emily Dickinson, Adrienne Rich*. Chapel Hill: University of North Carolina Press, 1984.

McConnell-Ginet, Sally, Ruth Barker, and Nelly Furman, eds. *Woman and Language in Literature and Society*. New York: Praeger, 1980.

Matthiessen, F. O. *American Renaissance: Art and Expression in the Age of Emerson and Whitman*. New York: Oxford University Press, 1949.

Miller, Cristanne. *Emily Dickinson: A Poet's Grammar*. Cambridge: Harvard University Press, 1987.

———. "How 'Low Feet' Stagger: Disruptions of Language in Dickinson's Poetry." In *Feminist Critics Read Emily Dickinson*. Ed. Suzanne Juhasz. Bloomington: Indiana University Press, 1983. 134–55.

———. "Marianne Moore's Black Maternal Hero: A Study in Categorization." *American Literary History* 1.4 (1989): 786–815.

———. *Marianne Moore: Questions of Authority*. Cambridge: Harvard University Press, 1995.

Miller, Nancy. "Changing the Subject: Authorship, Writing, and the Reader." In *Feminist Studies/Critical Studies*. Ed. Teresa de Lauretis. Bloomington: Indiana University Press, 1986. 102–20.

———, ed. *The Poetics of Gender*. New York: Columbia University Press, 1986.

Mitchell, Juliet. "Introduction I." In *Feminine Sexuality: Jacques Lacan and the École Freudienne*. Ed. Juliet Mitchell and Jacqueline Rose. New York: Norton, 1982. 1–26.

———. *Psychoanalysis and Feminism*. New York: Vintage, 1975.

Möckel-Rieke, Hannelore. *Fiktionen von Natur und Weiblichkeit: Zur Begründung femininer und engagierter Schreibweisen bei Adrienne Rich, Denise Levertov, Susan Griffin, Kathleen Fraser und Susan Howe*. Trier: WVT, 1991.

Moi, Toril. *Sexual/Textual Politics: Feminist Literary Theory*. London: Methuen, 1985.

Molesworth, Charles. *Marianne Moore: A Literary Life*. New York: Atheneum, 1990.

Monro, Harold. "Emily Dickinson—Overrated." In *The Recognition of Emily Dickinson: Selected Criticism since 1890*. Ed. Caesar R. Blake and Carlton F. Wells. Ann Arbor: University of Michigan Press, 1965. 121–22.

Monroe, Harriet. "A Symposium on Marianne Moore." *Poetry* 19 (1922): 208–16.

Montefiori, Jan. *Feminism and Poetry: Language, Experience, and Identity in Women's Writing*. New York: Methuen, 1987.

Moore, Marianne. *The Arctic Ox*. London: Faber, 1964.

———. "The Art of Poetry: Marianne Moore." Interview with Donald Hall. In *Marianne Moore: A Collection of Critical Essays*. Ed. Charles Tomlinson. Englewood Cliffs: Prentice-Hall, 1969. 20–45.

———. "Black Earth." *Egoist* 5.4 (1918): 55–56.

———. *Collected Poems*. New York: Macmillan, 1951.

———. *The Complete Poems of Marianne Moore*. New York: Viking, 1981.

———. *The Complete Prose of Marianne Moore*. Ed. Patricia C. Willis. New York: Viking, 1986.

———. "A Letter to Ezra Pound." In *Marianne Moore: A Collection of Critical Essays*. Ed. Charles Tomlinson. Englewood Cliffs: Prentice-Hall, 1969. 16–19.

———. *Like a Bulwark*. New York: Viking, 1959.

———. *A Marianne Moore Reader*. New York: Viking, 1959.

———. *Nevertheless*. New York: Macmillan, 1944.

———. *Observations*. New York: Dial, 1924.

———. *O To Be a Dragon*. New York: Viking, 1959.

———. *The Pangolin and Other Verse*. London: Brending, 1936.

———. *Poems*. London: Egoist, 1921.

———. *Predilections*. New York: Viking, 1955.

———. *Selected Poems*. New York: Macmillan, 1935.

———. *Tell Me, Tell Me: Granite, Steel, and Other Topics*. New York: Viking, 1966.

———. "To Be Liked by You." *Chimaera* 1.2 (1916): 56.

———. "To Browning." *Egoist* 2.8 (1915): 126.

———. *Unfinished Poems by Marianne Moore*. Philadelphia: Rosenbach Foundation, 1972.

———. *What Are Years*. New York: Macmillan, 1941.

———, trans. *The Fables of La Fontaine*. New York: Viking, 1954.

Mukarovsky, Jan. "Standard Language and Poetic Language." In *A Prague School Reader on Esthetics, Literary Structure and Style*. Ed. Paul L. Garvin. Washington, D.C.: Georgetown University Press, 1964. 17–30.

Murray, David, ed. *Literary Theory and Poetry: Extending the Canon*. London: Batsford, 1989.

Anon. "The Newest Poet." In *The Recognition of Emily Dickinson: Selected Criticism since 1890*. Ed. Caesar R. Blake and Carlton F. Wells. Ann Arbor: University of Michigan Press, 1965. 24–27.

Newlin, Margaret. "'Unhelpful Hymen!': Marianne Moore and Hilda Doolittle." *Essays in Criticism* 27 (1979): 216–30.

Nyquist, Mary, and Margaret W. Ferguson, eds. *Remembering Milton: Essays on the Texts and Tradition*. London: Methuen, 1985.

Olson, Tillie. *Tell Me a Riddle*. New York: Dell, 1961.

Ostriker, Alicia Suskin. "Marianne Moore, the Maternal Hero, and American Women's Poetry." In *Marianne Moore: The Art of the Modernist*. Ed. Joseph Parisi. Ann Arbor: UMI Research Press, 1990. 49–66.

———. *Stealing the Language: The Emergence of Women's Poetry in America*. Boston: Beacon Press, 1986.

Paglia, Camille. *Sexual Personae: Art and Decadence from Nefertiti to Emily Dickinson*. New York: Vintage, 1990.

Parisi, Joseph, ed. *Marianne Moore: The Art of the Modernist*. Ann Arbor: UMI Research Press, 1990.

Parsons, Frank Alvah. *The Psychology of Dress*. Detroit: Gale Research Company, 1975.

Pearce, Roy Harvey. *The Continuity of American Poetry*. Princeton: Princeton University Press, 1961.

Perloff, Marjorie. *Poetics of Indeterminacy: Rimbaud to Cage*. Princeton: Princeton University Press, 1981.

———. "Private Lives/Public Images." *Michigan Quarterly Review* 22 (1983): 130–42.

Phillips, Elizabeth. *Marianne Moore*. New York: Ungar, 1982.

Pinsky, Robert. *Poetry and the World*. New York: Ecco, 1988.

Plath, Sylvia. *The Collected Poems*. Ed. Ted Hughes. New York: Harper, 1981.

Pope, Deborah. *A Separate Vision: Isolation in Contemporary Women's Poetry*. Baton Rouge: Louisiana State University Press, 1984.

Porter, David. *Dickinson: The Modern Idiom*. Cambridge: Harvard University Press, 1981.

Pound, Ezra. "Doggerel Section of Letter to Marianne Moore." In *The Gender of Modernism: A Critical Anthology*. Ed. Bonnie Kime Scott. Bloomington: Indiana University Press, 1990. 362–65.

———. "A Few Dont's by an Imagiste." *Poetry* 1 (1912–13): 200–207.

———. *The Letters of Ezra Pound, 1907–1941*. London: Faber, 1951.

———. "Marianne Moore and Mina Loy." *Little Review* 4.10 (1918): 57–58.

———. "Remy de Gourmont." *Poetry* 7 (1915–16): 197–202.

———. "The Renaissance." *Poetry* 6 (1915): 84–91.

Ransom, John Crowe. *The World's Body*. New York: Scribner, 1938.

"Recent Poetry: Emily Dickinson." In *The Recognition of Emily Dickinson: Selected Criticism since 1890*. Ed. Caesar R. Blake and Carlton F. Wells. Ann Arbor: University of Michigan Press, 1965. 40–53.

Reichardt, Ulfried. *Innenansichten der Postmoderne: Zur Dichtung John Ashberys, A. R. Ammons, Denise Levertovs und Adrienne Richs*. Würzburg: Könighausen und Neumann, 1991.

Rich, Adrienne. *An Atlas of a Difficult World: Poems 1988–1991*. New York: Norton, 1991.

———. *Blood, Bread, and Poetry*. New York: Norton, 1986.

———. "Blood, Bread, and Poetry: The Location of the Poet." *Massachusetts Review* 24 (1883) 521–40.

———. *A Change of World*. New Haven: Yale University Press, 1951.

———. *Collected Early Poems, 1950–1970*. New York: Norton, 1993.

———. *The Diamond Cutters and Other Poems*. New York: Harper, 1955.

———. *Diving into the Wreck: Poems, 1971–1972*. New York: Norton, 1973.

———. *The Dream of a Common Language: Poems, 1974–1977*. New York: Norton, 1978.

———. *The Fact of a Doorframe: Poems Selected and New, 1950–1984*. New York: Norton, 1984.

———. "For Randall Jarrell." In *Randall Jarrell: 1914–1965*. Ed. Robert Lowell, Peter Taylor, and Robert Penn Warren. New York: Farrar, 1967.

———. *Leaflets: Poems, 1965–1968*. New York: Norton, 1966.

———. *Necessities of Life*. New York: Norton, 1966.

————. *Of Woman Born: Motherhood as Experience and Institution.* New York: Norton, 1976.

————. *On Lies, Secrets, and Silence: Selected Prose, 1966–1978.* New York: Norton, 1979.

————. *Poems: Selected and New, 1950–1974.* New York: Norton. 1975.

————. *Snapshots of a Daughter-in-Law.* New York: Harper, 1963.

————. *Sources.* Woodside: Heyeck, 1983.

————. *Time's Power: Poems, 1985–1988.* New York: Norton, 1989.

————. "A Tool or a Weapon." Rev. of *For You* and *The Clay Hill Anthology,* by Hayden Carruth. *Nation,* 23 Oct. 1971, 408–10.

————. "Voices in the Wilderness." Rev. of *Monster,* by Robin Morgan. *Washington Post Book World,* 31 Dec. 1972, 3.

————. *What Is Found There: Notebooks on Poetry and Politics.* New York: Norton, 1993.

————. *A Wild Patience Has Taken Me This Far: Poems, 1978–1981.* New York: Norton, 1981.

————. *The Will to Change: Poems, 1968–1970.* New York: Norton, 1971.

————. *Your Native Land, Your Life.* New York: Norton, 1986.

Rose, Jacqueline. *Sexuality in the Field of Vision.* London: Verso, 1986.

————. "Introduction II." In *Feminine Sexuality: Jacques Lacan and the École Freudienne.* Ed. Juliet Mitchell and Jacqueline Rose. New York: Norton, 1982. 27–59.

Ross, Andrew. "Viennese Waltzes." *Enclitic* 8.1–2 (1984): 71–82.

Rubin, Gayle. "The Traffic in Women: Notes on the 'Political Economy' of Sex." In *Toward an Anthropology of Women.* Ed. Rayna R. Reiter. New York: Monthly Review Press, 1975.

Sargeant, Winthrop. "Profiles: Humility, Concentration, and Gusto." *New Yorker,* 16 Feb. 1957, 38–72.

Scarry, Elaine. *The Body in Pain: The Making and the Unmaking of the World.* New York: Oxford University Press, 1985.

Schneider, Liz. "'Our Failures Only Marry': Bryn Mawr and the Failure of Feminism." In *Woman in Sexist Society: Studies in Power and Powerlessness.* Ed. Vivian Gornick and Barbara K. Moran. New York: Basic, 1971. 491–535.

Schulman, Grace, ed. "Conversation with Marianne Moore." *Quarterly Review of Literature* 16 (1969): 154–71.

————. *Marianne Moore: The Poetry of Engagement.* Urbana: University of Illinois Press, 1986.

Schweik, Susan. "Writing War Poetry like a Woman." *Critical Inquiry* 13.1 (1987): 533–56.

Scott, Bonnie Kime, ed. *The Gender of Modernism: A Critical Anthology.* Bloomington: Indiana University Press, 1990.

Sexton, Anne. *The Complete Poems.* Boston: Houghton, 1981.

Showalter, Elaine. "Feminist Criticism in the Wilderness." In *The New Feminist Criticism: Essays on Women, Literature, and Theory.* Ed. Elaine Showalter. New York: Pantheon, 1985. 243–70.

————, ed. *The New Feminist Criticism: Essays on Women, Literature, and Theory.* New York: Pantheon, 1985.

Sieburth, Richard. *Instigations: Ezra Pound and Remy de Gourmont.* Cambridge: Harvard University Press, 1978.

———. "In Pound We Trust: The Economy of Poetry/The Poetry of Economics." *Critical Inquiry* 14.3 (1986): 142–72.

Sielke, Sabine. "*Engendering the Body*: Kostümierung, Camouflage und *Cross-Dressing* als feministische Praxis." In *Gender Matters. Amerikastudien und Geschlechterforschung*. Berlin: John F. Kennedy-Institut, forthcoming 1997.

———. "Snapshots of Marriage, Snares of Mimicry, Snarls of Motherhood: Marianne Moore and Adrienne Rich." *Sagetrieb* 6.3 (1987): 79–97.

Silverman, Kaja. *The Acoustic Mirror: The Female Voice in Psychoanalysis and Cinema*. Bloomington: Indiana University Press, 1988.

Singer, Linda. "Erotic Welfare." *Sexual Theory and Politics in the Age of Epidemic*. New York: Routledge, 1993.

Slatin, John M. *The Savage's Romance: Marianne Moore's Poetry*. University Park: Pennsylvania State University Press, 1986.

Smith, Barbara Herrnstein. *A Study of How Poems End*. Chicago: University of Chicago Press, 1968.

Smith, Martha Nell. *Rowing in Eden: Rereading Dickinson*. Austin: University of Texas Press, 1992.

Smith-Rosenberg, Carroll. *Disorderly Conduct: Visions of Gender in Victorian America*. New York: Knopf, 1985.

Stapleton, Laurence. *Marianne Moore: The Poet's Advance*. Princeton: Princeton University Press, 1978.

Stonum, Gary Lee. *The Dickinson Sublime*. Madison: University of Wisconsin Press, 1990.

Suleiman, Susan Rubin, ed. *The Female Body in Western Culture*. Cambridge: Harvard University Press, 1985.

Tambimuttu, Thurairajah, ed. *Festschrift for Marianne Moore's Seventy-Seventh Birthday*. London: Frank Cass, 1966.

Tate, Allen. "New England Culture and Emily Dickinson." In *Critical Essays on Emily Dickinson*. Ed. Paul J. Ferlazzo. Boston: G. K. Hall, 1984. 81–93.

Todd, Janet. *Feminist Literary History*. New York: Routledge, 1988.

Tomlinson, Charles, ed. *Marianne Moore: A Collection of Critical Essays*. Englewood Cliffs: Prentice-Hall, 1969.

Van Doren, Mark. "Women of Wit." *Nation* 113 (26 Oct. 1921): 481–82.

Van Dyne, Susan. "Double Monologues: Voices in American Women's Poetry." *Massachusetts Review* 23 (1982): 461–85.

Vickers, Nancy. "Diana Described: Scattered Woman and Scattered Rhyme." In *Writing and Sexual Difference*. Ed. Elizabeth Abel. Chicago: University of Chicago Press, 1982. 92–109.

Vendler, Helen. *Part of Nature, Part of Us: Modern American Poets*. Cambridge: Harvard University Press, 1980.

Walker, Cheryl. *The Nightingale's Burden: Women Poets and American Culture before 1900*. Bloomington: Indiana University Press, 1982.

Weisbuch, Robert. *Emily Dickinson's Poetry*. Chicago: University of Chicago Press, 1972.

Welter, Barbara. *Dimity Convictions: The American Woman in the Nineteenth Century*. Athens: Ohio University Press, 1976.

Werner, Craig. *Adrienne Rich: The Poet and Her Critics*. Chicago: American Library Association, 1988.

Whitman, Walt. *Leaves of Grass*. Ed. Harold W. Blodgett and Sculley Bradley. New York: Norton, 1965.

Williams, William Carlos. *The Autobiography of William Carlos Williams*. New York: Random House, 1948.

———. "Four Foreigners." *Little Review* 6.5 (1919): 36–39.

———. *Imaginations*. New York: New Directions, 1971.

———. "Marianne Moore." *Marianne Moore: A Collection of Critical Essays*. Ed. Charles Tomlinson. Englewood Cliffs: Prentice-Hall, 1969. 52–59.

———. *Selected Essays*. New York: New Directions, 1969.

———. *The Selected Letters of William Carlos Williams*. Ed. John C. Thirwall. New York: McDowell, 1957.

Willis, Patricia C. *Marianne Moore: Vision into Verse*. Philadelphia: Rosenbach Museum, 1987.

Wolff, Cynthia Griffin. *Emily Dickinson*. Reading: Addison-Wesley, 1988.

Wolosky, Shira. *Emily Dickinson: Voice of War*. New Haven: Yale University Press, 1984.

Wright, Elizabeth. *Psychoanalytic Criticism: Theory in Practice*. London: Methuen, 1984.

# Index